P9-CEO-813

Re-Dressing the Canon

What theater can most powerfully represent is not the equivalence between performativity and performance, but their revelatory divergence. Indeed, that's what theatrical irony is: the startling contradiction of the stated by the shown.

(Introduction to *Re-Dressing the Canon*)

The writing and production of Western drama from the Greeks to the present has often been a patriarchal enterprise, yet dramatists, directors, and actors have always known that theater can question its own representational strategies, calling attention to and undermining the very ideologies it may also promote. How it does this is central to Alisa Solomon's canny readings of Western drama. Analyzing both canonical texts and contemporary productions in lively, jargon-free prose, *Re-Dressing the Canon* finds the feminist and queer fissures in the performance conventions of the Western dramatic tradition.

Solomon offers a performance-centered technique for investigating the relationship between theater and gender, showing how theater both reproduces and resists dominant culture. Combining theoretical analysis with performance criticism, *Re-Dressing the Canon* bridges theory and practice to make for a highly stimulating volume for theorists, students, contemporary performance-goers, and practitioners alike.

Alisa Solomon is a theater critic, teacher, and dramaturg in New York City. She is Associate Professor of English/Journalism at Baruch College–City University of New York, and of English at the CUNY Graduate Center. She is a staff writer at the *Village Voice*.

Re-Dressing the Canon
Essays on Theater and Gender

Alisa Solomon

London and New York

First published 1997
by Routledge
11 New Fetter Lane, London EC4P 4EE

Simultaneously published in the USA and Canada
by Routledge
29 West 35th Street, New York, NY 10001

© 1997 Alisa Solomon

Typeset in Times by M Rules

Printed and bound in Great Britain by
Biddles Ltd, Guildford and King's Lynn

All rights reserved. No part of this book may be reprinted or
reproduced or utilized in any form or by any electronic,
mechanical, or other means, now known or hereafter
invented, including photocopying and recording, or in any
information storage or retrieval system, without permission in
writing from the publishers.

British Library Cataloguing in Publication Data
A catalogue record for this book is available from the British Library

Library of Congress Cataloguing in Publication Data
Solomon, Alisa, 1956–
    Re-Dressing the canon: essays on theater and gender/Alisa Solomon
    p. cm.
    Includes bibliographical references and index
    1. Drama—History and criticism.   2. Women in literature.
    3. Sex role in literature.   4. Theater, Yiddish.
PN1650.W65S65   1998
792'.082'09–dc21
97-2805 CIP

ISBN 0–415–15720-X (hbk: acid-free paper)
ISBN 0–415–15721-8 (pbk: acid-free paper)

For Peter W. Ferran
incendiary teacher, cherished friend

Contents

Plates

Acknowledgements

Everyone knows that theater is a collaborative art. So are books about theater. Many people have helped to bring this one into being.

I am grateful to friends who leant me precious time and perspicacious thought, offering careful, critical responses to various parts of this book and helping immeasurably to improve it: Barbara Bowen, Elinor Fuchs, Marc Robinson, Gordon Rogoff. Framji Minwalla has been an unstinting source of comfort, good cheer, and keen editorial suggestions. Erika Munk not only supplied invaluable advice on several chapters, but also sustained me through this project with her boundless good humor and tough questions. My deepest thanks to them.

Others indulgently cajoled and encouraged, and passed along useful articles and ideas. I thank April Bernard, Roslyn Bernstein, Jill Dolan, Bob Gibbs, Don Mengay, José Muñoz, Tony O'Brien, David Román, and the late Robert Massa. Just as important have been friends and colleagues who remind me, through their work and in lively conversations, that theater can be – must be – a vital way of thinking about the world. For that I thank Jerri Allyn, Anne Bogart, Peter Brosius, Liz Diamond, Maria Irene Fornes, Rhea Gaisner, Mark Gevisser, Holly Hughes, Tony Kushner, Ruth Maleczech, Judith Malina, Deb Margolin, Zakes Mokae, Suzan-Lori Parks, Sinai Peter, Hanon Reznikov, Jenny Romaine, Rachel Rosenthal, Peggy Shaw, Carmelita Tropicana, Irena Veisaite, Lois Weaver, Mac Wellman, Sande Zeig. I also want to express my appreciation to my teacher Kaicho Tadashi Nakamura who, among many other things, has helped me learn to keep polishing. I am blessed with loving parents and siblings, whose support has always enabled my quests. This project is no exception. I thank them: Josephine Kleiman Solomon, Jack and Carolyn Solomon, Debby and Bob Simon, Michael Solomon, Rena Solomon.

I have received institutional support from Baruch College – City University of New York in the form of released time from teaching; I could not have completed this work without it. I warmly thank the MacDowell Colony, where this project, much described for ages, finally started taking shape on paper.

For their evocative photos, I thank Deborah Bright, Sheila Burnett, Malcolm Lubliner, Dona Ann McAdams, and Sylvia Plachy. For helping me acquire photos, I gratefully acknowledge the assistance of Stephanie Coen at *American Theater*, Tad Coughenour, Heidi Feldman at BAM, Kricya Fisher at YIVO, Maxine LaFantasie and Marvin Taylor at the Fales Library at New York University, and Peggy Shaw.

Some elements of this work appeared in earlier versions, and I am grateful to those who provided occasions for their development and wise counsel on their content: Lesley Ferris, editor of *Crossing the Stage*; Erika Munk, editor of *Theater*; Stanley Kauffmann, in whose honor an early version of the Ibsen chapter was affectionately penned; Michael Warner, who invited me to speak at the Rutgers Series in Lesbian and Gay Studies, where I first attempted "Notes on Butch;" and Richard Goldstein, Lisa Kennedy, Amy Virshup, and Ross Wetzsteon, editors (and former editors) at the *Village Voice*. Material originally developed there is reprinted by permission of the *Village Voice*.

I am grateful for permission to quote from: Joachim Neugroschel's English translation of Sholem Asch's *God of Vengeance*, copyright 1996 by Joachim Neugroschel. All rights reserved. "A Doll House" and "Hedda Gabler" from *The Complete Major Prose Plays of Henrik Ibsen* by Henrik Ibsen, translated by Rolf Fjelde. Translation copyright © 1965, 1970, 1978 by Rolf Fjelde. Used by permission of Dutton Signet, a division of Penguin Books USA Inc. Every effort was made to secure permissions for quotations where appropriate.

At Routledge, I warmly thank Talia Rodgers for her insights and enthusiasm, and Sophie Powell and Diane Stafford who were never derailed by wayward faxes and e-mails that are probably still floating somewhere in the ether.

I have dedicated this book to Peter W. Ferran, a teacher early on, who not only shaped my outlook and approach, but nurtured and inspired me. As only the best teachers do, he challenged me to find my own perspective and voice. He has remained an encouraging colleague and friend, providing support and feisty argument at crucial moments. I hope this work will stand as a fitting tribute.

Finally, though words can hardly convey the enormousness of my debt or emotion, I thank my partner, Marilyn Kleinberg Neimark, who makes everything possible.

The modern theater . . . needs to be questioned . . . not about whether it manages to interest spectators in buying tickets – i.e. in the theater itself – but about whether it manages to interest them in the world.

Bertolt Brecht

Introduction

How easy is a bush suppos'd a bear

THE GENDER GAP: IRONY AND MIMESIS

In the prologue to Aristophanes' *Thesmophoriazusae*, Euripides – the comic butt of the play – gives important advice to his old relative, Mnesilochus. "You can't talk about *hearing* things that you are going to *see*," Euripides says, rejecting Mnesilochus's simple demand that Euripides tell him where they are going. "The two concepts are, in the very nature of things, sharply differentiated."[1] In other words, Aristophanes begins his play that parodies genre and gender with a lesson in the basic principle of dramatic irony: in the theater, what you see isn't always what you get – and vice versa. Indeed, the comedy takes place in the gap between hearing and seeing, between what text declares and performance self-consciously fails to deliver. In both its satirical treatment of Euripidean tragedy and its sartorial travesties on the representation of women, *Thesmophoriazusae* points to, and mocks, theatrical process – the mimetic itself. In fact, the play's prologue, according to the Greek scholar Froma Zeitlin, contains the first technical use of the term *mimesis*.[2]

The term comes up when Agathon the poet, dressed in a flowing gown, defends his outfit to the sneering Mnesilochus. A poet, says Agathon, has to put himself in women's shoes, and the rest of her vestments, in order to capture her experience; that's the only way he can render it in his poetry truthfully. "If he's writing about a man," Agathon explains, "he's got all the bits and pieces already, as it were; but what nature hasn't provided, art can imitate" – or, more literally, mimesis can take care of.

With this original aesthetic invocation of *mimesis* Aristophanes acknowledges that his theater requires female impersonation – and also requires (and calls attention to) its inadequacy. (He makes it quite clear that Agathon's rendering of women isn't truthful at all.) In doing so,

Aristophanes underlines Euripides' instructions in irony: like theater in general, men in women's roles say one thing, but show something else. This impersonation, always incomplete on the non-illusory stage, yet always demanding acceptance if the play is to go on, stands metonymically for theatrical illusion itself. The point has permeated theater history for centuries. I'm interested in how feminist theater critics and practitioners might exploit it.

When Aristophanes wrote *Thesmophoriazusae*, probably in 411 BC, a century or two had already passed since men had given birth to Western drama by appropriating the women's part in proto-theatrical rituals, as Arthur Pickard-Cambridge argues. "The change to drama," he writes, "comes when men [instead of women] dressed up as maenads and sang the Resistance story."[3] As Aristophanes' satire on dramatic genre and dramatized gender demonstrates, the link between female impersonation and theater – indeed, their co-dependence – remained a visible and potentially risible feature of Greek theater for as long as we have records of it. Western drama's foundation in female impersonation can be felt to this day. Marjorie Garber offers merely a new spin on Pickard-Cambridge's assessment when she declares, in her 1991 compendium of cross-dressing, *Vested Interests*, "transvestite theater is the *norm*, not the aberration."[4] Indeed the mutability of human identity promised by theater, and figured by the norm of transvestism, is precisely what makes theater the queerest art, perennially subject to railing by those with a stake in promoting the "natural order" of the status quo.

While feminists have justifiably found theater's transvestic traditions to be suspect[5] – women were not deemed worthy of representing themselves, or, frequently, of spectating – it may be that Western drama's basis in this discriminatory practice has produced fissures where feminists can find footholds for producing deeper, more radical fractures. Certainly theater in patriarchal cultures has reflected and reproduced ideologies that shored up the power of those in control (whether or not women acted the roles of women – or even, sometimes, directed, produced, or wrote for the stage). But by questioning its own representational strategies, theater can also undermine those power structures. How that might happen is the central question posed in this book.

One clue comes from the art theorist Michael Fried, who disparages theater as a medium more concerned with the act of showing than with what it actually shows.[6] That, rather, is the feature to celebrate in theater, for it is the shifting perceptual ground from which theater's queer nature and feminist potential spring. As the quintessential mimetic art – Bruce Wilshire calls it "the art of imitation that reveals imitation"[7] –

theater can question the very means of its production, call attention to its own processes and limits, and, as a result, raise questions about the images and ideologies it may give stage and voice to. It can self-reflexively consider its own embeddedness in cultural institutions and historical moments. When it does so, theater – in Stuart Hall's terms – "negotiates" dominant culture, at once reproducing and resisting it: self-conscious theater self-deconstructs.

This happens most vigorously around the representation of gender. First, precisely because Western theater's originary mimetic activity was female impersonation, acting is bound up with "femininity." And second, because patriarchal culture has sustained an ideal of the artificial, malleable, and changeable woman, "femininity" is bound up with acting. That's why old-school sociologists, early feminists, and current queer theorists have relied on theatrical metaphors to describe the complex social behavior we've come to call gender, comparing it to role-playing, masquerade, and play-acting.[8] Of course this imagery has its limits: unlike the actor, we never get to make an exit, shedding our gender roles as we walk off the stage. Moreover, gender is not an individual accomplishment, but a social enactment, rigidly enforced by, and enforcing of, compulsory heterosexuality.[9]

Nonetheless, comparing gender to theater not only suggests that it is not an immutable or inevitable biological function. More important, the comparison reminds us of the spectator's role, providing a framework for recognizing our complicity in the social conventions that sustain a collective illusion. This move appeals especially to postmodern theorists, who use theatrical imagery most of all, preferring the medium's shifting truth-claims to the self-assuredness of master narratives. In recent years, "performativity" has become the buzzword of postmodern academic theory, invoked to describe the constructedness of a range of "marginalized identities" or "subject positions"; the particular phrase "gender performativity" has already become a hackneyed and much misused mantra of critical writing, its meaning becoming more diffuse even as the term acquires more buzz. As it has been seized by the critical industry, "performativity" has been uprooted from its origins in J.L. Austin's work on the relationship between utterance and action,[10] and has been whisked into the realm of theatrical metaphor. There, the performative – "the reiterative and citational practice by which discourse produces the effects that it names"[11] – has been translated, like Bottom in his ass's head, into a fancy synonym for performance.[12] That's a pity, because what theater can most powerfully present is not the equivalence between performativity and performance, but their revelatory divergence. Indeed, that's what theatrical irony is: the startling contradiction of the stated by the shown. My purpose, then, in part, is to ballast the proliferating performance metaphors with theater itself, to take up a challenge posed by Jill Dolan when she asks, "How can the liveness of theater performance *reveal* performativity?"[13]

So I return to the scene of the crime: the Western theatrical canon. Contemplating examples from the page, the stage, and the streets, I hope to reconnect a popular understanding of gender-as-performance to the source of its most provocative metaphor. I hope to re-enter the theater, that literal place of looking, and ask what happens – or at least what can happen – to gender when it is framed within and compared to the formal conventions of theater.

How are spectators engaged in a play, I ask, and how does that engagement reinforce gender regulation, or disrupt it, and how do some performance strategies produce that disruption? How can the gap that Euripides describes at the beginning of *Thesmophoriazusae*, especially as it is exposed and expanded through different types of female impersonation in the play, help us understand more about the relationship between gender and performance? Indeed, how can the fundamental ironic mechanism of Western theater, forged in the convention of female impersonation, inform and deepen a contemporary understanding of the staging of gender? And how can particular productions emphasize theater's ability to grapple with these issues – or to suppress them?

As I don't believe there is a single answer to any of these questions, this book does not offer a grand thesis that's stated here, and then demonstrated by the accumulation of examples in later chapters. Instead, taking a look at *Thesmophoriasuzae*, this introduction offers an approach to a feminist way of reading plays in theatrical terms, along with some ideas about why Western theater invites – or at least provides an opening for – such an approach. The essays that follow look at similar questions about gender and performance through different prisms. In some instances, the prism is a canonical play; in others, it is a contemporary production (or deconstruction) of a canonical play that deliberately puts gender issues in the foreground. I take as axiomatic that what happens in production can illuminate or respond to what happens in the academy, and vice versa; thus these essays make use of close reading, theoretical discussion, and specific performance criticism. The essays are related, of course, by virtue of the questions they engage; but they are related more like cousins than like a set of siblings arrayed in a line. Their family resemblance is feminist and thoroughly theatrical.

To attempt this sort of theatrical feminist criticism means, perhaps, beginning with assumptions that differ from those underlying some of the important work that has defined the field so far. For instance, if instead of conceiving of the feminist agenda as winning women's equal representation – in imagery as well as government and commerce – we subscribe to Gayle Rubin's utopian vision of feminism as the call to "liberate human personality from the straightjacket of gender"[14] altogether, theater begins to look like an even more disruptive device.

The sociologists Candace West and Don H. Zimmerman point out in their essay "Doing Gender," how the experience of the male-to-female transsexual, who has to learn the movements, postures, vocal intonations, and so on to pass muster as a woman, "makes visible what culture has made invisible – the accomplishment of gender."[15] So does much theater. On stage there's a radical synergy between theater that displays its performance conventions and makes the fact of theater part of its subject, and the real-life, theater-like conventions of gender roles. In such works, theater and gender take shape as critical images of one another, as mimetic – though not identical – twins. Exposing that relationship is the essential action of *Thesmophoriazusae*, a comedy that makes tragic form, female impersonation, and theatrical spectating its interconnected objects of revelatory ridicule.

MIMETIC TRUTHS AND PHALLUSES: *THESMOPHORIAZUSAE*

In *Thesmophoriazusae*'s prologue, Agathon offers his theory of mimesis, and then Euripides asks him to infiltrate the all-women's Thesmophoria festival, where the participants will ratify a plan to retaliate against Euripides for portraying women negatively in his plays. Invoking the language of theatrical disguise, Euripides says that smooth-cheeked Agathon will easily pass as a woman, and persuasively plead his case. But Agathon refuses, saying that he is too pretty and that the women will resent him for stealing their lovers. Hirsute old Mnesilochus will go instead, and Aristophanes stages his masking in broad detail: his face is shaved, his bare butt bent toward the audience as his genitals are depilated (in keeping with Athenian customs regarding feminine beauty – and for symbolic laughs, as a peek at Mnesilochus's pubis, depilated or not, would reveal his leather phallus). He is swaddled in a girdle, draped in a yellow gown (which conceals his phallus), and trussed with a wig – all accoutrements borrowed from Agathon.

Agathon explains why he possesses this wardrobe with his riff on mimesis: "A dramatic writer has to merge his whole personality into what he is describing." Aristophanes renders this theory suspect because it's so clear that Agathon is not merely putting on femininity for creative inspiration; the reason he can't help Euripides is that he already looks too much like an impersonated woman to pull off imitating one. That is, Euripides can't talk him into dressing like a woman because he is *already* dressed like one. Indeed, the total absorption demanded of Agathon's mimetic fallacy is the opposite of the mimetic experience theater offers, and that this play – and this moment in the play – points to: pleasure comes not from watching reality dissolve into what's staged, but from recognizing the dialectical tension between reality and representation. What Agathon says – just as Euripides predicted – contradicts what he displays. And yet, the play reminds us, he is merely an actor in the mask and androgynous costume of Agathon. In theater, especially in comedy, representation requires irony. Imitation is funny only if we recognize its inadequacy – and the exaggeration with which it attempts to compensate.

In juxtaposing different degrees of female impersonation, Aristophanes exposes femininity as an emblem of the mimetic, comically exploiting the ancient link between transvestism and tragedy. Several critics have noted Agathon's resemblance to Dionysus, god of theater and disguise.[16] In parodying Euripides, Aristophanes also calls forth the tragedian's image of Dionysus in *The Bacchae*, where Pentheus dresses as a woman in order to become spectator to a ritual of transformation – and ends up being transformed into the tragic spectacle. And Dionysus is also evoked in the setting of the Thesmophoria festival, which favors Demeter, goddess of fertility, over Dionysus, who looms behind the play as focus of the theatrical festival in which *Thesmophoriazusae* would have been a competitor. (Aristophanes does not stage an accurate replica of the Thesmophoria and thereby expose women's secret, separatist rites, as some critics have charged;[17] he offers a comically inverted notion of the women's ceremony, in which they effectively cross-dress again, conducting themselves like the men of a political assembly. This is not to say that the depiction is not belittling – most comedy is – but that it is not realistic.)

Gender is muddled yet again in the *parabasis*, the section of an old comedy in which the chorus makes a direct plea to the audience. Here, the chorus denounces male disparaging of women and declares women's superiority. Referring to objects they use that are homonyms in Greek for umbrella/shield and loomrod/spear, they pun, Laura Taaffe points out, on terms for "various accessories that mark each gender," but "are described with identical terminology."[18]

But it's through the on-stage creation and dissolution of female disguise that Aristophanes theatrically unwraps Western drama's ties to Western presumptions of the feminine as linked to the female body.

Mnesilochus – standing for the female impersonating actor – thinks he can pass if he acquires the appropriate costume and props. Thus Aristophanes presents femininity as a set of effects; suggesting that femininity does not require a woman's body, the play denaturalizes gender.

Mnesilochus's Dionysiac transformation is downright campy, especially as he is first established as a grisly stock figure, full of bawdy, homoerotic bombast and macho bluster. On first seeing Agathon, Mnesilochus demands to see the poet's "tool." Then he volunteers, should Agathon write any satyr plays, to "get right behind you with my hard-on and make it with you."[19] His costuming is linguistic as well as sartorial: he screams when the razor approaches his beard, and then curses, appealing to women's goddesses.[20] (Later, he will slip toward calling out to male gods – the stickier his situation, the shtickier his action.)

Mnesilochus's disguise is made up of the very elements of a typical stage costume for a female character on the Greek stage, and yet is extreme enough that it stands out from the less ridiculous versions of femininity represented in the play. The old man in drag contrasts both the two effeminate men who are mistaken for women – Agathon and, later, Cleisthenes (both played by the same actor) – and from the chorus of women at the Thesmophoria festival, played, of course, by men. The three types of figures – the man, reluctantly dressed as a woman before our eyes; the androgynous male; the male actor playing the woman's part – offer different versions of performed femininity. Under these circumstances, it's impossible to forget that women's roles are male creations. Even the chorus's self-deprecatory remarks early in the play – "There is nothing worse than a bad woman, except women in general" – are presented as men's comically self-serving idea of what they'd like to hear such women say, and more, as a comment on Mnesilochus's, and then the chorus's, acting ability.

When Cleisthenes brings the news that a man has infiltrated the festival and helps to search out the interloper, the scene becomes a near slapstick hunt for the offending phallus – an appendage the audience well knows can be found under any one of the *chitons* on stage, if not always in its detachable costume variety. Cleisthenes leads the hunt for the "big thing,"[21] and zeroes in on Mnesilochus. Searched from both sides, Mnesilochus hides his phallus between crossed legs, stuffing it behind, then pulling it toward his front, until it is discovered travelling back and forth like "a shuttle service across the Isthmus [of Corinth]." Some feminist critics have read a relieved celebration in the display of this errant phallus. Lesley Ferris writes:

just as Mnesilochus conspires with his phallus to prevent the women from discovering his true identity, so do the Athenian (male) citizens of Aristophanes' audience conspire with themselves and the actors: what joy, what gaiety our phallus brings, how it binds us, male performers and male audience, in the gleeful power of possessing one.[22]

Perhaps. But at the same time Aristophanes makes the phallus an object of ridicule and embarrassment. Most important, it's the object of Mnesilochus's undoing. The phallus is the "big thing" that prevents thoroughly convincing imitation, that gets in the way of total transformation and thus leaves a gap between what's staged and what's said; it's what makes theatrical mimesis possible. The phony phallus, in other words, is Aristophanes' ironic tool.

Throughout *Thesmophoriasuzae* Aristophanes offers variations on this idea of mimesis, linking female impersonation and parody, as Zeitlin suggests, as two kinds of "imitation with a difference."[23] For not only does the play present several mutually derisive versions of men playing women, it also dramatizes a series of spoofs of Euripidean drama. After the chorus of women at the Thesmophoria discover Mnesilochus, they hold him hostage while Cleisthenes runs for legal (male) authorities. Attempting to escape, Mnesilochus recites various rescue scenes from Euripides' plays – *Telephus*, *Helen*, and *Andromeda* – and awaits the tragedian's enactment of his notoriously clever finales. The play now shifts from a focus on imitating women to a focus on imitating tragedy, the two linked reflectively across the central axis of the *parabasis*.

Thwarted again and again, Euripides eventually makes a deal with the women, and wins his relative's release by dressing as a woman himself – a panderer – and distracting Mnesilochus's swaggering Scythian male guard with a naked dancing girl, a typical ending for a comedy. So the grand tragedian wins the day by employing the most lowly of comic devices (Aristophanes' comment, perhaps, on the way Euripides was encroaching on comic territory in his tragedies). What's more, the Scythian, so unschooled in theater that he doesn't have a clue who Echo is when she appears and starts repeating everyone's lines, falls for the dancer – a man in a body suit with female genitalia painted on it. Thus Aristophanes joins his critique of tragic form, female impersonation, and the theater spectator's ironic engagement in a final image of sexual and textual confusion – an image of theater's mimetic machinations.

AFTER ARISTOPHANES: FINDING THE FEMINIST FISSURES

Of course it's possible – some would say inevitable – that the subversions of Aristophanes' gender romp can serve the patriarchal presumptions they mock, just as carnival inversions historically redound to a restoration of the old order. And to be sure, Aristophanes, like other classical dramatists, is guilty of what Sue-Ellen Case condemns as "suppressing real women and replacing them with masks of patriarchal production."[24] But simultaneously, that is precisely what the play lays bare, or, to use Brecht's term, makes strange or alienates – that is, offers for critical regard. So, though as a feminist, I certainly recognize the misogyny within the Western dramatic tradition and resent women's frequent exclusion from that tradition, I am not ready to join some colleagues in ditching canonical plays as irrelevant or hostile to feminist concerns. I'd rather widen the openings that theater's denaturalizing effects provide to expose and exploit Western drama's revelation of gender's artificiality.

When Case brashly asserted in 1985 that "feminist practitioners and scholars may decide that [ancient Greek] plays do not belong in the canon – and that they are not central to the study and practice of theater"[25] her point was rhetorically important in its moment. But even agreeing that such plays tell us little about real women of the period (or of real men, I might add), I don't regard them, *a priori*, merely as offensive artifacts of a sexist, hegemonic tradition. I detect, in their showy theatricality, the possibility of an internal critique of the forces that govern the representation of women both on stage and off. The very obsession with gender conflicts on the Attic stage may even suggest a sort of guilty acknowledgement of the culture's relentless misogyny.[26]

Theater, like other cultural creations, certainly participates in constructing gender. As Teresa de Lauretis has written in a widely influential essay, gender is a product "of various social technologies, such as cinema, and of institutionalized discourses, epistemologies, and critical practices, as well as practices of daily life."[27] But because performance and femininity are so intertwined, exposing the mechanics of theatrical mimesis can also expose what de Lauretis calls these "technologies of gender." Thus plays that question their strategies of representation are ready sites for feminist resistance. But few feminist theater critics have staked them out.

Feminist theater theory over the last decade or so has raised important questions about the dramatic canon's composition and interpretation. It has introduced important ideas about the role of theater within a patriarchal political and social economy. It has brought analytical systems developed in feminist literary and film criticism to bear on theater texts and practices.[28] Surprisingly, though, so far feminist theater theory has had little to say about the workings of theater itself, about how the critical engagement demanded of dramatic spectators can trigger a parallel critical engagement with the world, and especially, women's place within in it.

One obstacle to looking at work this way has been that much contemporary theory, made myopic by the dominant modes of film and television, takes dramatic realism as its essential example, though this genre represents only a narrow slice of theater history – and, even then, doesn't always "hold a mirror up to nature" in any flat or simple way. Yet feminist critiques of theatrical mimesis often forget about irony (perhaps because without adjustment, they transfer to theater terms developed to analyze the very different genre of Hollywood film). They focus on theater that endeavors to hide its artificiality from the audience, that like a frowzy woman trying to keep her slip from showing tries to sweep its conventions out of sight.[29] More often, though, theater just lets it hang out. And sometimes – in the work that most interests me – theater brazenly parades around in its underwear.

When it does so, theater produces a critical distance between spectator and stage: the spectator sees the play, and sees herself seeing it. This basic Brechtian point can be bent in feminist directions by training it on images of femininity in metatheatrical plays, for they allow us to see ourselves seeing the theatrical construction of a social construction.

I'm proposing, then, an engaged criticism that moves beyond role-model feminism – the insistence that the stage present positive, or at least "realistic" images of women. (This view unwittingly lines up with a centuries-old tradition of assigning theater the task of moral instruction, and then linking its pedagogical success to verisimilitude.) After all, 2,500 years is long enough for gathering at the Thesmophoria festival to complain about the images of women in Euripides. I'm interested, rather, in a feminist criticism that investigates the way in which particular plays, presented in particular theatrical styles, encourage us to think about – and think against – social conventions of gender.

I'm interested, then, in an analysis that begins with an acknowledgement that theater, in J. L. Styan's words, deals with "emergent" rather than "immanent"[30] meaning. Instead of asking how the unconscious structures viewing – as most feminist criticism, based in psychoanalysis, does – I want to look at how a play, staged in a particular style, on the special social occasion of theater, structures viewing. This is hardly to say that the two structurings are mutually exclusive. Certainly spectators bring to the theater gender and other cultural scripts that overdetermine our unconscious. Indeed, this unmarked cultural backdrop is one thing feminist stagings often mean to make visible. So I don't intend to reject feminist theater theory that has come before, but to try starting from a different vantage point, one that puts the focus on the play's production of particular effects.

Following feminist film theorists, theater critics have, often uncritically, taken up Lacan's psychosemiotic proposition that psychosexual development – defined only in male terms – involves the child's movement from the prelinguistic stage of the "Imaginary," where he is one with the Mother, to the "Mirror" stage, where he acquires language and discovers his separateness, his self – a cultural entity whose entry into the "Symbolic" requires leaving behind a state of libidinal satisfaction, even as he recognizes that he possesses a penis and his mother does not. Fearful that if he remains with his mother, he might lose his penis too, he moves on; the phallus thus appears as the key to the "Symbolic."

Lacan's theory has been summarized and adapted by many writers,[31] so there's no need to rehearse the details here; for feminist theater critics, there are two important points derived from Lacan that were originally elaborated by feminist film critics. It is these that I want to challenge in theatrical terms.

First, briefly, feminists have argued that Lacan defines a representational system in which women can only be positioned as the fetishized "Other." Lacking the phallus, and thus access to the Symbolic order, they are denied subjectivity. Thus, women cannot be represented – only "woman," a construct of male desire, can be. It's easy to see how this notion applies to narrative cinema, which repeatedly represents women as erotic objects, and all the while, in E. Ann Kaplan's words, "perpetuates the illusion that spectators are being shown what is 'natural.'"[32]

On stage, however, "woman" may be *re*presented, but at the same time a living, breathing woman can be *pre*sented. And most important, it's possible for her to comment on the character or image she represents, that is, to make those quotation marks around "woman" visible. In semiotic terms, she can widen the distance between signified and signifier by calling attention to that gap. Thus she *breaks* the illusion that spectators are being shown what is natural. In traditions in which males play women's roles, they, too, can denaturalize gender by pointing to its artificiality on stage, as occurs in *Thesmophoriazusae* (and, as I argue in Chapter 1, in Shakespeare). When men play women, it's even more difficult to sustain the idea that in these traditions – all nonnaturalistic – the male actor *becomes* the fetishized female.

The Lacanian idea of women's "unrepresentability" has been used to bolster the claim that "mimesis is not possible for [women]."[33] This claim, however, relies on a faulty notion of theatrical mimesis, one that posits (like Plato) a Truth behind a representation, and that then rejects this totalizing Truth as inherently misogynistic. On the contrary, theatrical presence displays the absence of any prior cap-T truth; there is no thing that theater copies. In a play, there is no doer behind the deed – Mnesilochus, say, exists only through his actions on stage. *That's* why Plato distrusted theater so much: It wasn't just that theater offered a pale imitation of an imitation; it hinted that there was no ideal standing beyond its representation and ordering the universe. As Herbert Blau puts it, theater "implies no *first time*, no origin, but only recurrence and reproduction."[34] Echoing this observation, Judith Butler asserts, "the original identity after which gender fashions itself is an imitation without an origin . . . it is a production which . . . postures as an imitation."[35] It is in this sense that gender – like theater – is automimetic. Both are imitations of an action, and action is always already mimetic.[36]

The concept of the "male gaze" has been even more readily appropriated by feminist theater critics, though film theorists have been careful to specify its narrow application to Hollywood movies. In coining the phrase in 1975, Laura Mulvey explicitly stated that the voyeurism and scopophilia evoked by film are products of its particular apparatus. She writes:

> cinema builds the way [a woman] is to be looked at into the spectacle itself. Playing on the tension between film as controlling the dimension of time (editing, narrative) and film as controlling the dimension of space (changes in distance, editing), cinematic codes create a gaze, a world, and an object, thereby producing an illusion cut to the measure of desire.[37]

Building on this definition, E. Ann Kaplan asserts that the scopophilia generated by the male gaze

> is activated by the very situation of the cinema: the darkened room, the way the gaze of the spectator is controlled by the aperture of first, the camera and second, the projector, and the fact that the spectator is watching moving images rather than either static ones (painting) or live actors (theatre), all help to make the cinematic experience closer to the dream state than is possible in the other arts.[38]

Obviously, the theater – again, the non-naturalistic theater least of all –

neither induces a dream state nor controls the spectator's gaze like a camera. Nonetheless, the "male gaze" has been imported to the theater, where it has come to mean, essentially, "male point of view," a far less precise term, and one that may accurately describe certain sociological features of theater (and of everything else, for that matter), but does not characterize a particular spectatorial exchange with the stage. Sue-Ellen Case, for one, reduces the meaning of the "male gaze" to the notion that "representations of women are perceived as they are seen by men."[39] She continues:

> When the *ingenue* makes her entrance, the audience sees her as the male protagonist sees her. The blocking of her entrance, her costume and the lighting are designed to reveal that she is the object of his desire. In this way, the audience also perceives her as an object of desire, by identifying with his male gaze.

Case is referring to only one genre of theater here, though she implies that she is encompassing the entire art. Of course not every play has an ingenue – and not every play operates primarily, or at least entirely, through unbroken identification with a male protagonist. Never mind that blocking, costume, and lighting can be deployed to opposite effects. Even within the conventions of her example, the spectator's gaze is far freer than the moviegoer's.

Certainly theater viewing is not entirely unlike cinematic viewing. Indeed, from Renaissance perspectivalism to fourth-wall naturalism, theater has influenced the cinematic apparatus – and, in turn, been influenced by it. Yet (like some experimental film) theater contains, and frequently employs, the means to disrupt the uniocularism it might simultaneously encourage. How, for instance, can the male gaze be understood as having anything to do with an outdoor theater seating 14,000 spectators, where male actors play both male and female characters, in amplified masks and cothurni, and declaim verse in a highly presentational style? Or in a walled, open-roofed theater with a huge thrust stage, where adolescent boys play women, and frequently comment on that fact? Or in the epic theater, where the actor seeks to draw attention to the very distinction between herself and her character which, if she were in a play by, say, Marsha Norman, she would seek to overcome? Do such plays participate in the "technology of gender" in patriarchal cultures? Do they represent male ideas of women? Do their plots often relegate women characters to traditional roles? Of course. But the fact that they can *prohibit* the cinematic male gaze through self-conscious theatricality enables them, at the same time, to undermine the rigidity and stability of gender. As Kristina Straub has written, in a discussion of Charlotte Charke, the commodification of cross-dressed women on the late seventeenth-century English stage "cannot be reduced to the specularization of women within the structuring principle of the masculine observer and the feminine spectacle, an epistemological and psychological principle which may have been only emergent at this moment in history." Rather, "the cross-dressed actress is less a confirmation than a challenge to modern assumptions about the gendering of spectacle."[40] I would extend her observation beyond seventeenth-century plays with cross-dressed heroines to any plays in which stage conventions and theater-like social conventions are compared.

ABOVE THE STREAM: SPECTATING AND CRITICAL CONSCIOUSNESS

To develop a more wide-ranging understanding of gender and spectacle, the gaze to begin with, then, is the one Mikel Dufrenne refers to in *The Phenomenology of Aesthetic Experience*, when he describes the special perceptual attitude that turns the "work of art" into the "aesthetic object." He writes, "What the artist has created is not yet completely the aesthetic object but only the means for that object to exist whenever the sensuous is recognized as such by the proper gaze."[41] With that gaze, the spectator completes the play by perceiving it in a particular way, by engaging it in a special, conscious manner. It's my contention that how that engagement is evoked, directed, left free to wander, and, especially, asked to engage itself, determines the gender critique a play might make. Put bluntly, a play's feminist meaning is to be found not in what happens to a character, but in what happens to the audience.

I'm aware of the snags of such a claim: there's no universal spectator, nor even a universal feminist spectator. And there's no way to know, in a sociological sense, how any individual audience member, or an audience at large, reacts to a play, especially one produced in another era. But my aim is not primarily sociological. And in any case, *all* critical writing about theater (including feminist writing[42]) makes assumptions about the audience's response – we couldn't talk about plays if we didn't. Concepts like suspense or the comic rest on ideas of audience reaction. Obviously they rely on cultural assumptions – and often some audience members will resist them. There's plenty of misogynist comedy, for example, that makes me squirm in my seat while all around me roar with laughter, an experience Jill Dolan captures and analyzes well in *The Feminist Spectator as Critic*. Nonetheless, the feminist critic still recognizes the way the comedy works on a non-resistant audience;

indeed, that is precisely what she seeks to describe. In other words, a feminist, more phenomenological theater criticism doesn't assume that every single spectator has the same experience, or interprets her/his experience in precisely the same way. Rather, it looks at how performance produces itself in the temporal event of theater, all the while instructing its audience in a means of regarding it.

That doesn't mean that the spectator must follow the instructions. The critically unconscious spectator may be incapable, unable to "suspend disbelief" because social prejudices overpower the aesthetic frame of the event. On the other hand, the critically conscious spectator may *deliberately* oppose the instructions. In both cases, the representation of gender is a likely factor.

In New York in 1993, I actually witnessed a case of the old saw about the man rushing onto the stage to save Desdemona – or at least a case like it. The oft-told Desdemona story, even if apocryphal, reveals how social attitudes about race and gender inhibit a white man from sustaining an aesthetic attitude. At a women's bodybuilding show called *The Most Awesome Female Muscle in the World*, it was the staged flouting of gender laws that finally busted one muscleman's "proper gaze," leaving him as taken in by a false but familiar feminine image as was the Scythian guard in *Thesmophoriazusae*.

Equal parts carnival, sport, performance art, and follies, the one-night extravaganza set out, according to producer Laurie Fierstein, to "celebrate women's power. It's a format where women can display their strength without being objectified,"[43] where they can flex and pose without having to play to the male judges of traditional bodybuilding competitions. Those sports events seem to be a venue for valuing female strength, Fierstein says, but they end up replicating the general cultural imperative that women look a certain male-sanctioned way. Even in the pumped up precincts of bodybuilding the prejudice prevails: women can get *too* muscular. Often judges favor the fit, kittenish look – the 1992 national Schwarzenegger Classic title went to a woman who was 5–7 and weighed 123 pounds.

Fierstein's basic point was that "a woman's body should be whatever *she* wants it to be," and she invited women to create their own vignettes to display themselves in whatever terms they wished. (The idea that women *could* control their own display was a radical assumption of Fierstein's experiment.) One performer, Nicole Bass, decided to play out a rescue fantasy. The curtain rose on an adolescent girl positioned under a big, silly, papier mâché rock, and the girl started screaming for help. Our hero, 6–2 and 204 pounds, sinews glistening under her satin cape, was to sweep in, toss the rock aside, sling the girl onto her shoulder, and whisk off. Just before Bass entered, a beefy man in the audience started down the aisle, muttering about the girl needing help, and was almost up the stairs to the stage when a couple of ushers guided him back to his seat. Despite a roomful of women with bulging biceps, despite a hoaky theatrical frame, he could not enter into a "fiction" that posited him as superfluous. He refused the perceptual terms of the performance to retain his social role.

A different dynamic operates when, on the other hand, the spectator consciously rejects the terms of a performance. Rather than being prevented by ideology from adopting the aesthetic attitude, she recognizes – and takes issue with – the ideological implications of the aesthetic object. Feminists in literature have for decades now recommended "reading against the grain" to expose the centrality of male experience and the masculinist (and heterosexist) assumptions of the traditional canon; Judith Fetterly introduced a much-adopted term in 1978 when she urged the feminist critic "to become a resisting reader rather than an assenting reader."[44]

In theater, too, feminist critics have taken up the call for resistance, also to encourage much-needed acknowledgement of the narrowness that has passed for "universalism" in the canon. But more than that, because the feminist attitude is essentially a critical consciousness, a way of seeing that gender (and other) orders are not natural or absolute, it has much in common with the particular aesthetic attitude demanded by theater. Theater that periodically catapults spectators out of the world of the play and into the world of the theater encourages them, in Brecht's parallel phrase, to think "above the stream."[45]

Thinking against the grain or above the stream is endemic to theater precisely because theater depends on a kind of double vision. We see two things at once – the actor and the character, the setting and the scenery, and so on. It's Wittgenstein's old duck/rabbit trick: the drawing that looks both like a duck and like a rabbit invokes a perceptual engagement he called "seeing-as."[46] We see something as something other than what we know it to be – or, as something *more* than what we know it to be. Such double vision is essential to theater viewing – as several centuries of vain efforts to overcome it attests.

Wittgenstein's definition of "seeing-as" doesn't entirely fit the experience of theater viewing. In his example, one is incapable of seeing the figure simultaneously as both a duck and a rabbit, but rather, switches back and forth between the two perceptions while maintaining an awareness of the potential duck lurking within the apparent rabbit, and vice versa. In theater, on the other hand, we can see both (or more) layers of fiction and reality at the same time. What's important about the comparison, though, is Wittgenstein's observation that "seeing-as" is "subject to the will. There is such an order as 'imagine *this*' and also 'Now see the figure like *this*' but not 'Now see this leaf green.'"[47]

Still, as modern painting has vibrantly demonstrated, the aesthetic frame does, in fact, allow us to see this leaf green – or purple or blue as the case may be. In theater, especially, where everything is a sign and reality is always contingent, the imperative to "imagine *this*" can be subjected to further self-examination. To imagine, say, this young man as Hamlet requires the same act of the will as to imagine that young man as Ophelia. What's more, to register that fact is to catch ourselves in the act of imagining, and to recognize an analogy between performance and gender.

There's an affinity between the double vision ignited by "seeing-as" and the critical consciousness of feminism (or other exogenous stances, like DuBois's "double consciousness" experienced by African Americans, or the "camp sensibility" celebrated in queer culture). For instance, an undergraduate textbook called *Feminist Frontiers III* uses the idea of "double vision" to explain a feminist perspective: "Women's lives are seen simultaneously through the old lens of patriarchy and the new lens of feminism."[48] The cultural critic Ann Powers elaborates: "[Feminists'] awareness decenters them, lifts them out of the place of 'woman' in society; but the fact that they still operate in and through society means they don't settle anywhere else."[49]

In other words, it's not just that there's something performance-like about femininity. At the same time, the double vision that enables us to recognize – and inhabit – that quality of gender is analogous to the double vision evoked by self-conscious theater.

I am not drawing a simple one-to-one correspondence between gender and theater. Indeed, I'm challenging the current trend for asserting that "gender is merely performance," first of all by pointing out that there's nothing *mere* about performance – it's an intricate, complex, and elaborate practice that produces different meanings and effects depending on its particular form and context. (For example, despite Garber's all-encompassing claims, a drag queen carries different significance when framed within a naturalistic play from when parading in a gay pride march, or camping in an after-hours club, or mincing on a TV sitcom: Ru Paul does not equal an Elizabethan boy-actress, neither equals the transvestite prostitutes cruising half-a-dozen blocks from where I sit, none of them equals Milton Berle in a dress, and so on.)

Still, plays that place issues of representation at the forefront – often by putting a character in cross-dressed disguise – remind us of the disarming possibility that our own guarded identities, even those that feel as intimate as skin, must be aggressively and institutionally enforced if they are to be sustained. Thus, through their mimetic apparatus, such plays denaturalize gender even as they may narratively represent patriarchal images of femininity and masculinity.

In the essays that follow, I hope to examine the first half of this contradictory dialectic. I don't reject the second half – but over the last fifteen years, it has been amply addressed. So without necessarily denying how certain narratives reinscribe sexual difference, I try to focus on the disruptions that, at the same time, threaten to obliterate it.

I turn first to three canonical playwrights to look at the self-consciousness of their theatrical styles and ask whether their own stagings of gender performance may disrupt these naturalized categories of identity. (Other categories such as race and class are also at times presentationally performed, and may also be destabilized in the process, but it's gender that is most implicated and undone by theatrical mimesis.) Using close reading and performance criticism, I start with Shakespeare's *As You Like It*, asking how cross-dressed boy-actresses, frequently commenting on their double disguises, raise the possibility – as anti-theatrical railers warned – of "adulterating" gender.[50] Next I turn to Ibsen, whose realism has long been used to dismiss feminist readings of his plays – and vice versa. I suggest that Ibsen frequently points to the devices of this dramatic style in *A Doll House* and *Hedda Gabler*, linking that system of representation to the artificiality of women's roles. Finally in this section, I reread Brecht's *Good Person of Szechwan*, to suggest that gender – especially in this play with a cross-dressed hero – is one of the social conventions made strange by epic style.

I begin with these dramas not in spite of their classical status, but because of it. These familiar plays have been largely rejected by feminist theater critics; I think it's time to look at them again. Numerous other plays by dead white men would have served as well: plays by Calderón, Marivaux, Molière, Genet, and others draw the analogy between the social convention of gender and the aesthetic convention of theatrical illusion. But those I've chosen are more frequently studied and (with the exception of Brecht) most frequently produced in the US.

In the second section, I look at contemporary productions of canonical plays that take some feminist, queer, or postmodern principles of identity and gender for granted, and reread them, through performance, back into classic texts. I consider three canonical crossings with different aims, approaches, ideologies: the Mabou Mines production of *Lear* in which the genders of all the characters were reversed, Charles Ludlam's performance as Hedda Gabler at the American Ibsen Theater in 1984, and the Split Britches-Bloolips deconstruction of *A Streetcar Named Desire*.

These two sections are connected – or perhaps, divided – by an essay on turn-of-the-century Yiddish theater and other instances of Jewish performance. It asks: if some canonical plays can, through their questioning of theater's representational strategies, raise questions about social conventions of gender, and if some contemporary productions can read these questions back into canonical plays by pointing up themes relating to the representation of gender, what might a theater, produced by a subculture that was regarded by the dominant culture as feminized and foreign, and that operated both against and within the Western canon, reveal about performance and gender (and their relationship to racial construction) both on and off stage?

So, like a Yiddish stage star interrupting the action of a play to deliver a show-stopping monologue, I insert this discussion of the Yiddish stage *mitn dirinen* to shift the focus, skew the angle, queer the questions. Thus, this interlude doesn't provide a logical stepping-stone from the first section of the book to the chapter of contemporary performance criticism, but jarringly joins them, to borrow the phrase of the late eighteenth-century Hasidic leader Rabbi Nachman of Bratslav, by a narrow bridge.

Finally, I offer an epilogue, "Notes on Butch" (originally delivered as a talk), that contemplates butchness as an epic performance of gender.

As this outline suggests, these essays orbit around issues of gender, representation, metatheater, performance, and sexuality rather than proving, by incremental demonstration, a thesis. To assert a grand theory and then attempt to demonstrate it across centuries and cultures, requires sweeping, totalizing generalizations that my grounding in cultural materialism militates against. Instead, I begin with the vexing questions articulated here – questions raised as far back as Aristophanes – and with them, interrogate a series of texts and performances.

As an unreconstructed Brechtian, I am firmly convinced that self-conscious theater can reveal the artificiality of gender, but I certainly can't leap from there to the faith that theater will bring down the patriarchy, any more than Brecht expected epic theater to dismantle capitalism. But I do think that Brecht was right about theater's capacity to teach us a way to see critically, and to apply that critical consciousness to the world.

The all-important question, which Judith Butler raises in *Bodies That Matter*, is "whether the denaturalization of gender norms is the same as their subversion."[51] As she points out, some parodies of gender (such as misogynistic drag shows) may denaturalize the category's norms, but never call them into question. The issue, then, is whether the parody – or any other sort of metatheatrical gender display – effects, through its performance style, the double vision of critical consciousness, that is, the means by which subversion can at least be imagined. It's one thing to recognize that there are theater-like aspects of masculinity. It's another to feel authorized to assume the strength and self-sovereignty masculinity claims.

One anecdote making the rounds of the women's self-defense community painfully suggests that knowing that gender is theater-like has little bearing on one's ability to flout its rigid rules. The martial arts instructor Nancy Lanoue told me about a student who enrolled in a self-defense course taught by Lanoue's colleague[52] and insisted that she'd signed up just for the hell of it, for she had never experienced any threatening situation in which she thought self-defense techniques might have been helpful. After hearing some of the tales told by other students, this woman allowed how "there was this one time," and went on to describe an encounter she'd had with a man she saw daily at her local bus stop. They greeted each other for months, so by the time he invited her to have coffee with him one afternoon, she didn't regard him as a stranger.

As they sat in a cafe, she told the class, she felt his hand creep onto her thigh. She squirmed a bit, but the man did not relent. Feeling more and more uncomfortable as the man's gropes intensified, she cleared her throat and widened her eyes imploringly at the man at the next table, in a vain effort to get his attention. "What did you want that man at the next table to do?" the self-defense instructor asked. "I wanted him to say," she replied – and here she thrust out her chest, stood tall, and dropped her voice into its deepest register – "'TAKE YOUR HANDS OFF THAT WOMAN!'"

1   Much virtue in if

Shakespeare's cross-dressed boy-actresses and the non-illusory stage

When Rosalind lifts her wedding veil to tie up all the romantic loose ends of *As You Like It* by revealing that she is really a girl, her father and her betrothed respond in astonished joy: "If there be truth in sight," exclaims the duke, "you are my daughter." "If there be truth in sight," echoes Orlando, "you are my Rosalind." And Phebe, granting "If shape and sight be true," concludes, "Why then my love adieu" (V, iv, 117–120).[1]

But as the play has amply and antically demonstrated, those are pretty big *If*s. Sight and shape be *not* true, especially in matters of love – both erotic and filial. In the forest of Arden, the girl Rosalind becomes the boy Ganymede, romantic tutor to Orlando and unwitting heart-throb to Phebe. In the court, greed perverts brotherly affection, translating devotion into treason.

And yet the theater, where sight and shape are most false, has the power to reveal what's most true. In love, like in theater, sight and shape – how we look at things, how they appear – are as much a function of the excited imagination as of any material fact. A girl masquerading as a boy pretending to be a girl turns out to be, according to ever self-conscious early modern stage conventions, a boy. Orlando might be marrying someone in a dress in the quadruple wedding finale, but he has learned, as we have, that a dress is just a costume, and anybody can wear it.

That, at least, is what director Declan Donnellan brought out in his all-male production of *As You Like It* with London's Cheek by Jowl Company (which toured to New York in 1991 and 1994.) In that final scene, Rosalind lifts her veil and Orlando reels when he looks at her face and sees Ganymede, shocked with the fact of gender's artificiality. He then paces halfway around the stage, his mouth agape in disbelief – and delight. Finally, he circles back to sweep her (him) into his arms.

By far the clearest, most crisp, and sexiest *As You Like It* I've ever

Plate 1 Celia (Simon Coates) and Ganymede (Adrian Lester) in Cheek by Jowl's *As You Like It*, Brooklyn Academy of Music, 1994. Photo by Dan Rest.

seen, the production dives headlong into the play's sing-along metaphor – "All the world's a stage." Jacques recites the famous line at the beginning of the play as the actors – all in black pants, suspenders, and white shirts – take their places (and he repeats the line later in its appointed place). This little prologue may unnecessarily trumpet the play's reveries and revelries on role-playing, but it sets the terms of Donnellan's theatricalized Arden, where, as Touchstone remarks, there is "much virtue in If" (V, iv, 102).

Such virtue is made most potent in this production precisely because all the parts are played by men. Donnellan seeks neither to hide this fact in the guise of "meaningless" convention, nor to trivialize it with campy elbow jabs and winks.[2] Most important, Donnellan and his fourteen athletic actors romp joyfully on the play's rampant homoeroticism.

Rosalind (played by lovely Adrian Lester) sends sparks flying when s/he leans against Celia's shoulder, or, as Ganymede, conversing with Jacques, deliciously lays a hand on his eager arm. And in scenes with Orlando, whether dressed as girl or boy, passion is palpable – ever more so because whether Lester is dressed as girl or boy matters so little.

The production sweeps along on the erotic exuberance of this perfect androgyne. Actors' exits overlap others' entrances across the bare stage, as if the entire company just can't wait to get to the consummating end. Music fuels this driving motion. The songs (there are more than in any other Shakespeare play) issue organically from Arden, where courtly constraints of all kinds are banished, and *a capella* harmonies from a quartet of men twine through deepest bass to angelic falsetto. Even Jacques' departure from the final revelry is turned around in this lusty production; he and the singer Amiens make a fifth couple.

The celebration takes on both depth and dubiousness because Donnellan sets up a formal, architectural stage picture, with all the couples lined up in an eager row, Hymen on an upstage platform, and then Rosalind revealed down center; then he lets it all collapse into anarchy, with actors dancing and then taking turns playing accompanying music on horns; winding sinuously around the stage in an Argentine tango, dancers trade roles as leaders and followers. (Throughout the play Donnellan establishes beautiful, symmetrical stage pictures, and then explodes them, a visual device that comments upon the play's comic artificiality.) In addition, this ending feels both celebratory and cautionary because Donnellan and company play the first half of *As You Like It* at full emotional tilt. Often, Acts I and II are rushed through, treated as so much dull but necessary exposition that sets up those cute wooing scenes in Arden. But here, the brawling between Orlando and Oliver is dangerous, and the wrestling match with

Charles is downright menacing, the men of the court circling around the fighters and whooping like frat boys. Orlando finishes Charles off with a series of kicks to his groin, and comes out of the bout panting and scared. Similarly, Rosalind reacts to the order of banishment with shock and dismay, crying and barely able to sputter out her rebuke to her uncle. Bringing out the darkness of these scenes, the all-male cast highlights the viciousness of a masculinist vision of social order.

But the most startling aspect of the production is Rosalind/ Ganymede's epilogue, a speech much commented upon in the recent surge of Shakespeare criticism that focuses on issues of gender and sexuality.[3] Stepping out of the celebratory dance, Rosalind addresses the audience:

> It is not the fashion to see the lady the epilogue; but it is no more unhandsome than to see the lord the prologue. If it be true that good wine needs no bush, 'tis true that a good play needs no epilogue. Yet to good wine they do use good bushes; and good plays prove the better by the help of good epilogues. What a case am I in then, that am neither a good epilogue, nor cannot insinuate with you in the behalf of a good play? I am not furnished like a beggar, therefore to beg will not become me. My way is to conjure you, and I'll begin with the women. I charge you, O women, for the love you bear to men, to like as much of this play as please you. And I charge you, O men, for the love you bear to women – as I perceive by your simpering none of you hates them – that between you and the women the play may please. If I were a woman, I would kiss as many of you as had beards that pleased me, complexions that liked me, and breaths that I defied not. And I am sure, as many as have good beards, or good faces, or sweet breaths, will for my kind offer, when I make curtsy, bid me farewell.
>
> (V, iv, 198–220)

It's the epilogue's last six lines that have provoked the most critical scrutiny in recent years, and for good reason. Echoing the denouement in which Rosalind reveals herself as a woman, the performer now reveals himself as a boy. Echoing the play's frequent sojourns on an If, once again a conditional statement – "If I were a woman" – allows us to follow through to a pleasing, playful conclusion. The remark spirals back into the play's conflation of gender and performance, pointing, as Joel Fineman has written, "to the play's last disguise and to the conditional that is the premise of the play itself."[4] Of course, the conditional is the premise of *any* play – and, as Jacques reminds us, of all the world as well. (Much virtue in If, indeed.)

This final unmasking also troubles the resolution of Rosalind's marriage. Preventing the nuptials from having the last word, the epilogue calls into question the presumed naturalness of the orderly heterosexual pairings and the tidy restoration of courtly order for all "According to the measure of their states" (Duke Sen. V, iv, 174). (Donnellan's addition of Jacques and Amiens underlines this disruption. As he told me in an interview, "You tend to see the four happy couples at the end as incipient nuclear families and nuclear families have been capitalized into some repressive idea of basic virtue. It seemed only morally decent to put Jacques there to raise some questions."[5])

The epilogue takes this disturbance of order another step, as it reminds the audience of the histrionic elements of love. The boy-actress speaking is not a beggar only because, led in by Hymen in wedding finery, he is not "furnished" as one. His way – because he is an *actor* – is to conjure, that is, to put notions in our heads, to persuade us, for a couple of hours anyway, that sight and shape be true, or at least true enough.

What's more, the boy-actress's own gender ambiguity is projected onto the audience, reopening, in the last moments, the play's many erotic permutations. "I would kiss as many of you as had beards that pleased me, complexions that liked me, and breaths that I defied not" is traditionally and most obviously understood to mean, "If I were a woman, I would kiss the men I found appealing." But the gender of the recipients of those kisses is not actually named, and those beards have a bawdy female resonance, too – underscored by the Petrarchan references to sweet breaths and lovely complexions. Thus we have a boy – still in a wedding dress – also telling us that if he were a woman, he'd have sex with women.

This makes the actor's charge to the women all the more ironic, as women are asked "for the love you bear to men" to like the play just as much as you like it. In other words, the love women bear to men is to have *no* bearing on their love of the play. As far as the men are concerned, for their love of women, they are asked merely that the play find some pleasing position *between* men and women. There's ambiguity in that "between," too. Not only does the epilogue suggest that because men love women, the play should please both of them, in addition, the actor offers the play both as a mediator between men and women, and as an event that separates them from each other. It may even suggest that there is some territory, neither male nor female, *between* men and women, some non- or anti-gendered space that the boy-actress both occupies and signifies. Thus in these last forty lines, the play's pretty endings come unglued, heterosexual closure is rendered suspect, and erotic options become diffuse again, even extending to the audience.

Most of these polymorphous possibilities are lost in contemporary productions where a woman plays Rosalind. Frequently the epilogue is cut out entirely, or the line "If I were a woman" is changed to "As I am a woman," closing off the sexual ambiguities that vibrate between the boy-in-a-dress and those he addresses. At the Cheek by Jowl production, on the other hand, I experienced the epilogue with a heightened, almost giddy, awareness of gender's provisionality.

What made this effect most startling was that the basic *gestus* (to borrow Brecht's term) of Adrian Lester's delivery was similar to that of the many female Rosalind's I've seen: he was flirting with men in the audience. Though the text names women (a radical recognition in Shakespeare's time of the recent, controversial admission of middle-class ladies into the playhouse), and the bawdy references were plain, I felt that he wasn't really talking to me. As appealing as I found Lester to be, I existed outside this particular erotic exchange between actor and spectator. Along with Arden's intensely homosocial world, the play's homoeroticism remained – despite Phebe's infatuation with Ganymede and Celia's blatant love for Rosalind – fulsomely male; it didn't assume me as a player in its sport. And because I never thought of Lester's Rosalind (nor Celia, Phebe, and Audrey) as a woman – but always as a "woman" – the play's heterosexuality was as artificial as a Petrarchan poem, an imposed structure, its compulsoriness made to be broken, honored, as it were, only in the breeches.

This is not meant as a negative criticism – most *As You Like It*s I've seen have no sexual charge at all. (And besides, it is the men to whom the epilogue finally appeals.) Rather, my response raised heady questions about spectatorship, sexuality, and gender. Watching Lester deliver the epilogue, I was reminded of contemporary gay male performers – Tim Miller, Jeff Weiss – whose work often seems pitched to a gay male spectator, but that still reaches me with a taboo-smashing promise of erotic variety and sexual adventure. Conversely, I thought of productions at New York's lesbian theater, the WOW Cafe, where a lesbian spectator is constructed because she is assumed. (Of course I don't mean that there is any such thing as *the* gay male or *the* lesbian spectator; rather, that the works I have in mind take same-sex desire as a given, not as something to be explained, apologized for, or agonized over.) Like some of these works, Donnellan's *As You Like It* felt exhilarating, even liberating, despite my exclusion from one of its most high-voltage currents.

The reason, I believe, extends beyond the all-male cast, to the production's bare-stage, fast-paced, non-illusory style – which, of course, is intricately connected to the all-male cast. It didn't much matter that Lester's lust wasn't aimed directly at me because its eroticism was less a function of representing male homosexual and homosocial desire than of the demands made on the spectator's active and conscious imagination, and further, of the self-conscious display of the imagination as necessary to the construction of character and dramatic event. In short, the production recognized, displayed, and celebrated theater itself as seduction. Setting up an analogy between the as-if convention of theatrical roles, and the as-if convention of social roles, it aroused the possibility of breaking through ordinary, often constraining, categories of identity, even categories as intimate and naturalized as sexuality and gender.

Obviously I don't want to claim that what I experienced in Stonybrook, New York in 1991 (and again in Brooklyn in 1994) must be the same thing that spectators experienced at the newly opened Globe some 400 years earlier. But I do agree with Jonathan Dollimore that some of our postmodern preoccupations with the instability of identity represent new variations on "what the early modern period knew but in a quite different form: identity is *essentially* informed by what it is not."[6] And Barbara Freedman makes a compelling case for the way "both Renaissance and postmodern models of representation undermine the humanist impulse to 'stand / As if a man were author of himself' (*Coriolanus* V, iii, 35–36)."[7]

Perhaps, then, looking at this recent all-male *As You Like It* and the conundrums it raises around sexuality, gender, and representation might reveal something about how transvestism on the Renaissance stage, as Susan Zimmerman puts it, unleashes "an erotic dynamics that deconstructs gender itself, leaving conventional categories of sexuality blurred, confused – or absent."[8] Or at least, it might reveal something about how such dynamics are unleashed in the postmodern theater when a contemporary company queers a canonical play by reviving a sexist old stage practice.

In the last decade or so, there has been an explosion of scholarship investigating the representation of gender on the early modern stage, the role of the boy-actress, and the relationship of a cross-dressed theater practice to a world undergoing rapid and profound social change. Feminists, new historicists, cultural materialists and queer theorists have pulled Shakespeare and his contemporaries out of a modernist, universalist stratosphere, and reread their plays in the light of contemporary attitudes toward women and sexuality, and in the context of a stage practice repeatedly railed at for its threat of disrupting religious, class, and gender hierarchies. Certainly, there is much disputing among these critics, but they share an important corrective impulse to demystify and demythologize, to restore plays to their place in a culturally and politically specific moment, to return them, that is, to the theater, a public site of immediate social interaction and reaction.

The popular stage, banished along with other perverse practices to the "liberties" outside of London, occupied a liminal (and to some, criminal) space between carnival and court, between the elite world of literary text and the street world of punishing ritual performances like the skimmington and charivari, in which gender transgressors (adulterous or domineering wives, cuckolded or wimpy husbands) were displayed for public ridicule. The theater's in-between, fringe status is self-consciously echoed in so many Shakespeare comedies where fecund realms outside the city limits provide the space for new erotic tingles – and tangles.

In anti-theatricalist diatribes, the playhouse itself was figured as a kind of Illyria, den of illusion and romantic delirium, of deception and degeneracy – both because the mere act of spectating was considered sexually dangerous, and because the theaters were situated where, it was whispered, sexuality ran amok. Here, as Puritans frantically warned, women ventured out in public where they could be the whore-like objects of men's gaze – and more subversively, as Jean Howard has suggested,[9] could themselves take up the role of spectator. Here, she adds, social hierarchy was displayed in the seating arrangement, for the first time determined by what was in one's pocket, not by what coursed in one's veins. And here, most alarming to Phillip Stubbes and his ilk, boys masqueraded as women, a practice, he cautioned, that threatened to "adulterate" gender altogether. How could social mobility be held at bay when the public saw commoners play kings? How could sex roles stay within their Levitical limits when female characters defied fathers, pursued lovers, and generally trounced around by themselves? And how could gender be accepted as an intransmutable, God-given set of distinct qualities when boys played women – and men wooed them?

In sum, this was an arena where rigid role definitions discandied, on stage and off, reflecting – and stirring – the anxiety of an age when social mobility reared up from an emerging market economy.[10] Within this political, cultural, and economic mutation toward "the modern," many critics have noted, gender relations were transformed too. As always, those with the most to lose – landed men – sought to stave off such developments, often targeting women and their increasing (though still severely limited) freedom, as the touchstone for all that threatened the status quo. (It's no accident, notes David Underdown, that this was the period of the most virulent witchhunts.[11])

Much of the controversy was played out over clothing. As Puritans crusaded to shore up collapsing sumptuary codes (primarily as they regulated the display of wealth and rank), gender roles were fiercely debated, the proper comportment of wives and young ladies pronounced and contested in an increasingly vituperative series of pamphlets.[12] Some critics point to the Galenic model of sexuality current at the time, which posed that there was one sex, the adult male, and that women (and, in another way, boys) were partially cooked or inverted versions of his biological completeness. This unisex biological model provided justifications for strict social divisions between men and women, though – or precisely because – that distinction seemed to be in an unsettling state of flux. In 1547 William Harrison complained "that with ear-ringed men and doubletted women," he couldn't tell one sex from the other.[13]

Cross-dressing was a burgeoning fad in this period, especially among women, and as Ania Loomba suggests, the fad was bound up with theater: in the early modern period, "female cross-dressing functions as a version of theatricality that extends disguise from the playhouse to the social space . . . [while] the public controversy over gender roles was becoming increasingly theatricalized."[14] After all, banished from the stage, women who wanted to act – and act up – had to make the streets their platform. Indeed, the controversy was as much about women claiming a place in the public sphere as about their attire.

Though the virgin queen herself had once asserted, "I know I have the body but of a weak and feeble woman, but I have the heart and stomach of a king, and a king of England too,"[15] she issued countless proclamations enforcing the dress codes that made the social hierarchy legible. Under James, many of these sumptuary laws were repealed; nonetheless, in 1620 he sought an end to ever more popular gender insubordination among women, instructing London's clergy to "inveigh vehemently and bitterly in theyre sermons, against the insolencie of our women, and theyre wearing of brode brimd hats, pointed doublets, theyre haire cut short or shorn."[16] The king's command was soon defended in the quasi-literary form of the pamphlet: *Hic Mulier; or, the Man-Woman* warned that by donning male attire a woman unacceptably signalled her sexual availability. A week later, in dialogue form, *Haec-Vir; or, the Womanish Man: Being an Answere to the late Booke intituled Hic-Mulier*, rebutted that rejection of cross-dressing.[17]

It's difficult – maybe impossible – to draw any one-to-one correspondences between the theatricalized display and disruption of gender categories in the streets, and plays (especially in the Jacobean period) that made such display and disruption their theme. What does seem clear, at least, is that for decades before this culminating debate over cross-dressing the stage reflected and egged on anxieties over the stability of categories like gender and social status, simply by virtue of having a non-illusory, transvestic style. While the controversy over women in broad-brimmed hats was played out in pamphlets, sermons, and speeches, in the theater, it was the cross-dressed boy-actress who provided continual fodder for Puritanical frothing. One of the most panicked claims of the anti-theatricalists was that, because of their costumes, boy-actresses would *become* women – both in the eyes of their beholders, who would be aroused into sodomy, and in some more profound, externally rendered, internal way. In *The Overthrow of Stage-Playes* (1599), John Rainolds warns:

> the apparell of wemen . . . is a great provocation of men to lust and leacherie: because a womans garment being put on a man doeth vehemently touch and move him with the remembrance and imagination of a woman: and the imagination of a thing desirable doth stirr up the desire.[18]

Going further, in *Histrio-mastix* (1633) William Prynne asserts that boy-actresses "metamorphosed into women on the Stage."[19] (This anxiety persisted into our own century. Before Yale University went co-ed, its undergraduate drama club enforced a rule against boys playing women's roles more than twice in a row.[20])

Shakespeare's plays, especially, take on such vexations as self-conscious subjects, raising relentless self-referential questions about representation, role definition, and social hierarchy. With Falstaff impersonating the king, Portia masquerading as a lawyer, Sir Toby capering like a gentleman – to name only a few of the legion instances – Shakespeare repeatedly draws an analogy between the actor's art and the transgression of social boundaries. But whether his theater gave license to, or ultimately vitiated rebellious energies is a matter of much debate, especially when it comes to women.

As feminist critics have pointed out, the comedies often engage the popular controversy over women, referring explicitly to contemporary sermons and marriage handbooks that counseled women to stay indoors and to abide by the dictates of their husbands or fathers, and to the arguments battled out in the pamphlets.[21] For instance, Viola/Cesario and Orsino echo the debate familiar to theater-goers from contemporary treatises when Orsino avers that no woman "Can bide the beating of so strong a passion / As love doth give my heart; no woman's heart / So big to hold so much; they lack retention" (II, iv, 95–97). And in the debate as presented in *Twelfth Night*, anyway, Viola/Cesario clearly wins – largely because the staged action, more than Viola/Cesario's remarks, contradicts the duke's self-loving claims. In *As You Like It*, Rosalind/Ganymede practically quotes from a misogynistic pamphlet on the inconstancy of women: "Make the doors upon a woman's wit, and it will out at the casement; shut that, and 'twill out at the keyhole; stop that, 'twill fly with the smoke out at the chimney . . . O that woman that cannot make her fault her husband's occasion, let her never nurse her child herself, for she will breed it like a fool" (IV, i, 152–167). Here, of course, the remarks are satirically distanced, both because Rosalind/Ganymede is patently plying this argument against Orlando's peachy Petrarchan views, and by the quadruple irony that he is a boy playing a girl disguised as a boy impersonating a girl: whose side is s/he really on? That is the question – and the question is the point.

Despite the comedies' conscious engagement of contemporary debates about women, and despite female characters' frequent flouting of the rules laid down in marriage manuals, some critics argue (offering tamed Katherine as the most pathetic example) that Shakespeare's tales of gallivanting heroines fortify gender divisions in the end, retrieving upstart women into a suffocating patriarchal embrace in their fifth-act resolutions, countermanding and foreclosing any promise of liberation that the cross-dressing narratives may have offered. The "patriarchal bard,"[22] they contend, lets steam out of the pressure cooker but never dares to open the lid. Their conclusions, however, rely on the dynamics of gender display on the page, not on the stage.

These critics often point to the moments when female characters dressed as boys refer to "how much [they] lack of a man" as Viola does (III, iv, 308), or to moments when feminine behavior uncontrollably leaks through their male disguise, such as when Rosalind/Ganymede swoons at the sight of blood. But surely seeing boys in these roles – dressed as boys – deconstructs gender essentialism rather than reinforces it, by alienating it. After all, in an all-male production of *As You Like It*, the first time we see Ganymede, we don't see a pert female ingenue swaggering around adorably in a pair of breeches – the image typically offered on the contemporary American stage. Rather, we see an *un*disguised boy. The exaggerated descriptions of Ganymede's underlying femininity – "I could find in my heart to disgrace my man's apparel and to cry like a woman. But I must comfort the weaker vessel, as doublet and hose ought to show itself courageous to petticoat" (II, iv,

3–6) – are a necessary means of identifying the character and sparking the play's central irony. These lines and the vision we behold tell us: this is and is not Rosalind. Indeed, Ganymede's swoon is critically distanced by Rosalind/Ganymede's thrice uttered excuse: "this was well-counterfeited" (IV, iii, 167). That not only sets up Oliver's ironic instruction that Ganymede "take good heart and counterfeit to be a man" – to which Ganymede replies, "And so I do" (IV, iii, 173–175). In addition, the entire exchange works as a comment on acting: swooning would have been among a boy-actress's best tricks.

The comedies constantly make the boy-actress visible as such, reminding the audience not only of the presumed gender disguise involved in all staged women, but specifically comparing the boy-actress's gender indeterminacy to his actual adolescence. In a much overlooked essay on the profession of the boy-actress in *Twelfth Night*, Matthew H. Wikander demonstrates how that play constantly comments on the performer playing Viola/Cesario as himself "in standing water, between boy and man" (I, v, 161). "The positive androgyny seen in Viola by feminist critics," Wikander writes, "the fluid adolescent sexuality seen by psychoanalytical critics, the marginal liminality seen by anthropological critics are all aspects of the real adolescent playing the role."[23] As their small-pipe voices began to crack, and their whiskers began to peep through their damask cheeks, these young actors stood on the verge of maturing into performers who could play adult male roles, or, perhaps, lose their livelihoods. Of course Viola/Cesario was "sick for a beard:" the boy's future in the theater depended on it.

When Ganymede offers to cure Orlando of his lovesickness by pretending to be his mistress, s/he explains:

> I, being but a moonish youth, grieve, be effeminate, changeable, longing and liking, proud, fantastical, apish, shallow, inconstant, full of tears, full of smiles for every passion something, and for no passion truly anything, as boys and women are for most part cattle of this color.
>
> (IV, iii, 397–403)

Boys and women, perhaps. But most of all, boys who *play* women. Ganymede has described the skills required of an apprentice who might someday grow into one of the King's Men.

Perhaps that's one reason the comedies with cross-dressed heroines interrogate masculinity just as vigorously as femininity. The very worry of the adrogynous adolescent boy-actress as he contemplates his future – poised, as Wikander notes, "at a critical moment in a professional progression from 'woman's part' to 'man's estate'"[24] – mirrors the cross-dressed heroine's concern that she be recognized as a man. At the intersection of this double-crossing – the boy as girl and, in turn, the girl as boy – *both* genders are revealed as actor-like constructions (though most recent arguments for the comedies' deconstruction of gender concentrate on their representation of women).

Comic hay may be made of Cesario or Ganymede's failure to sustain convincing performances as males – Viola/Cesario flees from dueling, Rosalind/Ganymede swoons at the bloody napkin – but their efforts, frequently compared to acting, display masculinity as a series of effects, ironized by the fact that they appear on the stage as undisguised youths, laboring to show themselves as men. Katherine Kelly is right that "In inviting his spectators to see in the breeches parts a microcosm of the actor's art, Shakespeare also invited them to view themselves as gendered subjects acting out a drama of sexual difference."[25] But more than that, in pointing to the boy-actresses in the breeches parts, at once masked and unmasked, Shakespeare presents the drama of sexual difference as a comedy of unstable roles – for women and men alike.

It's not only Ganymede who must learn to swagger with "a swashing and a martial outside" (I, iii, 116), nor only Cesario who must bear up and draw a sword. These cross-dressed heroines struggling to demonstrate their masculinity are juxtaposed against male characters played by grown men, who must also learn to act like men. In addition to deconstructing femininity, *As You Like It* and *Twelfth Night* criticize the construction of manliness – and, especially, of *gentle*manliness.

Orlando's complaint against his brother isn't merely that Oliver has horded their joint inheritance, but that he has "trained me like a peasant, obscuring and hiding from me all gentleman-like qualities" (I, i, 67–68). In *Twelfth Night*'s heuristic subplot, Sir Aguecheek practices all the arts that men of his means are expected to master, and yet cannot be taken seriously as a gentleman; similarly, Malvolio strives for upward mobility by exaggerating his gentlemanly "virtues." In both plays, masculinity is bound up with class status; those who fail to persuade with courtly graces (Aguecheek, Malvolio) or who reject them (Jacques) are effeminated.

But this equation is repeatedly undermined by the actions juxtaposed against it. In *As You Like It*, machismo is revealed as so much posing – the martial outside something "many other mannish cowards have / That do outface it with their semblances," as Rosalind/Ganymede remarks (I, iii, 117–118). Charles the huge, mocking wrestler is outfoxed by the slender, tender Orlando; in the forest later on, Orlando self-consciously performs masculinity, admitting, "put I on the countenance of stern commandment" to get food (II, vii, 108–9) though, as Duke Senior tells him, "Your gentleness shall force, / More than your force move us to gentleness" (II, vii, 102–103). The contrast between force and gentleness – figured in the dichotomy between court and Arden – is extended further in Jacques' grief at the killing of animals, a grief associated with his scorn for showiness and insincerity, all of it adding up to a distaste for masculinist theatrics. In his description of the seven ages of man – set off by Orlando's martial display – Jacques paints a portrait that is entirely male, yet barely "mannish": only the "soldier, / Full of strange oaths, and bearded like the pard, / Jealous in honour, sudden and quick in quarrel, / Seeking the bubble reputation / Even in the cannon's mouth" (II, vii, 149–153) is "swashing" – and Jacques ridicules him for it. And the "justice, / In fair round belly, with good capon lin'd" is pedantic and trite. At the other stages, Jacques's man is mewling, whining, woeful, and emasculated by his "shrunk shank" and "big manly voice / Turning again toward childish treble," until finally he collapses into "second childishness and mere oblivion."

The famous speech bears quoting at length because it presents so severe a critique of manhood. Though the speech has traditionally been regarded as presenting a melancholic view of *human* progression (or degeneration), Jacques does not universalize his description into a general critique of the futility of human life. Rather, his portrait of human development is blatantly gendered, exposing notions of noble masculinity as a sham, much as Ganymede and Phebe satirize Petrarchan images of women. Phebe's hilarious demonstration that her eyes neither wound nor murder Silvius, and Ganymede's remark that "men have died from time to time and worms have eaten them, but not for love" (IV, i, 101–103) say as much about the histrionics of male wooing as about the artificial construction of an ideal female love-object.

In playing Rosalind for Orlando in the love cure, Jean Howard has argued, Ganymede:

> acts out the parts scripted for women by her culture, [thereby revealing] the constructed nature of patriarchy's representations of the feminine and shows a woman manipulating those representations in her own interest, theatricalizing for her own purposes what is assumed to be innate, teaching her future mate how to get beyond certain ideologies of gender to more enabling ones.[26]

But because the actress is a boy, sometimes invoking and sometimes blatantly throwing off the representations of the masculine scripted by his culture, that performance also reveals "male" behavior as a set of poses, gestures, and tropes. The first time Rosalind/Ganymede, Touchstone, and Celia/Aliena come upon Corin in Arden, for example, Ganymede faces a test: can s/he pass for male? It's a comically ironic challenge given that he *is* an undisguised male. In the Cheek by Jowl production, Lester clears his throat before speaking, trying to land his voice in a lower register – though it hadn't been in much of a high one to begin with. And in response to Corin's scornful glance at his feet, Ganymede slides them from a dainty closed stance into a wide, but still slightly demure posture. Such an action is common in productions with female actors playing Rosalind, but here, the move is alienated and funnier, revealing that masculinity is as consciously performed by Rosalind, as femininity is by Lester – and vice versa.

More than that, in exposing male courting as a series of performance conventions, Rosalind/Ganymede draws attention to the self-conscious self-display that Touchstone, Silvius, Oliver, and Orlando take on, too, when they set to wooing.

Indeed, in *As You Like It* (and in *Twelfth Night*) male lovers are likened to women because they are *acting* – though Ganymede accuses Orlando of not acting well because he is "point device in [his] accoutrements." The bloody napkin that excuses Orlando's absence a scene later, and indicates both his bravery and brotherliness, also associates him with menstruation – a fitting foil to Ganymede's swoon.

How, though, did these conundrums take on significance in the early modern playhouse – and beyond? Jean Howard puts the question well when she asks:

> Did theater . . . with its many fables of crossdressing also form part of the cultural apparatus for policing gender boundaries, or did it serve as a site for their further disturbance? If women off stage seized the language of dress to act out transgressions of the sex–gender system did theater effectively co-opt this transgression by transforming it into fictions that depoliticized the practice? Or was the theater in some sense an agent of cultural transformation, helping to create new subject positions and gender relations for men and women in a period of rapid social change?[27]

The answer to all these questions, as Howard acknowledges, is Yes. Tensions between social disruption and social integration are dialectical, all the more so when represented on stage. Regardless of the heterosexual comic closure at the ends of such plays, denouements aren't delivered up – or received – as incontrovertible summations; what counts is the experience of a play over time, and that experience may by turns challenge, reinforce, contradict, or throw into confusion the tidy untanglings that restore wife or daughter to husband or father's charge.

That's especially the case in Shakespeare's comedies, where emphatically moldy tales[28] point up the very artificiality of the restorative ending, at once sentimentally satisfying and ontologically unsettling. And often, the comic closure is far less closed than it looks: *Twelfth Night* ends with Viola still disguised as Cesario, and Malvolio, who has the key to the trunk containing her "women's weeds," vengefully vanished – all topped off by Feste's final song about contingency. As already noted, the epilogue of *As You Like It* knocks the legs out from under the smugly reconstructed social and gender orders.

More important, the simple fact that live actors present these stories confounds the either/or nature of Howard's queries. Her questions about "fables of cross-dressing" assume a response to female *characters*; they need, rather, to be addressed in terms of male *actors*.

It's rare that contemporary critics put the question of representation of gender *together with* the fact of who played the female parts: discussion of the former tends to remain at the level of the plot, often referring to the "subjectivity" of, say, Viola or Rosalind,[29] and at most nodding to the adolescent boys who inhabited the roles. On the other hand, critics who concentrate on the homoeroticism unleashed by the boy-actresses[30] have little to say about their impact on conveying – and commenting upon – images of women.[31]

This gap results from the reluctance of even the most inspiring new Shakespeare scholars to regard the plays fully as events taking place on the stage. In a sophisticated and persuasive reading of the homoerotics in Shakespeare's comedy, Valerie Traub, for instance, suggests that Rosalind/Ganymede initiates and encourages Phebe's affections because s/he speaks to Phebe first.[32] But Rosalind/Ganymede's line – "Why do you look on me?" – is obviously not an uninvited come-on, but an implied stage direction, a response to an action: Phebe *has* been looking on Rosalind/Ganymede, gawking, even leering. (Of course it's possible to direct the scene toward the effect Traub assumes, by instructing Phebe not to look in a goopy or lascivious way at Rosalind/Ganymede – or even not to look at all. That could comically implicate Rosalind/Ganymede in deliberately creating more sexual conundrum, and it could extend the hint of lesbianism as an erotic option that's suggested in the Rosalind–Celia intimacy.)

When current critics do take performance into account, they often fail to consider the non-illusory nature of the early modern theater. While the social conditions of the theater and the circulating anxieties of the times are evoked powerfully in their work, there's scant attention to the way an audience might, as a function of a specific style of stage-craft, critically take in – and take issue with – tales of adventuring females reined in at the end. Granted, in any sociological sense this is probably impossible to accomplish; nonetheless, the obvious fact that early modern dramaturgy made different demands on an audience than the prevailing realism of today's theater must be brought to bear on speculations about the social impact of the plays. When a contemporary reviewer complains, for instance, that the off-stage bed trick in *Measure for Measure* is not persuasive if a white actor plays Isabella and a black actor plays Mariana because, as Michael Feingold once charged, "running his fingers through the woman's hair would show Angelo he's been had,"[33] he reveals how hegemonically – and absurdly – realism constrains our experience of a more perceptually polymorphous drama.

Shakespeare's plays don't demand that the audience *believe* such events in any literal sense, but merely that they *accept* the as-ifness of the situation, that, like Orlando taking Ganymede as "if thou wert indeed my Rosalind" (IV, i, 187–188), they agree to a conditional, that they go along with a proposition that says, *if* this, then that. After all, like the bed trick, theatrical representation depends on the substitution of one thing for another. What matters isn't some sort of scientific accuracy in the substitution, but its effect: the *if* coils things up so the *then* can unwind. We grant it knowingly for the sake of the result. Indeed, the pleasure in this type of theatrical spectating comes from consciously entering into the mimetic contract, whose terms are recalled and displayed again and again. Frequent metatheatrical moments in Shakespeare's plays bring the play between engagement and distance to the surface, reminding the audience of its double-consciousness, and of its role in effecting theatrical representation.

With all the textual references to boy-actresses, it's hard to imagine that the audience forgot altogether that they were actively participating in the theatrical event by consciously taking one thing for another. Indeed, the comedies often stage this act of imaginative substitution, eroticizing spectatorship by comparing it to the emotional acrobatics of young lovers. As already noted, *As You Like It* – to paraphrase Maynard Mack on *Hamlet*[34] – takes place in the conditional mode: its wooings, its plot tangles, its resolutions all depend, like theatrical representation itself, on If. That virtuous If provides Ganymede's – and Shakespeare's – escape hatch: "I will marry you if ever I marry a woman, and I'll be married tomorrow," s/he tells Phebe. "I will satisfy you, if ever I satisfied man, and you shall be married tomorrow," s/he tells Orlando (V, ii, 114–117). Two scenes later, all are satisfied – but not until Touchstone offers his own disquisition on If, explaining how one may avoid the "Lie Direct . . . with an If. . . . Your If is the only peacemaker: much virtue in If" (V, iv, 95–102). Of course he's commenting

Plate 2 "O blessed bond of board and bed." The wedding scene in Cheek by Jowl's *As You Like It*, Booklyn Academy of Music, 1994. Photo by Dan Rest.

not only on the proceedings at hand, but on theater itself – the ultimate Lie Direct avoided with an If. Early modern dramaturgy did not seek to sweep the audience out of their senses, but pointed repeatedly to its own fictiveness and to the devices that drove its plots: the pleasure comes in being caught in an If.

The boy-actress is the most pointed emblem of this perceptual process. Two things at once – male and female, actor and character – he stands as an overdetermined icon of non-illusory theater. Often, Shakespeare calls attention to the boy-actress's slippery status, using his heightened, both-at-once position to test the limits of gender, role-playing, and representation.

This happens in a most pronounced fashion, suggests Peter Stallybrass, when plots call for boy-actresses to undress on stage, often to reveal a breast. In such scenes, Stallybrass discerns:

> a radical oscillation between a sense of the absolute difference of the boy from his role and the total absorption of the boy into the role. In other words, if Renaissance theatre constructs an eroticism that depends upon a play of differences (the boy's breast/the woman's breast), it also equally conjures up an eroticism which depends upon the total absorption of male into female, female into male.[35]

Stallybrass is right that "at moments of the greatest dramatic tension the Renaissance theater stages its own transvestism," sparking off "not so much a moment of indeterminacy as of contradictory fixations."[36] But that is a function not only of the shifting gender of the boy-actress, but of theater itself. Heightened though they may be, scenes where breasts are named or bared are hardly the only moments when "two contradictory realities are forced to peer into each other's faces."[37] Indeed, the perceptual engagement demanded of the non-illusory stage is precisely the always apparent clash of at least two contradictory realities. The heroine's breast is not the only thing that is both present and absent. The same is true of forests, castles, horses, sunsets. They exist because the language insists upon them, not because they actually appear. The spectator holds at least two things in mind at once: the engaging fictive world taking shape in word and action, and the framing theatrical artifice that enables that fictive world. As the dramaturg in Brecht's *Messingkauf Dialogues* exclaims, Shakespeare's theater is full of *V-effekts*.[38]

Perhaps the most pointed instance of this complex clash of realities comes in the last scene of *Twelfth Night*, where Viola/Cesario and Sebastian – an adolescent actor and a full-grown man – peer into each other's very different faces, which are taken throughout the play to be identical. Barbara Bowen has argued that *Twelfth Night* explores how seeing twins is like seeing theater because both depend on the simultaneous apprehension of likeness and difference.[39] Indeed, this "natural perspective that is and is not" depends precisely on a likeness that is imagined *in spite* of difference, so that the play more specifically explores how agreeing to see actors who don't resemble each other as twins lays bare the particular demands and pleasures of the non-illusory theater.

In other words, on the non-illusory, early modern stage, the primary, privileged means of conveying information is not scopic. Despite the Petrarchan certainty that upon seeing the beloved, ardor could pass directly from eyes to liver, in Shakespeare's dramaturgy, the dangerous orifice is the ear. Like Othello, we may demand ocular proof to believe what we're told, but, as in his case, what we see takes on value only *because* of what we've been told.

Of course by engaging the world of the play, we accept that a character, represented by a male, is female, but it's the performative language that creates that performed fictional fact. And as that fact contradicts what we see (or at least what we know), the language must be emphatic. Just as there are no red-gelled Leko lights gradually brightening to demonstrate how "the morn in russet mantle clad / walks oe'r the dew of yon high eastward hill" (*Hamlet* I, i, 171–172), Ganymede's identity as Rosalind (or, for that matter, any actor's identity as any character) exists in the space of the imagination where word and image collide, sometimes in contradiction, sometimes in collusion, and often both at once.

The non-illusory stage, then, provides a heightened space for examining what postmodern theorists call the "discursiveness" of identity formation, the notion that we are produced by and limited to what is said about us. In addition, the modern idea that there is an ultimate "authentic" or "natural" self that is bound to or contained within the body is called into question by a self-consciously transvestic stage practice. Modern, humanist readings of Shakespeare's cross-dressing comedies have long suggested that the heroines costume themselves for a journey toward self-discovery that culminates in a resolution between outer appearance and inner essence.[40] Leaving aside the point that Viola and Rosalind never really are restored to any female essence (Rosalind breaks away from it in the epilogue; Viola remains disguised as Cesario – and Orsino addresses her as "boy" when proposing marriage), if one recognizes that on the non-illusory stage characters have no inner essence – they exist only through what is shown and said to us – the postmodern notion of gender as performative, constituted by citational behavior, becomes a more compelling lens through which to interpret these plays. The early modern theater serves as a crystallizing example of what Judith Butler describes as the exteriorizing of gender, the inability to appeal to any interior, *a priori* identity because it simply doesn't exist.[41]

Even Rosalind/Ganymede's allegedly essentializing description of male machismo and female weakness is expressed in terms of clothing – "Dost thou think though I am caparisoned like a man I have a doublet and hose in my disposition?" (III, ii, 191–193) – calling attention to the transformation of the boy-actress we last saw in a petticoat, as well as referring to contemporary anxieties around the ability of clothes to make the man – or woman.

The Cheek by Jowl *As You Like It* played cleverly with this idea in the second wooing scene (IV, i), using an apron as a sign of femininity – and for the idea of gender as performance-like. After Orlando objects to Ganymede's suggestion that Rosalind might cuckold him some day, Ganymede tries to win back his attention by plucking the apron off Aliena, tying it around her/his own waist, and lifting her/his eyebrows into an expression of flirtatious docility. S/he uses the apron to draw Orlando back into accepting Ganymede's performance as Rosalind – much as Rosalind's Act I costume (in this production, a vaguely nineteenth-century long blue gown) works for us. Then, when Ganymede instructs, "you were better speak first, and when you were gravelled for lack of matter, you might take occasion to kiss" (IV, i, 70–72), s/he takes the male suitor's part and demonstrates on Orlando, tying the apron around *him*. Finally, Ganymede drapes the apron over her/his face, letting it cascade as a veil for the mock wedding ceremony.[42]

In this charming and complicated maneuver, the apron serves as shifting signifier, indicating domesticated femininity, marriage, gender instability, the artificiality of "woman," and, finally, the synecdoche that underlies theatrical representation in general. The apron, that is, becomes an emblem of the boy-actress himself.

Throughout the production, Donnellan highlights the engendering of gender with such devices, offering as a corollary to its playful permutations of gender display, a critique of a masculinist court. At the same time – indeed, as a consequence – the production offers a powerful illustration of the fluid polyeroticism of Shakespeare's comedy.

But what does it mean nowadays to figure femininity, "woman," eroticism, and theater-viewing through the boy-actress, through, that is, a man in drag? On the one hand, as I've argued, the play's critique becomes more pointed than in productions with women because femininity is ironized, revealed as completely artificial. And the play becomes sexier. Yet, just as Shakespeare can no longer be regarded as the pan-historical, universal, value-free Bard, Cheek by Jowl's production can hardly be read outside its own contemporary conditions. The production operates both within and against literary and performance traditions in England and in America, and it functions very much within the economy of mainstream institutional theater throughout the Western world.

I'm not interested in pronouncing the production "misogynist" or, for that matter, "feminist" or "radical." But I do think it's disingenuous – if not impossible – to suppose that its critique of gender, theater-viewing, and sexuality can be read as though the performance exists outside material relations involving gender, theater, and what we've come to call homosexuality.

On the one hand, Cheek by Jowl queers Shakespeare, thus displacing the heterosexist assumptions at the center of traditional productions. At the same time, its staging style blatantly rejects the grand, fussy business and looming scenery that often seem to stand for interpretation. With these moves, Cheek by Jowl situates itself as an alternative to dominant traditions.

Yet it can be authorized in doing so by appealing to Authenticity. You don't like seeing men in dresses? You don't like seeing a play without a beautiful set? But that's how Shakespeare did it. I'm not attributing this rejoinder to Donnellan, nor charging him with an academic attempt to present museum Shakespeare; I'm simply aware that historical precedent relieves the company of defending its choice of an all-male cast. Imagine the justifications that would be demanded if an all-woman production were mounted. Could one be? Would it be presented at international festivals and the Brooklyn Academy of Music? Would it be any good? By whose standards? And if not, why not?[43]

Certainly Donnellan does not bear the responsibility of answering such questions, any more than he must apologize for BAM being funded by Philip Morris (who, in the very week Cheek by Jowl opened, urged BAM officials to lobby its City Council representatives against pending anti-smoking legislation). I cite these commercial facts and political contradictions not to denigrate the performance in any way, but to step back from it and ask of a production in our own day what is being asked of plays in Shakespeare's time: how does it negotiate dominant culture especially around issues it addresses on stage – among them, gender and sexuality? How is today's theater a site of reproduction and resistance?

These are vexing questions and I don't pretend to have the answers myself. But I do see the Cheek by Jowl *As You Like It* straddling a number of contemporary contradictions. Playing in America in the early 1990s, it simultaneously tweaks the neocons by queering Shakespeare, whom they uphold as the much-maligned pillar of the Western canon, and legitimates queerness by revealing that it resides within Shakespeare – and without even changing a word of the text. (Indeed, precisely because it is Shakespeare, there is often room for experiment that is not tolerated elsewhere. That's why in the academy, Shakespeare studies has often been the testing ground for new literary approaches, from New Criticism to Queer Theory.)

This *As You Like It* – at least in New York – takes place at a moment when drag performance has become tame enough for Hollywood kiddie pics, even as homosexuality – and lesbians and gay men – are targeted by the ascending religious right as the prime enemy in America's culture war, a moment when Ru Paul records sales go off the charts in Colorado even as citizens of that state vote to outlaw statutes protecting lesbians and gay men from discrimination. Perhaps this merely reflects the failure of artworks to affect public opinion on policy matters, or perhaps the ease with which we live contradictions.

Shakespeare, like the Bible, has long been claimed for one political side or another. And like the Bible, he has most successfully been wielded as a conservative force, serving British nationalism and colonialism,[44] and in the US, even corporate interests. (Shakespeare stands as the centerpiece of a corporate training institute in upstate New York, where, according to management professor John K. Clemens, business students and corporate managers study "mankind's greatest texts to enable them to become better leaders." Question number seventeen in the Classic Leadership Case on *Henry IV* and *V*: "What do the *Henriad* and *Iacocca* show us about a leader's need to develop team spirit among those he leads?"[45])

It's tremendously appealing and satisfying, then, to experience a queer *As You Like It*, even if I hardly expect it to advance the cause in practical terms, any more than I would expect, say, an anti-fascist *Julius Caesar* or a feminist *Troilus and Cressida* to make any legible political impact. This is not simply a question of being produced in mainstream not-for-profit institutions. Indeed, given how few people actually go to noncommercial theater in the US, and how much experimental work aspires to be produced in the same institutions, terms like "mainstream" and "avant-garde" or "countercultural" have lost much of their value. Rather, it's a question of what it even means to imagine that a play *could* challenge hegemonic culture.

When radical critics deal with Shakespeare, we can easily fall into the very totalizing traps we are striding over when we read against the grain: we, too, expect Shakespeare to be everything, to contain everything. One colleague, for instance, less taken with this *As You Like It* than I was, complained to me about its "erasure of women." But to be erased, women have to be there in the first place. Certainly they are absent. But is a typical production, with four women in the four female roles, any more feminist? Why do we expect it to be?

Similarly, that racial difference is not remarked upon in the production – Adrian Lester and several other actors in the cast are black, the rest appear to be white – can be read as a liberal integrationist gesture (i.e. race doesn't matter) or as the dominant group wielding its prerogative to dismiss racial identity, which others, as bell hooks has written, are constantly reminded of.[46] But again, unless we hang onto an image of the all-knowing, pan-cultural, pan-historical Bard, why should we expect to find within Shakespeare's text a repudiation of racism?

It may be that Shakespeare, by virtue of the boy-actress and the non-illusory stage, is quintessentially queer, that a critique of heterosexism inheres in Shakespeare's plays and their performance tradition. Pointed interrogations of other categories require more deliberate interventions. For example, a forthcoming adaptation of *King Lear* by Reginald T. Jackson called *House of Lear* paints the tragic hero as the AIDS-afflicted mother of a fashion house in the African-American gay community – or, as an announcement for the production put it, it sets "Shakespeare's epic tragedy of betrayal" in "the glittering world of vogue houses and the legendary drag queens that rule them!"[47] I attended an early rehearsal and was struck by the adaptation's ability to use the play's investigation of humanness as a springboard to an investigation of gender, sexual, and racial identities as they are socially formed and maintained. When Lear asks Kent, "Do you know me?" Kent replies, "No. But there's something about you I respect." "What's that?" asks Lear. Kent says, "Realness." (The gender-reversed *Lear* produced by Mabou Mines in 1990 is discussed in Chapter 5.)

To be sure, in approaches to Shakespeare, as in the lesbian and gay liberation movement, "queer" can elide women and people of color, and end up merely referring to hip gay middle-class white guys. But as it's posed in queer theory at least, the term suggests an outsider stance that positions itself not only against heterosexism, but against all the exclusive practices that are accounted "normal" in the land of Gingrich. Queer politics, then, rejects assimilationism in favor of subverting – if not overthrowing – the bastions of dominant normality.

Theater can shake up our notions of those fixed structures through its inherent queerness. A production like the Cheek by Jowl *As You Like It* doesn't radicalize Shakespeare for ever after, nor wield him as an anachronistic banner for queer liberation. But it does participate in what Jonathan Dollimore calls "transgressive reinscription" which produces "not an escape from existing structures but rather a subversive reinscription within them, and in the process their dislocation or displacement."[48] That is, it exercises the imagination, enabling us to carry beyond the theater the virtue in If.

2 The New Drama and the New Woman

Reconstructing Ibsen's realism

After Nora dances her liberating tarantella at the party in *A Doll House*, Torvald criticizes it for being "a bit too naturalistic – I mean it rather over-stepped the proprieties of art."[1] Torvald doesn't mean that he believes his wife had really been bitten by a tarantula and was trying desperately to shake off death (though we know how much her "life was at stake"). Rather, he's commenting on the indecorousness of her frenzy. Unable to contain her passions in a more genteel form, Nora, we assume, danced at the off-stage party with the same abandon we witnessed in her rehearsal a few scenes earlier. Then, stage directions assert, "Nora dances more and more wildly . . . she seems not to hear [Torvald's instructions], her hair loosens and falls over her shoulders; she does not notice, but goes on dancing." Her performance is "naturalistic" not because Torvald mistakes it for the real thing, but because it depicts the deepest, most ineffable experience in a way that breaks past conventions. Alarmingly, Nora has exceeded expectations, just as Ibsen burst the seams of the well-made play and perfected a realistic drama that seethes with inexplicable emotion.

The shocking actions of Ibsen's female heroes parallel his shocking actions as a playwright. And both, in turn, respond to contemporary crises over the representation of women – in affairs of state (would they vote?) and stage (would they remain dainty, decorous, and in distress?). Ibsen investigated both kinds of representation by framing and refiguring contemporary dramatic forms. It wasn't just that the actions of Ibsen's female protagonists crossed the bounds of ladylike conduct. (The conservative critic Clement Scott complained after *A Doll House* premiered in England in 1889, Nora is not "the pattern woman we have admired in our mothers and sisters"; Hedda, he charged a few years later, "has glorified an unwomanly woman."[2]) At the same time, these characters overstepped *dramaturgical* bounds, displacing the male protagonist and claiming a central place in the action. Juxtaposed against these women, Ibsen's men, as Shaw sadly noted, exposed "the shameful extremity of a weak soul stripped naked before an audience looking to him for heroism."[3]

Ibsen's disruption of dramatic and social conventions challenged contemporary assertions about the inevitability and incontrovertibility of gender roles. Even as the New Woman emerged in *fin-de-siècle* Europe, staking a claim for equality and inclusion in the public sphere, science was slamming the door on her exit from the home. Both Freud and Havelock Ellis, for all their differences in approach and ideology, promoted the idea that anatomy is destiny, that biology determines gender. Marriage and motherhood had nothing to do with choice or social pressure, they asserted; these functions were hardwired into a woman's body. To resist the roles of wife and mother, then, was to be "abnormal," "psychotic," "monstrous."

Despite the now commonplace notion (first promulgated by Zola) that the period's realistic drama lined up with the drive for this scientific "objectivity" (and its corollary biological determinism),[4] Ibsen's prose plays negotiated these dominant currents, reproducing them, perhaps, but also (maybe even for the purpose of) resisting them. In doing so, Ibsen's innovative dramatic structures, the new acting style his work demanded, the resonance of his settings, and his invocation and rerouting of well-made strategies are as important as the stories the plays tell and the characters they represent. And certainly, all of these are more important than anything Ibsen said to defend or contradict the aims of the women's movement. In sum, Ibsen's plays engaged the roiling controversy over gender through their self-scrutinizing dramatic actions, questioning the representation of women by questioning the means of representation itself.

From our vantage point today, it's hard to think of realism as a form that oversteps the proprieties of art – indeed, we tend to think of it as doing quite the opposite, as strictly delineating, and then hiding the marks of, those proprieties. That's the first bias that must be overcome in approaching Ibsen's prose plays. Too frequently they're measured according to a standard calibrated by the most debased instances of the genre – contemporary psychological realism that dominates American drama on stage, film, and TV.

Accordingly, we expect an Ibsen production, with precise period costumes and picture-perfect wallpaper, to convince us that it represents nineteenth-century reality – and then we belittle it for failing to sweep us into that world with the illusionistic power of a film, or of a "virtual reality" computer game. Or, if we're Lacanian-influenced feminist

48   *Reconstructing Ibsen's realism*

theorists, we belittle it for succeeding – thereby objectifying women in a "prison-house of narrativity."

Experienced this way, as any stagestruck undergraduate will tell you, Ibsen, compared to say, Beth Henley or August Wilson, seems stodgy, old-fashioned, and fake. Of course that says less about Ibsen than about how we teach (and, too often, produce) him: as the progenitor of the form that so transports such students in these more "real" and "relevant" expressions. Indeed, if students learn anything about Ibsen, it's that his plays follow a clear progressive trajectory from overwrought verse dramas to realistic paragons, the prose plays themselves evolving like an ever more fit species, shedding soliloquies, asides, and all the integuments of the well-made play as they creep, then crouch, then culminate in the upright masterpiece, *Hedda Gabler*. (Ibsen's last plays leave proponents of this model speechless. That Lugne-Poe seized on them immediately for his symbolist theater counts as an embarrassing reversion, an affront to everything we should most prize in our father of modern drama.)

This grand narrative, as a number of contemporary Ibsen scholars have suggested, is at best misleading, supporting a handy teleology at the expense of Ibsen's poetic vision. The Hegelian, mythic, or metaphoric readings offered by these critics – among them Brian Johnston, Richard Gilman, Robert Brustein, and Orley Holtan – are not only illuminating; they open Ibsen up to expansive critical approaches usually reserved for Shakespeare. But instead of pointing out how our own saturation in a tiresome, formulaic realism prevents us from encountering Ibsen's complex, self-referential use of the form, they dismiss his dramatic style as a sort of necessary evil, as the most convenient conduit to Ibsen's "higher" concerns.

Gilman has written, for example, that "the seeming naturalism of *Hedda Gabler* is . . . a ground for the play's true action: its movement into a realm of existential, or ontological being and its vision of crucial values at stake and at war."[5] In *To the Third Empire* Johnston goes further in characterizing Ibsen's dramaturgy as a kind of trick, a way of pandering to bourgeois audiences before sneaking some metaphysics into their entertainment. He writes, "only by inserting such [realistic] details can Ibsen cunningly infiltrate the full content of his dramatic concept into the play and most cogently and adequately present his full dramatic 'argument'."[6] But the "dramatic argument" is the event that happens in the theater. And it happens not *in spite* of the style of Ibsen's prose plays, but *because* of it. Ibsen's realism doesn't compete with or merely provide the ground for mythopoeic content, patterned action, metaphoric meanings. It is absolutely integral to these achievements.

Ibsen does not need to be rescued from the dramatic artifices of his day, but from the unexamined aesthetic assumptions of our own.

Yet rescue from realism is very much evident in the tone of these influential critics. Like Solness, who triumphantly decides to build "castles in the air" instead of houses for people to live in, these critics sweep Ibsen to an artistic height "above" realism, at once saving him from this debilitating art form and from the related, anchoring weight of social concerns. There's plenty of irony, I believe, in the pinnacle achievements of Solness, Rubek, Borkman – not only because they bring death, but also because they depend on renunciation (usually of a woman, of a child, of a socially engaged life). Still, the efforts of anti-realist critics Johnston most of all – seem to depend on an exultant reading of these dubious endings. On the other hand, when Ibsen's protagonists are women, they are whisked into metaphoric abstraction so that they *can't* be read as triumphant, for to find glory in the final acts of Nora, Hedda, or Ellida Wangel is to verge on a feminist reading, and that, these critics contend, is the social concern from which Ibsen requires deliverance most urgently of all.

The history of Ibsen scholarship reads, at times, like an argument against feminist (or proto-feminist) interpretations of Ibsen's plays, or at least of *A Doll House* and *Hedda Gabler*. For nearly 100 years, critics have resented, as Robert Brustein puts it, that "Ibsen has been expropriated by the women's movement."[7] To stave off such hostage-taking, they insist that we overlook the gender of Ibsen's female characters, that we leap immediately to a supposedly neutral image of the universal human being. Thus such proclamations as: Ibsen "was completely indifferent [to the woman question] except as a metaphor for individual freedom";[8] *A Doll House* "has nothing to do with the sexes";[9] Ellida Wangel's free choice to remain with her husband instead of running off with the controlling Stranger at the end of *Lady from the Sea* represents humanity's tragic need "to remain *this* side of the third empire of the spirit";[10] "Hedda Gabler isn't a woman, she's a human being."[11]

So it seems necessary, if absurd, to point out that if Hedda, Nora, and Ellida were not female, there would be no dramatic action. Lona Hessel might be addressing Ibsen scholars when, in *Pillars of Society*, she tells Bernick, "This society of yours is a bachelors' club. You don't see women."[12]

It makes sense that those who dismiss the obvious critique of women's subjugation in the plays are the same critics who denigrate their dramatic style. For if to some extent Ibsen's plays with female protagonists are feminist – at least at the level of the stories they tell – it's because they are realistic. They refer to a recognizable world in which women's lives are confined, constrained, controlled. While they don't make an agit-prop argument for changing that world, they evoke it critically, revealing its consequences. That is, they play on a feminist field, sexist bourgeois values providing the fateful background of Ibsen's mythic work. Anti-feminist critics imply that feminists confuse this background with the plays' foreground; rather, these critics do away with the circumstantial realm that determines the plays' actions, never asking *why* Ibsen's female protagonists make such great metaphors for the human condition. Henry James said that Ibsen's characters were "caught in the fact,"[13] an observation later critics have cited, reasonably enough, to evoke the existential yearning that pleads through the plays, the cry for what Ibsen called "a revolution of the human spirit."[14] But the characters are first caught in facts on the ground – or, more precisely, facts on the stage. For whatever metaphoric value words, props, or characters might take on, because they are on a realistic stage they first have *literal* meanings. Flowers may stand for death or nature; first they function in the drama as flowers. (Think of how Hedda derides the bouquet sent by Thea.) Hedda may be a tragic or mythic figure; first she is a woman. And she can have tragic or mythic resonance *because* she is a woman.

To be sure, the association between Ibsen and women's rights movements is not a paranoid invention of those who insist on its irrelevance. We know from a number of Ibsen's own activities and remarks that he considered the issue important.[15] It's impossible to imagine, in fact, that the first productions of *A Doll House* could have been received without reference to the "woman question." As Joan Templeton notes in "The *Dollhouse* Backlash: Criticism, Feminism, and Ibsen," her exhaustive analysis of anti-feminist "defenses" of the play, Nora's doorslam resounded through the West in the 1880s, initiating a spate of articles from America, England, France, Italy, Germany, and Scandanavia, in daily papers and highbrow weeklies, describing *A Doll House*'s theme as "the subjection of women by men."[16] Nora's long, justificatory speech in the last act practically quotes, as Templeton points out, texts that pleaded the case for women's rights, such as those by Mary Wollstonecraft, Margaret Fuller, and Harriet Martineau. In the 1890s, she adds, *A Doll House* was recognized "as the clearest and most substantial expression of the 'woman question' that had yet appeared."[17]

Of course Shaw has been much blamed for this widespread recognition, even though he claimed Ibsen for a wider socialist agenda than feminism (and even though the Fabian Society – and Shaw himself – as Jill Davis has shown, had rather dubious attitudes about the proper place of women, using fiery new terms to relegate them to the same old roles as mothers and men's helpmeets[18]). In England, especially, Ibsen (along with Shaw and Tolstoy) was seized on by the *critics* of the New Woman movement – as though women couldn't have come up with the demand of equality themselves. A satiric 1894 *Punch* cartoon, for example, depicts a "Donna Quixote" perched in an armchair, squinting into a book over her homely spectacles, as she hoists a tell-tale latchkey over her head. At her feet lies the head of "Tyrant Man." Behind her an amazon battles the dragon "Decorum" as another waves the banner of the "Divided Skirt." A third tilts at the windmill of "Marriage Laws." Books are strewn around her, among them a volume of Ibsen.[19]

If this cartoon version of the New Woman was nowhere to be found outside the imaginations of those she threatened, the actual New Woman did, in fact, keep volumes of Ibsen around – specifically the New Woman who worked in the theater, one of the few realms where women could enter public discourse. It's no coincidence that during this period, Ibsen was championed – and more important, produced – by the Free Theater movement that began on the European continent and then caught fire in England, and that these were the theaters from which female actor-managers emerged most powerfully, developing a new style of acting to meet the demands of Ibsen's innovations. Janet Achurch was a producer of the *Doll House* in which she played Nora in 1889 and the *Hedda Gabler* in which she starred in 1891; Florence Farr produced and performed in *Rosmersholm* in 1891; Elizabeth Robins staged and acted in *Hedda Gabler* in 1891. As Shaw noted, all four women who were Ibsen's strongest supporters, producers, and actors (at least in English) – Achurch, Farr, Robins, and Marion Lea:

> were products of the modern movement for the higher education of women, literate, in touch with advanced thought, and coming by natural predilection on the stage from outside the theatrical class, in contradistinction to the senior generation of inveterately sentimental actresses, schooled in the old fashion if at all, born into their profession, quite out of the political and social movement around them – in short, intellectually naive to the last degree.[20]

These new women had to create a new acting style – a new actress – to meet the demands of Ibsen's characters, who slammed the door on melodramatic mincing and well-made miracles, who staged themselves with a new and liberating self-consciousness, demanding for women on stage, as well as off, a new way to act.

Plate 3 Elizabeth Robins, as Hedda Gabler, burns Lovborg's manuscript, London 1891. Photo courtesy of the Fales Library, New York University.

So it's no surprise, either, that for some twenty years, as Ibsen produced his cycle of prose plays, the mainstream press throughout Europe carried debates about him. Each new opening presented another occasion for discussion, denouncement, applause, analysis – not only of performances and dramatic design, but of ideas. No doubt then, as now, some of the daily reviewers were dunderheads, often failing to note the most profound and innovative aspects of Ibsen's work. But it doesn't follow that the raging discussions lessened a great dramatist into a *pièce-à-thèse* hack. On the contrary, for all the narrowness and outrage of many contemporary Ibsen critics, their assumption that drama engages and affects the most urgent issues of its times would be a welcome remedy to so much of today's theater writing, which makes a proud point of detaching drama from the world it inhabits. Indeed, the solution to reductive readings of Ibsen is not to drain his plays of their social content, as though it were some enfeebling venom injected by dramatically indifferent parties, but to recognize the inextricable relationship of that content to Ibsen's metaphoric and theatrical invention.

There's a related, more profound way in which Ibsen's realism offers a feminist critique: through its implosive critique of dramatic form. After Nora declared that she must forsake husband and children to "become a human being,"[21] Ibsen was, of course, vehemently denounced. Today's critics are divided over why Ibsen's contemporaries were scandalized by his plays. Most suggest that they recoiled from Ibsen's unspeakable subject matter, and ignored, as Meyer puts it, "the technical originality."[22] On the other hand, Johnston insists that the rejection of Ibsen may have *seemed* like a revulsion toward his dangerous topics, but was really "the condition of vertigo" instilled by a dramatic style that made "the 'reality' purportedly presented (our world), and the artistic standpoint from which that reality might be judged" feel as though they were dissolving beneath the audience's feet.[23] Both, of course, are right: the one is not detachable from the other. All the more so when issues of gender are involved, for Ibsen's innovative dramaturgy reveals the artificiality of the well-made play, and, as a consequence, the artificiality of the era's well-made woman. It questions the reliability of the artistic order and, as a result, the reliability of the social, even epistemological, order. Indeed, in contemporary reviews of Ibsen's plays, the critique of Ibsen's dramaturgy often takes the terms of a critique of Ibsen's representation of women – and vice versa. For example, a review of *Hedda Gabler* in 1891 declared:

drama, in its present state of technical development can only present comparatively simple characters. . . . Everything that should make this curious being [Hedda] intelligible to us, her development, her secret thoughts, her half-sensed misgivings and all that vast region of the human mind which lies between the conscious and the unconscious – all this the dramatist can no more than indicate. For that reason, I think a novel about Hedda Gabler could be extremely interesting, while a play leaves us with a sense of emptiness and betrayal.[24]

Those who were most disturbed by Ibsen's unseemly ideas railed like their Puritanical predecessors, unconsciously attaching Ibsen's internal critique of theatrical form to his critique of gender roles. Clement Scott (who coined "Ibsenite" as a term of opprobrium) was easily the Phillip Stubbes of his day. His accusation that anyone who *attended* an Ibsen play was guilty of gender dysfunction, recalls the seventeenth century's most virulent condemnation of theater as a site of sexuality run amok. Ibsen's audiences, he wrote, were:

> The sexless. . . . The unwomanly woman, the unsexed females, the whole army of unprepossessing cranks in petticoats. . . . Educated and muck-ferretting dogs. . . . Effeminate men and male women. . . . They, all of them – men and women alike – know that they are doing not only a nasty thing but an illegal thing . . .[25]

Ibsen's plays could provoke such a response precisely because they make social conventions seem as hoary and artificial as theater conventions. In other words, it wasn't just that Ibsen sympathetically represented female characters in untenable social situations. Pointing to the limits of theatrical form, he commented on the limits of middle-class, patriarchal values. Scott's tirade responds to a deeper and more subversive feminism than that carved on the surface of their stories, one that conjures a complex critique in the interplay between presentational and representational dramatic styles, between the mechanisms of melodrama and the tarantellian promise of a new realist form.

Traditional Ibsen criticism makes much of the way Ibsen catapulted drama beyond the well-made play. More recently, mythopoeic interpreters of Ibsen have highlighted his self-conscious use of the more formulaic genre, demonstrating how, as Johnston puts it, "Ibsen is alerting us, not just to inadequacies in our idea of the world, but also to inadequacies in our idea of the *theater*; that is, of the way the world conventionally is represented in the theater."[26] Benjamin Bennett goes further in linking Ibsen's social critique to his metatheatricality. Ibsen, he says, employs artificial theatrical devices:

which are meant to be recognized as devices, as an arbitrary and disturbingly familiar theatrical language which reminds us, by its nature as a language, that the theatrical performance is an organized communal event in which we are participating. As real life interferes with the play's ideality and calls attention to our status as individuals, so an obvious theatricalness interferes with the play's objectivity and calls attention to the communal conventions we are involved in.[27]

Though both writers cite *A Doll House* and *Hedda Gabler* particularly to illustrate how Ibsen relies on a melodramatic model, mocking it as he moves beyond it, neither critic recognizes a relationship between Ibsen's obvious theatricality and the obviously theatrical communal convention both plays challenge: femininity. But it is in this confluence of theatrical performance and social performance that Ibsen's realism creates a current for the "liberating realm of imagery and reference" that Johnston calls the "supertext."[28]

Think again of Torvald's misgivings about Nora's tarantella. Her dance is too "naturalistic" because it is unbecoming, that is, it is inappropriate behavior for a respectable wife – and for a character in the new realism, as many critics of the day complained. William Archer sounds a bit like Torvald when he chides that the tarantella scene "belongs to an inferior order of dramatic effects."[29] He approved of Eleanora Duse's decision to replace the manic whirling with more contained action, in which she "dons the crown of roses, seizes the tambourine, makes one sweep round the stage, then drops powerless with emotion and fear in a chair."[30] Even Elizabeth Robins charged that the tarantella was too stagey, "Ibsen's one concession to the effect-hunting that he had come to deliver us from."[31]

Archer and Robins derided the dance most likely because they recognized it as a standard occasion for a star turn, an actor's chance to pull out all the stops on a big emotional number, never mind how tenuously it relates to the plot. But Nora's frenetic dance is not merely an outward manifestation of inner desperation – stagey effect-hunting, indeed. Rather, it announces itself as a remnant of that old staginess, and then goes it one better. Not a *concession* to the old effect-hunting, Nora's tarantella is an *appropriation* of it.

Audaciously, Ibsen calls *twice* on this effect from an inferior dramatic order – first in the staged rehearsal at the end of Act II, then in Nora's off-stage performance, which Torvald reports on near the beginning of Act III. Not only does the dance relate to the plot – in both instances,

Nora's dervishing forestalls Torvald's trip to the mailbox – it structures the action. Melodramatically, it serves as a relentless, ticking clock. Nora counts the hours until Torvald will learn her terrible secret: "Five. Seven hours to midnight. Twenty-four hours to the midnight after, and then the tarantella's done. Seven and twenty-four? Thirty-one hours to live." In marking out the end of her life in the tarantella, Nora reverses – or so we think – the traditional image of the dance as a remedy, a means of discharging poison. And in this reversal, the tarantella takes on its metaphoric meaning, for it also marks the ferociousness with which she must overstep proprieties if she is, in fact, going to live.

Act II ends with Nora's anticipation of doom. She finishes the tarantella rehearsal, pulls herself together, ties up her hair, and goes in to supper to give the performance of her life, chirping, "Here's your little lark!" So we await her return in Act III, events wound up in intricate well-made fashion. (Of course, Ibsen's six years as a stage manager and director at the Christiana Theater taught him such mechanics well; he directed some 145 plays there, half of them by or in imitation of Scribe.) Ibsen delays the unravelling of these events. Act III opens with Kristine and Krogstad's romantic reunion. What's more, this reunion gives the well-made devices another twist: though Krogstad agrees to ask Torvald to return his letter unread, Kristine talks him out of it, subverting the savior function the old dramatic style assumed.

When Nora does enter, she's dragged in by Torvald, pleading with him from off-stage for just another hour – as though teasing the audience by trying to put off the resolution it awaits with such pent-up certainty. Finally she arrives, wearing the tarantella costume we've seen displayed, passed among women's hands, stitched – and now, worn. The dress itself has enabled much of the dramatic action, serving as Nora's excuse to keep Torvald out of the room, to invite Kristine over for a confidential chat, and to shoo her away. The costume, too, is the instrument through which Rank's feelings about Nora become known, in the famous "stocking scene" (which Duse and La Galliene cut for its immodesty). But the dress, having gathered so much meaning as an image of liberation, impending disaster, and theatrical gear-grinding, acquires most significance in its removal. "What are you doing in there?" Torvald asks, when Nora walks out on his declarations of forgiveness. She replies from off-stage: "Getting out of my costume." While she does so, Torvald prattles on about how safe and snug he'll make her now, promising to be both "conscience and will to you." She returns, of course, in her regular street clothes, dressed for a stunning exit.

More than in this literal sense, the tarantella serves as Nora's ennobling and enabling act. It exemplifies how profoundly her life – like the well-made play – has been a series of histrionic effects. This is not a sudden realization – at least not for the audience. Ibsen prepares that shocking doorslam with a web of imagery as wide as Shakespeare's, yet moored by realism to the literal accoutrements of a bourgeois life.

Throughout the play Nora is associated with secrecy, deception, and disguise. The very first word she speaks is "hide"; and in the first moments of the play we watch as she sneaks some macaroons and "steals over and listens at her husband's study door." She plays hide-and-seek with her children. Torvald fantasizes that she is his "secret darling." Most important, of course, she holds a terrible secret. (Not only that she borrowed money and forged a signature, but that she *worked* – unfit activity for a married woman of her class. Note that Torvald's first question to Kristine when Nora says her friend needs a job is, "I suppose you're a widow?" Indeed, what Nora liked most about working was that "It was almost like being a man.")

But in another contortion of the well-made form, Ibsen does not make Nora ashamed of her subterfuge. Her ability to borrow money and pay it back through her own labor and sacrifice was "something I've . . . got to be proud and happy for." The lie that drives the old-style plot, in other words, is not the lie that matters in the end. Ibsen provides the expected melodramatic resolution: Krogstad returns the forged note and Torvald ecstatically rips it up and throws it in the fire. But that reprieve merely makes way for a more shattering liberation.

The revelation of Nora's instrumental lie discloses another, at once more political and more existential: her marriage is a sham. Being a twittering little lark of a wife and mother is to have a role, not an identity. This ontological fact cannot be extricated from the social conditions that give rise to it, any more than Ibsen's "supertext" can resonate without the sympathetic vibrations of his self-conscious dramatic style: Ibsen's realism trembles to life in the tension between melodrama and metaphor .

Nora's association with the New Woman – and with performance – is hinted at throughout the play because she is repeatedly characterized as an actress. She tells Kristine how much Torvald "enjoys my dancing and dressing up and reciting for him." Sewing trimmings on the tarantella dress, Kristine remarks, "So, you'll be in disguise tomorrow." Later, Rank suggests that at next year's party, Nora could masquerade as "charmed life" by "going just as she is." Foreshadowing the play's ending, Torvald complains that Nora didn't understand when it was time to leave off dancing. "An exit should always be effective," he says, "but that's what I can't get Nora to grasp." In the theater of his own mind, Torvald casts her as a melodramatic damsel in distress when he imagines her "in some terrible danger, just so I could stake my life and soul and everything, for your sake." But of course, this is not a melodrama, so that miracle cannot take place. Finally, in her last-act speech, when Nora makes her most honest, unmediated statements about herself, Torvald ironically believes she is acting. "Ah, none of your slippery tricks," he demands. "No more playacting," and "Oh, quit posing."

Nineteenth-century critics of the play – as well as more recent writers who insist on a "universal" reading of the protagonist – tend to regard Nora's little squirrel act as her most authentic expression of self, and thus to condemn her actions as the thoughtless iniquities of a naive, immoral hysteric. This, as Templeton shrewdly suggests, is to see Nora through Torvald's eyes.[32] She quotes the Norwegian scholar Else Host, arguing that it is the "childish, expectant, ecstatic, broken-hearted Nora" who makes the play immortal while the coldly analytical character of the last act is psychologically unconvincing and wholly unsympathetic.[33] In a 1925 study, Herman Weigand, insisted that *A Doll House* had to be read as a comedy, because surely Nora would fly back home and "revert imperceptibly to her role of song-bird and charmer." After all, he reasoned, Nora is:

> an irresistibly bewitching piece of femininity, an extravagant poet and romancer, utterly lacking in sense of fact, and endowed with a natural gift for play-acting which makes her instinctively dramatize her experiences: how can the settlement fail of a fundamentally comic appeal?[34]

More enlightened readings rely on similar essentialist assumptions. For Johnston, Torvald's affectionate nicknames associate Nora with a "strong 'animal' identity," supporting his interpretation of her as a woman unable "to take the universal ethical realm into consideration at all," and as a representative of the "presocial, instinctual, feminine and familial" side of the great Hegelian conflict between feminine and masculine principles.[35]

Such commentary ignores not only the way language reveals Nora's femininity as a role, but the way Nora's behavior changes depending on whether Torvald is – or might be – watching her. In the face of all the acts we know Nora to be capable of – striking a deal with Krogstad, working to pay off her debt, consciously manipulating Torvald by playing the infantalized charmer, resolving not to ask Rank for assistance since he has romantic designs on her, staunchly standing up to Krogstad and admitting that she forged her father's signature when she could have lied, determining to leave the imprisoning "playpen" that her marriage has become – in the face of all this, it's impossible to reduce Nora to Torvald's little squirrel. Yet the myth persists, rather like the cliché that Hamlet is incapable of acting, though we see him setting the Players' show as a trap, throwing off Ophelia, confronting his mother, killing Polonius, arranging for the execution of Rosencrantz and Guildenstern, and so on.

Several times, we see Nora alone and on these occasions she is no mere little lark. She opens and closes the first two acts, framing their hurtling events with her efforts to situate herself safely outside them. The play begins with her giddy entrance. Stage directions call for her to be "humming happily." She unloads her Christmas packages and gives the boy delivering the tree an enormous tip, then surreptitiously munches some macaroons before listening for Torvald, like an actor peeping through a curtain to see if the audience has arrived. Her merry disposition may seem, at first, merely to correspond to the imminent holiday. And once we see her interact with Torvald, who greets "my little lark" and "my squirrel," it may seem, simply, to characterize her. Soon, though, Ibsen gives us a concrete reason with which we can correct our impression, and understand her exuberance in retrospect: Torvald will be starting a new, lucrative job and, Nora exults, "Won't it be lovely to have stacks of money and not a care in the world?" But still later, Ibsen lets us catch ourselves in the act of seeing her through Torvald's eyes by parceling out the true explanation for Nora's happiness, the conclusion of what she calls "the big thing": she saved her husband's life by borrowing money, then stealthily worked and scrimped to pay off the debt. Now it will soon be paid in full. No wonder she feels like a lark.

And no wonder she ends the act frightened: Krogstad, like a classic melodramatic villain, has crawled out of the past right on cue, and threatened to blackmail her. On top of that, Torvald has proclaimed that the sins of the parents ruin the lives of their children (a theme underscored by Rank's condition – and taken up by Ibsen's next play, *Ghosts*). Though Nora challenges Torvald's suggestion that the mother is the one to blame, she takes his words to heart when he retreats to his study, leaving her once again in private. "Hurt my children – ! Poison my home?" she wonders, "pale with terror." And then she rejects this mechanistic view and gets on with the show. In a telling stage direction, Ibsen instructs, "A moment's pause; then she tosses her head." And Nora says, "That's not true. Never in all the world."

Yet, the curtain goes up with Nora alone again, this time pacing restlessly past the Christmas tree, now "stripped of ornament, burned-down candle stubs on its ragged branches." She frets, anticipating that

Krogstad will arrive with that Scribean essential – the incriminating letter. She's drawn out of her anxiety only by the maid's entrance with the box of masquerade clothes, which, Nora says, "I'd love to rip . . . in a million pieces." Her predicament is bound up with her performance. As already noted, the last time we see Nora alone, she's counting the hours until the tarantella is done. Then she bucks up – indeed, *larks* up – and makes a grand entrance into supper.

These moments are worth noting in detail because they so sharply contrast the image of Nora that Torvald maintains, and that pervades the play more generally. Kristine imposes a similar interpretation: despite Nora's clear statements that having a rich admirer to bail her out is a fantasy, Kristine can't imagine Nora taking care of herself. But the audience holds the privilege of irony, of double-vision, weighing Kristine and Torvald's reactions against our own heightened percep- tions. Nora's no-nonsense moments alone, her clearly manipulative way of stringing along Kristine and seducing money out of Torvald, demon- strate that this is no frail little fledgling, but a woman who has learned her part expertly. Indeed, Nora doesn't really panic until her perfor- mance fails to persuade: despite her virtuoso pleas, Torvald rejects her suit that Krogstad be reinstated in his job.

In more subtle ways, too, Ibsen associates Nora with the profession of acting. In the "stocking scene," where she flirts with Rank, she unabashedly displays a pair of flesh-colored stockings – exactly the costume item that was scandalizing critics of Europe's popular theater forms. As the theater historian Tracy Davis notes, pink-colored tights were "the article most heavily invested with indexical signification of skin, eroticism, and sexual stimulation," in pornographic novels, ballet, pantomime, opera bouffe, burlesque, music hall, and acrobatic perfor- mances of the period.[36] "The female leg, naked in tights," she says, "became synonymous with the female performer, with enjoyment, and with the theatre itself."[37]

Ibsen even goes so far as to intimate the common association of the period between actresses and prostitutes. Describing to Kristine the odd jobs she's taken, Nora lists "needlework, crocheting, embroidery, and such – (Casually.) and other things, too." And when Krogstad asks her if she knows of some sure, quick ways of getting money, Nora replies, "None that I'm willing to use." Finally, on hearing what she's done, Torvald accuses his wife of being a "hypocrite, liar . . . [and] criminal" – a series of epithets not far from contemporary railing about actresses.

The actress served as a heady, even cautionary, image of the New Woman. Ibsen invokes her as a double-emblem of the question blazing inside the theater and beyond: how should – how could – women act?

For nowhere was the critique of gender constraints and theatrical representation more available than in the tension between old and new styles of acting. Despite our 1990s assumptions about internal, naturalistic, cinematic acting, the most successful Ibsen performances a century ago came from what Tracy Davis calls the combining of "realistic characteristics with sensational behavior," the striking of "the right balance between truthful embodiment and theatricalized effect in accordance with the audience's taste for modernism and their long experience of presentational acting."[38] As Davis notes, Achurch's Nora was generally more acclaimed than Duse's understated performance. Duse's "dread of becoming melodramatic," Archer explained, resulted in her failure to be "legitimately dramatic."[39]

Ibsen's stage directions periodically call for actors to smile "almost imperceptibly" or for even more subtle actions, like "suppressing an involuntary smile."[40] Surely these instructions are most telling in what they mean to counteract: the actor's temptation to make points. They contrast, rather than negate that possibility, marking the places where high-flown histrionics are not appropriate.

The tension between the two styles provides a means of pointing to characters as themselves self-dramatizing – a feature of Ibsen's men as well as his women. Nora certainly does this when she puts on her larkish behavior to cajole Torvald, tease Kristine, or flirt with Rank. And in doing so, she reveals the performance-like nature of femininity. But she is no match for Ibsen's diva of self-dramatization, Hedda Gabler, who stages her predicament most violently by quoting grand theatrical gestures.

Perhaps Johnston sounds a bit like a true-believer who's seen the face of Jesus in a pizza pie when he suggests that Nietzsche's *Birth of Tragedy* is concealed within *Hedda Gabler*,[41] but Hedda's appeal to classical models is undeniable. As Johnston and Elinor Fuchs[42] have shown, Ibsen's references to Greek mythology reach beyond Hedda's dreams of vine leaves in Eilert Lovborg's hair to produce an imagistic atmosphere that rings with Attic echoes.

More immediately, as Johnston notes, *Hedda Gabler* evokes Scribe as the art of the past. Indeed, in *Hedda Gabler* Ibsen out-Scribes Scribe, forcing immense, mythic subject matter into an intolerable confinement.[43] Even more than in *A Doll House*, Ibsen oils the machinery of the well-made play with irony, setting up the form's devices, then deflecting them toward open, inexplicable ends. To take just one example, the possibility that Lovborg will compete with Tesman for his academic post – apart from offering Hedda a frisson of spectatorship introduces a conflict that could drive the plot of this play had Scribe or one of his imitators written it. Ibsen intimates, then steers away from this plot when Lovborg announces, to Tesman's relief and Hedda's dismay, that he will not make his splash until after Tesman's appointment is secured. Ibsen thus arouses his audience's anxiety in a familiar way, only to yank it in new directions. For if the contest between Tesman and Lovborg is not over a job – nor over a woman, as Hedda quickly rejects Lovborg's assumptions of intimacy – our attention is focused on something else. Indeed, the dramatic action turns out not to center on the conflict between two male rivals at all, though the play's first mention of Lovborg sparks just that possibility when, in the first scene, Aunt Julie uncharacteristically gloats that Tesman's former competition has fallen miserably and is "lying there now, in the bed he made – poor, misguided creature." Yet that creaky conflict is denied. And what brings relief in the old drama brings Hedda nothing but boredom.

In this, and so many other instances of roused and rerouted expectations, Ibsen trains attention on Hedda's response to the action, offering a point of view through which we might consider the limitations of a plot that once satisfied. It's a complicated ruse, for we see Hedda desire a melodrama for her own amusement and recognize her disappointment as a more fascinating and mysterious subject than the melodrama itself. But Hedda, too, realizes the inadequacies of the narrative she would impose. So she tries to shape events into a grander form, or at least to give the sordid old plot the trappings of classical significance. But even those corny vine leaves can't confer heroism on bourgeois banalities. By the time Hedda hands a pistol to Lovborg, she tells him, "I don't believe in vine leaves any more." For Hedda can't find diversion, much less salvation, in forms of the past that just won't shape themselves to the petty concerns of the drawing room (though we, of course, *can* find it in Ibsen's staging of this tension). She yearns for – but can't quite imagine – a form of the future, where she can play protagonist in her own life. Ibsen has put her at the center of a new drama in which she labors vainly to make herself the center of an old action.

Straining toward both past and future to find meaning is an essential action – and process – of *Hedda Gabler*. The play moves forward along this vigorous, sublime tension as it attenuates – but never obliterates – the dramatic present. The unfulfilled rivalry between Tesman and Lovborg centers on this cosmic contest – Tesman studies handicrafts in the Brabant in the Middle Ages, Lovborg has given birth to a visionary treatise on the future. Of course we never do learn the substance of

Lovborg's prophecies (in an early draft of the play, Ibsen revealed that his work presaged a true camaraderie between men and women) because Hedda herself expresses no interest in the book's content. Still, Lovborg's grandiose work seems as distant and unreal – as academic – as Tesman's pedantic research. But the present – that uncatchable moment made palpable in the theater – is precisely what everyone but Hedda ignores. While others locate themselves between what's come before and what they hope is yet to transpire, Hedda gets little thrill from memories, and even less from expectations. Indeed, *expecting*, in both senses, is just what Hedda cannot stand to be. She hungers for an unmediated immediate, in short, for a theater of her own devising. Yet when faced with the yawning emptiness of the present, she has nothing to fill it with. That's when "these things come over me, just like that, suddenly, and I can't hold back." Such rashness, as she says, has consequences, each of them more dire than the last – her marriage to Tesman, their acquisition of the Falk house, her pregnancy, her destruction of Lovborg's manuscript, her suicide.

Ibsen parallels this restlessness for – and restlessness in – the present with his retrospective and anticipatory method. Intensifying and deepening the suspense of the well-made play, Ibsen creates a pull between past and future in our experience of viewing his drama. Expository material is meted out only as it has the capacity to excite our expectations. Information about the past or about off-stage events – for example, Aunt Rina's illness, Thea's escape from her lifeless marriage, Lovborg and Hedda's former tête-à-têtes (re-enacted in the photo album scene) – does much more than the ordinary work of filling in the dramatic world or rounding out its characters. It creates a state of guided apprehension, our readings of past events changing as new information is provided.

In this way, we perceive events and then, in an ongoing process of reconsideration, revise our understanding of them as more and more details accumulate. Thus Ibsen recreates the very idea of dramatic sequence, allowing events to proceed in overlapping succession, like runners staggered for a relay race. Encouraging us constantly to reassess our conclusions, this innovation calls melodramatic conventions into question, and with them, the gender conventions they inscribed.

Ibsen points this imbricated sequence in two directions. For example, Aunt Rina's sickness makes us expect her death and anticipate that she will be replaced, as Aunt Julie suggests, with someone else who needs care. At first, we think, that will be Hedda's child, but that presumption is deflected toward Thea. Rina's death, when it does come – and the stage full of people dressed in mourning it brings with it – foreshadows the deaths of both Lovborg and Hedda. (Even the letter announcing Rina's last moments, which the maid brings in after the night of Lovborg's debauch, seems, at first, as though it will bring news about him.) Similarly, Thea's past stirs questions about Hedda: will she – can she – flee? Thea's line of action, of course, overlaps the others. Her loss of respectability puts her in need of Aunt Julie's ministrations; her collaboration with Lovborg recalls Hedda's intimacy with him. And so on. Every gesture, every line of dialogue, every event, takes its place in an action tugged inexorably forward toward a future implied by an ever-changing past.

This sense that the action is being pulled along is emphasized by what Rolf Fjelde refers to as the play's stichomythic dialogue.[44] If this phrase recalls the Greek echoes in the play, it also describes the way so much of the exposition is elicited by means of interrogation. As Hedda once goaded Lovborg to tell her about his demimonde adventures, she questions Thea about her arrival in town, and Brack about Lovborg's comportment. Aunt Julie examines the maid about Hedda and Tesman. Brack questions Hedda about her marriage. The play thus acquires an interrogative mood, encouraging our process of taking in, retrospectively reviewing, and modifying our responses.

Lovborg, man of the future, exists almost entirely in the past: though he makes two much-ballyhooed appearances, we learn most about him by report. What we actually *see* him do – chat with Hedda over the album, change his mind about going to Brack's party, lie to Thea about the loss of his manuscript, confess to Hedda and go off with her pistol – is orchestrated by Hedda. Though he'd be the hero in a more traditional drama, here he's a figure in a drama Hedda is stagemanaging. In this respect, she's rather like the duke in *Measure for Measure*, who reneges on his responsibilities, puts a tyrant in his place, and then manipulates the action he has unleashed, steering it toward a comic ending. Hedda's manipulations don't bring such a felicitous, if phony, outcome; she aims for tragedy. Still, just as critics have labored to understand the duke's motivation, they have psychoanalyzed Hedda, searching for explanations for her impossible actions.

From the sympathetic diagnoses of Lou Andreas Salomé,[45] to the more consciously feminist analyses of Gail Finney, who sees Hedda as "the personification of the hysterization of the female body, or the reduction of the woman to her status as female,"[46] Hedda's womanhood has supplied a clinical explanation for her actions. (Even non-feminists have drawn such conclusions: Michael Meyer suggests that Hedda "should have been born a boy";[47] director Mel Shapiro, who cast Charles Ludlam as Hedda in a 1984 production at Pittsburgh's short-lived American Ibsen Theater, justified this decision by arguing that Hedda was "trapped in the wrong body."[48]) But plausible as some of these interpretations may be (though Shapiro and Meyer might remember that craving male privilege is not the same thing as wanting to be a man), none of them is big enough to contain Hedda. As Hedda herself says, dismissing the very idea of motivation, "Oh – reasons –." Her suicide is so overdetermined, that any explanation, taken alone or in sum, feels insufficient. It's not just the boredom, the baby, Brack's blackmail, Lovborg's botched nobility, Thea's new partnership with Tesman, or Hedda's last-ditch attempt to see something done beautifully. None of these explains the size of her gesture, at once self-destructive and self-aggrandizing. And yet that gunshot rings with inevitability.

Critics in Ibsen's day complained precisely of this fact. When it premiered, *Hedda Gabler* received the most venomous notices of any of Ibsen's prose works. One reviewer chided, "We do not understand Hedda Gabler, nor believe in her." Another called her "a horrid miscarriage of the imagination, a monster in female form." A third resented that "Certain traits are perhaps truthfully portrayed, but the psychological combination of these traits is without logic."[49] What's noteworthy about these criticisms isn't simply that the writers made the right observation, but the wrong judgment about it, but that from today's vantage point, we assume they are comparing Hedda to "real women," when in fact they are complaining about a new kind of dramaturgy. At a time when the theater, in Joseph Donohue's words, was "crowded to overflowing with images of yielding, often helpless, feminine women"[50] (and with cardboard villains), they rejected Hedda not because she was unlike any actual person – a criterion that was hardly operative (or relevant) – but because she didn't behave like other female *characters*.

This distinction is important if Hedda's gender is to be understood as something more than the symptom psychoanalytic critics make of it. True, on one level she is a woman trapped in social conditions that leave no room for her individual expression, much as she is a figure trapped in the wrong kind of play, and a human spirit trapped in the mundane degradations of the material world. But our understanding of these suffocations – and of their mutually reflecting nature – come from recognizing Hedda's, and *Hedda*'s, divergence from a melodramatic norm. Gay Gibson Cima persuasively argues that seen in the light of the new performance style wrought by Elizabeth Robins and other female actor-managers, "Hedda simultaneously mocks and enacts the role of woman as ideal victim."[51] Balancing the "realistic" with the "melodramatic," Robins's performance as Hedda, says Cima, "attempted to enact and kill off the melodramatic image of the self-sacrificing woman, to show the ludicrousness as well as the seductiveness of her very sacrifice."[52]

Without diminishing the contributions of Robins and other actors to this subtle critique of women's depiction on the turn-of-the-century stage, I think it's fair to credit Ibsen with the play's ability self-consciously to deconstruct. The play's self-referentiality, its constant provision of alternative interpretations, make subversive readings of representation possible, rather than, as Cima suggests, promoting "the dominant ideology almost as fiercely as melodrama had."[53] (However, performance traditions that ignore the metatheatrical pointings of the play may very well promote dominant ideology.) As in *A Doll House*, the gender critique is opened up in part by the comparison of the protagonist to an actor.

Like Nora, Hedda refuses to play her traditional role, while those around her take refuge within the "character types" that cozily dictate their behavior. Like Nora in her stocking scene, Hedda is associated with the icons of actress and theater when Brack guesses that she won't jump off the figurative train of her marriage because someone on the platform will look at her legs. When Tesman finally catches on about his wife's pregnancy, Hedda blurts out, "Oh, I'll die of all this." Tesman asks, "Of what?" and she replies – in Fjelde's translation – "of all these absurdities." But James McFarlane translates this line as "of this *farce*,"[54] reinforcing Hedda's refusal to take her place within a suffocating and decaying dramatic form, a form which by definition denies her honor, heroism, and action. Hedda's final exit is her most self-consciously theatrical gesture of all. Retiring to her inner space, her own little stage behind a curtain, she pokes out her head in a that's-all-folks sort of salute, promising "from now on I'll be quiet."

Responding to the play's metatheatrical pulses does not have to lead to a reading that merely spirals back on itself, nor to one that turns it into an abstraction, a symphony that has no discursive meaning, as Rick Davis would make of it.[55] On the contrary, feeling the claustrophobia of the proscenium enables us to feel Hedda's claustrophobia of polis and personhood. And it should enable feminist critics to reconsider assumptions about the possibilities of realistic drama – or at least of Ibsen's realistic drama. Ibsen, especially, deserves such a circumspect review, for the gender critique implied in his bending and breaking of realistic form, may yet be as powerful as the most postmodern queer performance.

In recent years, productions of Ibsen have begun to fasten on this possibility. For more than a decade, pioneering directors have tried to pry Ibsen loose from the encrusted habits and cherished convictions of audiences and producers alike. Offering versions of the plays that break out of box set illusionism, they've attempted to retrieve Ibsen from the yoked constraints of canonical reverence and an enervated realism. If Robert Brustein's 1978 production of *The Wild Duck*, for example, went too far in literalizing Brustein's metaphorical reading – the upstage wall was a humongous camera shutter – it did help catapult Ibsen out of the museum. More successfully, Travis Preston's 1984 *Little Eyolf* at the American Ibsen Theater in Pittsburgh, with its presentational acting, dance-concert side-lighting, abstract set (a boat stood vertically on end, as though planted into the floor, throughout Act III) and open stage, created a chilling tone in which the human experiences of loss, grief, recrimination, and guilt acquired the weight of spiritual disintegration – and renewal. Both encouraged a willingness to regard nineteenth-century realism as a deliberately self-conscious form, one that, as Gordon Craig remarked in 1911 was just another "example of a new artificiality."[56]

But it's not surprising that the most powerful productions have been those that have grounded their metatheatricality in a heaving, hortatory realism, nor that they have been the plays that most directly take on gender. Ingmar Bergman's *Doll House* and Deborah Warner's *Hedda Gabler* seemed to begin from an understanding that Ibsen's realism never demanded total immersion in the fictive world of the play: to peer into a recessed box at the end of a darkened theater and grant plausibility to the events that took place there was not to relinquish awareness of artifice; to identify setting and the behavior of characters as comparable to one's everyday environment and actions was not to surrender critical faculties and enter a dreamworld with a life of its own. Realism's aim, J.L. Styan has written, "was to create the illusion of natural space within the unnaturally rigid frame of the proscenium arch."[57] Like Ibsen, both productions acknowledged that blaring, gilded, unnaturally rigid frame, which tugs against the very illusion within it, defining an experience of both engagement and detachment. As a result, Ibsen – and these directors – drew attention to the rigid frames that constrain human fulfillment, among them those erected by the sex–gender system.[58]

Bergman's 1981 *A Doll House* (seen in New York ten years later), streamlined the play and set it on a sparsely furnished, island-like platform. Behind this stage-upon-a-stage photographs of intricate interiors were projected onto a giant screen. Actors sat outside the platform's perimeter, watching the action until it was time to join it. Pernilla

Ostergren played a spirited and sensual Nora, leaping onto a tabletop – another stage surface – to dance a wild tarantella. Bergman's bold intervention was to split the final scene, setting Nora's farewell in the couple's bedroom where, we can't fail to assume, they have just had sex. Bergman even implies that Torvald may have forced Nora. The second half of the scene begins with Nora entering the bedroom dressed in travelling clothes and carrying luggage and rousing her husband to announce her departure. Torvald, naked in bed, modestly pulls the sheets to his chin, an ineffectual shield against his wife's astonishing argument. In a startling, ambiguous image, Bergman has the couple's daughter (he replaces the play's three children with one girl) creep quietly into the bedroom and stand as silent witness to this horrifying – yet somehow promising – primal scene. Nora makes her final escape from her suffocating home/stage by fleeing into the audience.

The most thrilling Ibsen I've seen was Warner's *Hedda Gabler* at Dublin's Abbey Theater in 1991. Departing from two traditional takes on Hedda – solving the psychological puzzle of her enigmatic personality, or presenting her as simply unimaginable within the terms of her society – Warner and actor Fiona Shaw sculpted a muscular hero who was all too imaginable within her constraining world.

Like many before her, Warner introduced Hedda in a silent prologue. (Shaw prowled the stage in the wee hours of the night, checking her nightgown for signs of her period, striking her belly, and weeping with pregnancy.) Hedda was portrayed not as a monster, but neither as a didactic victim of a society that offers her no options but motherhood.

The production was played at a breathtaking pitch, with an all-out but controlled eruption of emotion. Tesman hovered near hysteria as he realized he was financially over his head. Lovborg was virtually operatic in his grief. Most exciting, Thea became a gathering force of strength and action, a potent contrast to Hedda's entrapment.

As for Shaw, she was an elegant wild horse refusing to be broken. She hauled furniture around the stage, flinging chairs here and there, as if trying to make her domestic prison – and theatrical prison – somehow inhabitable, as if trying to break through its frame. With each scene, the room became sparser and sparser. The final moments were played on an almost barren stage. When Hedda burned Lovborg's manuscript, rather than deliberately peeling it apart, sheaf by sheaf, she hurled it into the fireplace in a single, desperate gesture. When she gave Lovborg one of her pistols, it was as shocking as it was inevitable.

By the last act, the accumulated tension had reached a level that was absolutely unbearable. I found myself not only waiting for Hedda's gun to go off, but *wishing* for it, longing, like Hedda, for the release that final blast would bring. When Judge Brack remarked "People don't do such things," he might as well have been talking about Ibsen. It's no way to end a play – unless, as Warner and Shaw so stirringly demonstrated, it's the only way.

3 Materialist girl

The Good Person of Szechwan and making gender strange

Like most social activists who believe in theater as an instrument of change, feminists have both claimed and rejected Bertolt Brecht, joining in the critical tug-of-war that has characterized his reception in America since the Theatre Union introduced him to this country with its ill-conceived (and disastrous) production of *The Mother* in 1935. Brecht has been described as the great poet whose plays no longer work, the genius dramatist whose theatrical theory doesn't fit, the artist whose politics hardly matter, the idealist who decayed into an opportunistic creep. Feminist critics, going further, have pointed to a series of seeming contradictions to prove or discount Brecht's usefulness: most of his major plays feature female protagonists; he portrayed women stereotypically. He assumed the emancipation of women was part of socialism; he paid little attention to the vibrant women's movement of the Weimar period. Throughout his career, he surrounded himself with trusted female collaborators; he owes his career to brilliant women he treated as a harem – and screwed professionally as well.

All this invoking, dismissing, extolling, and reviling has often missed the deepest feminist implications of Brecht's epic theater. And it has done so for the same reason that, more generally, Brecht in America has been reduced to two solid misconceptions: that he didn't want any emotion in the theater and that his plays fail because they don't convert anyone to Communism (or to communism). These caricatures, long elevated to the status of unshakable cliché, rely, as do many feminist quibbles with Brecht, on a simplification that culminates in a smarmy certainty about the "Brechtian" – a grungy, grudging didacticism produced through a predictable set of stage effects (projected scene titles, bright lights, music hall band, scowling actors). This conception has little to do with the plays themselves or with the intricate performance style Brecht built into them, and elaborated in his theoretical writings.

Now, with the 1994 publication of John Fuegi's *Brecht and*

Company,[1] there's renewed frenzy – falsely claimed as feminist – for deflecting attention away from Brecht's dramatic genius onto his nasty person. As soon as it appeared, Fuegi's missionary tome, which asserts that much of the work Brecht published under his own name was written by his exploited and discarded lovers, was immediately debunked by Brechtians across the political spectrum – Robert Brustein, Erika Munk, Ronald Speirs, Carl Weber, John Willett – for its sensationalized, grandiose claims and its shoddy, and often downright erroneous, scholarship.[2] Nonetheless, Fuegi's oft-repeated (and ludicrous) litany of "Hitler, Stalin, Brecht" sets off new momentum for discarding Brecht; *Brecht and Company* is being assigned in drama and women's studies courses at campuses across the country, defining Brecht for another generation of students never called upon to encounter his plays.

Of course Brecht's plays are difficult for Americans because they assume knowledge of, and draw much of their dramatic complexity from, classical sources like Shakespeare, Schiller, and Goethe. More than that, they run up against the abiding cultural assumption that art and politics are mutually destructive, that the poetic realm is of necessity sullied and simplified by specific social concerns, while political action is stymied by the resonant ambiguities and universalist impulses of the aesthetic. Thus, for example, a *New York Times* article extolling novelist Toni Morrison for winning the 1993 Nobel Prize for Literature takes pains to point out, "Although works like 'The Bluest Eye' and 'Sula' give the reader an exacting portrait of an entire community and way of life, Ms. Morrison is not really concerned with social conditions."[3]

The notion that social conditions are an embarrassment to art masks, of course, how work that doesn't explicitly address social conditions usually assumes that they are acceptable, or at least inevitable. To question them is to be relegated to the inferior category of *political* writer and dismissed for didacticism. So it has gone for poor BB – who made things even worse by writing theoretically about his experiments in epic theater.

Brecht's years in America from 1941 to 1947 hardly provided the opportunity for his work to offer the proof of the pudding, as James Lyon has detailed.[4] Despite Brecht's frantic efforts to keep working, his refuge in the US amounted to a series of misadventures – dozens of screenplay projects that (with one exception) never materialized, performance plans that became drawn out disasters (the Laughton *Galileo* at least came to fruition eventually, but was a critical failure). Strangely, Brecht didn't seem to grasp that America – especially Hollywood, where he made his home, and Broadway, where he yearned for theatrical success – was temperamentally and aesthetically unprepared for the dialectical demands of his art. Celebrating the individual, wallowing in sentiment, involving the spectator vicariously in a hero's journey toward self-knowledge, the American theater could hardly make sense of – much less room for – Brecht. By the time Brecht fled the US, right after his appearance before the House Un-American Activities Committee, he had lost whatever chance he might have had to influence theatrical development in this country.

In the years that followed, McCarthyism drove the wedge between art and dissidence ever deeper. Brecht's own productions with his own company would never be seen here, not even in 1986, when the Berliner Ensemble, by then classically tame, toured to Toronto. Canadian producers looked for US producers, eager to set up some performances here, but found no takers. While the Berliner Ensemble toured London in 1956, and again in the late 1960s, inspiring a generation of politically engaged playwrights like Howard Brenton, Caryl Churchill, and Steven Berkoff, here Artaud and Grotowski were inflaming a generation of theatrical shamans without the counterbalancing weight of Brecht's "scientific" approach. Along with the Method mania of the mainstream, these gurus could support a presumption that would leave no room for Brecht: intellect – and thus Brecht's critically-based work – does not belong in the theater.

Thus was Brecht relegated to the realm of myth, cliché, and casuistic complaint, his plays going unstudied and unproduced in any but the most simple-minded of ways. To this day, reviewers – and worse, directors – of American Brecht productions approach his work with received ideas that are at best limited, and limiting. America's – and American feminists' – ability to skim Brecht for confirmation of the old platitudes and leave the rest for waste depends, in sum, on a fundamental failure to recognize the complex achievement of Brecht's dramatic art.

Nowhere is this failure more apparent than in recent readings of the play most frequently cited by feminists, *The Good Person of Szechwan*, in which Shen Teh, the prostitute who "can never say no",[5] opens a small tobacco shop with money she receives from three gods in search of a good person after she puts them up for a night. When freeloading neighbors, among others, exploit her generosity, Shen Te transvests into her male cousin, Shui Ta, whose entrepreneurial shrewdness should enable her to make ends meet – and remain good. These critics – among them John Fuegi, Iris Smith, Gay Gibson Cima, Anne Herrmann – scold Brecht for his "stereotypical" portrayals of femininity as good and masculinity as evil, and see only a "metaphor" in Shen Teh's "crossdressing." Cima goes so far as to suggest a biographical staging that casts a "Brecht lookalike" as the First God and Shen Te's lover Yang Sun, and his many mistresses as multiple Shen Tehs.[6] But these critics have neglected to examine the play's dialectical action in any but the most superficial of ways. This knee-jerk approach, laying a tendentious template over a work of art to see where it lines up, is particularly frustrating in the case of Brecht because it is so unnecessary. Epic theater's basic effort to make the familiar strange, show the world as alterable, hold events at a temporal distance and, as Brecht writes, reveal the human being as "the sum of all social circumstances,"[7] contains a profoundly feminist impulse (even if the social relations defined by gender were not the ones that particularly interested Brecht). It can make gender strange – that is, startle us with a recognition of gender's artificiality, divulging how something we took to be natural is in fact a construction.

As with any zealous critical school, in the most egregious cases preconceived conclusions can blind critics even to the most essential, obvious facts of a work. One call for a feminist refashioning of *Good Person* goes so far as to miss the play's theatrical crux, "The Song of Defenselessness of the Gods and the Good People." In a 1991 article in *Theatre Journal*, Iris Smith complains of "the *unseen* creation of the male figure, who seems to appear *sui generis* on the stage." She goes on to suggest that "At some point, perhaps in Scene Seven . . . the costuming of Shui Ta could be done in full view of the audience."[8]

Of course Shen Te *does* costume herself as Shui Ta in full view of the audience in the "Song of Defenselessness," which follows Scene Four. Moreover, this careful, complicated scene offers important clues about epic acting, the relationship between gender and epic acting, and indeed about gender *as* epic acting. For the Brecht scholar Peter W. Ferran, this interlude represents "Brecht's epic theater in its quintessence."[9]

The song comes nearly halfway through the play, several scenes *after* we've seen Shen Teh disguised as her shrewd cousin, Shui Ta. Clearly, its function is not to *reveal* that Shui Ta is Shen Teh's invention, but to show how that invention is assembled, how the contradiction described in the song – that goodness can come about only if militarily enforced – both demands and defeats the use of the disguise, how dramatic character (and, by extension, social character) is artificially manufactured, how our sympathies and antipathies can be evoked and manipulated. The demonstrated *construction* of Shui Ta, presented through the action of a baleful and defensive song, *deconstructs* notions of character, social role (including gender), dramatic inevitability, and the easy distinction between good and evil. Most important, the interlude substantiates, through the actor's combined action of delivering a song and putting on a costume, the play's elemental disjunction: one actor stirs both our empathy with Shen Teh and our disgust with Shui Ta. Thus the interlude calls attention to our own dialectical activity in the epic theater, the act of complex seeing, which demands that we perceive things as they are and, at the same time, as other than they are.

The song immediately follows a busy scene in which all the intertwining threads of the plot get tangled up: Shen Teh, newly in love with the pilot Yang Sun, praises the "glorious" morning, cheerfully dishes out rice to the freeloaders who exploit her generosity, and buys a shawl – the slightly damaged one – from the old couple with a long-standing marriage. But her romantic haze is ironically framed: before her entrance there's malicious gossiping about where Shen Teh has been all night, and the barber Shu Fu smashes Wang the Waterseller's hand; after her entrance, the old woman reminds Shen Teh that she owes rent to the exacting Mrs Mi Tzu. Worse, the freeloaders refuse to testify for Wang against Shu Fu, which prompts Shen Teh to declare, in verse: "Oh you wretched people! / Your brother suffers violence and you close your eyes." In the space of some 100 lines, in the face of glaring selfishness, Shen Teh's giddiness (as she describes it) transforms into anger (as a stage direction puts it). Yet here, as throughout the play, Shen Teh is not as thoroughly good and kind as those who accuse Brecht of flattening her into an object lesson charge. Early in the scene she closes her own eyes to Wang's suffering, so absorbed in her infatuation that she fails to notice it. (Later, she betrays Wang more directly.)

In the same compact space, the play further complicates its representation of love as an economic transaction, and its depiction of men's commodification of women. (An early working title for the play was *Die Ware Liebe*, "Love for Sale" or "The Commodity, Love;" playing on the pun of *Ware* and *wahre*, the title could also mean "True Love.") Before getting silver from the gods, of course, Shen Teh survived as a prostitute. But in one of Brecht's many ironic undoings of this self-conscious dramatic archetype, Shen Teh does not get ripped off by a man until she gives herself to him. Yang Sun demands the price of his trip to Peking and of his bribe for a pilot's job in exchange for his love. At the end of Scene Four, Shen Teh hands over to him the $200 lent her by the old couple for rent.

Playing against this inverted romance, this scene also introduces the idea of the wealthy barber Shu Fu as a husband for Shen Teh. Seeing her in the rosy splendor of the morning – when she's flushed with love for Yang Sun – Shu Fu falls in love with her. In addition to setting up the later transaction between Shen Teh and the barber, this moment also reminds us that Shen Teh met Yang Sun while on her way to a tête-à-tête with a marriage prospect – one who could cough up the rent money. Here, and in the later negotiations with Shu Fu, marriage is compared to the whoring Shen Teh thought she could leave behind by becoming a businesswoman – or businessman. Indeed, as Shui Ta, Shen Teh serves as her own pimp, becoming, as Brecht's working notes put it, "both goods and saleswoman."[10]

To sum up, Scene Four ends with Shen Teh in love with a man and disappointed in humanity, standing under an accelerating cascade of troubles: the rent, and now the old couple, still owed; Wang injured and abandoned; the freeloaders ever demanding; Shu Fu waiting to pounce. The audience is left in a frame of mind to urge, like the free-loaders in the first scene, "Cousin! Cousin!" But rather than simply satisfy this by now obvious response to Shen Teh's problems, Brecht interrupts (to use Walter Benjamin's word for the process of epic devel-opment[11]) the action, casting into relief our mounting empathy for Shen Teh's plight and uncovering the conditions that lead to her extreme solution.

"Shen Teh enters," the stage direction reads, "carrying the mask and clothes of Shui Ta, and sings 'The Song of Defenselessness of the Gods and the Good People'." After the first verse, "She puts on Shui Ta's clothes and takes a few steps in his manner." After the second, "She puts on Shui Ta's mask and continues to sing in his voice."

Who sings this song? That is, what stage persona commits the action of – in Brecht's words – "handing over" (*zeigen gestus*)[12] "The Song of Defenselessness"? Of course the text assigns the song to the character Shen Teh, but, as Brecht has written, "When an actor sings, [s]he under-goes a change of function."[13] This is doubly true here. At the most literal level, the singer presents a character in transition, changing her function from portraying Shen Teh to portraying Shui Ta. But we see more than one character changing into the costume of another. The actor's function changes also because by singing, as Brecht writes, "[s]he who is showing should [her]self be shown."[14] The actor demonstrates how she performs both the role of Shen Teh and the role of Shui Ta. And at the same time she demonstrates how she performs another role, which parallels her pointed-to actorly effort: Shen Teh *playing* Shui Ta. In other words, revealing the process by which she takes steps in Shui Ta's manner and sings in his voice, the actor calls attention to the anal-ogy between her activity and Shen Teh's.

In describing this "transformation scene before the curtain" in a journal entry, Brecht emphasized that it "is not in any way mystical but merely a technical solution in terms of mime and a song."[15] A solution to what? In the plot's terms, to Shen Teh's plight – up to a point. But more important, to the dilemma Brecht describes while working on the play: whether it will "have a straight-forward conflict *gods-ligung-laogo* [early names for Shen Teh and Shui Ta], which would keep it all on a moral plane and allow two conflicting principles (two 'souls') to figure separately," or to "have a plain simple story about how li gung masquerades as her cousin"[16] which seems necessary, he concludes, if the device of Shen Teh's pregnancy will eventually force her to give up the game. The "Song of Defenselessness" provides the "solution" *by virtue* of being technical. Showing the mechanism of the transformation, instead of allowing it to remain mystical, Brecht can develop *both* approaches – using the "simple story" about the masquerade to pitch the parable along a moral plane. Shen Teh and Shui Ta can function both as "conflicting principles" that "figure separately" *and* as two incarnations of the same being.

The song achieves this dialectic because, through the analogy it draws to all acting, it grants Shen Teh and Shui Ta the same level of credibility. We always perceive Shui Ta as an impersonation performed by Shen Teh; simultaneously, we understand that Shen Teh is herself an impersonation created by the actor; therefore, she elicits no more unexamined empathy than does the less affecting Shui Ta, despite her more appealing qualities.

This equilibrium is maintained through a sly paradox of acting: Shen Teh's character, in conventional theatrical terms, is "unbelievable" – could anyone really be so naive, we have to ask in the face of her unmitigated generosity toward the exploitative freeloaders. But Shui Ta's character, the familiar ruthless businessman, is completely believable (*because* it is so familiar). Indeed, in a 1970 *New York Times* review of a Lincoln Center production starring Colleen Dewhurst, Walter Kerr chides the play for precisely this contrast. Explaining that "we lose patience with these figureheads [the freeloaders] long before the lady does," Kerr concludes, "if we ever side with anyone, we tend to side with her tough-minded 'cousin'."[17]

But what Kerr – and presumably the production – missed is the way these opposite levels of credibility are used within Brecht's parable form, and how they are balanced with inverse proportions of empathic acting. Acquiring intimacy with the audience through soliloquies, and given downright sentimental speeches about love and motherhood (which are soon punctured by various ironic devices), Shen Teh demands more "Aristotelian" pity than does Shui Ta, who never addresses the audience, and remains emotionally at arm's length because of our double awareness of him as an effective figure in the parable, and as Shen Teh's creation. The *type* of character Shui Ta represents is more believable than the *type* Shen Teh represents, yet we experience Shui Ta from a greater distance.

To keep wide this distance from the evil character we can so easily compass – and to close the distance on the good character we can hardly accept – Brecht repeatedly reminds us that Shui Ta is being played by Shen Teh. In the first scene, it's the freeloaders who come up with the idea that a wily cousin can get Shen Teh out of her jam with the unpaid Carpenter, and then with the landlady Mrs Mi Tzu: "My dear Shen Teh, why don't you turn the whole matter over to your cousin?" After repeated promptings, Shen Teh relents: "slowly, with downcast eyes," the stage direction reads, Shen Teh declares, "I have a cousin." (Michael Hofmann's 1989 translation of Brecht's Santa Monica version of *Good Person* goes so far as to have a freeloader think up the name Shui Ta.[18]) After the claimants leave – and more relatives of the freeloaders arrive – Shen Teh's imposing guests have a facetious laugh over the mythical cousin, "the imposing Mr. Shui Ta." The scene ends with more knocking on the door, threatening that still more relatives will overtake Shen Teh's shop.

When knocking is heard again, at the top of the next scene (following an interlude where Wang presages Shen Teh's later betrayal), it announces the quick-fix to the rapidly multiplying relatives: "a young gentleman," as the stage directions say, Shui Ta. At first the freeloaders dismiss him: "But that was a joke." But almost at once, they come to grant him the authority of his imposing presence. As an onstage audience to Shen Teh's performance, they offer one model of a response to her acting. For them, the performance of Shui Ta is "Aristotelian" – that is, they believe in it completely and are swept away by it; for us, the performance is epic, always experienced with complex seeing. The onstage audience's reaction works like a lens that intensifies our double vision – and that mirrors our more sympathetic response to Shen Teh.

Later in the scene, after Shui Ta wheedles the Carpenter out of his fee, the freeloaders repeat the event, quoting – in a style reminiscent of the acting Brecht calls for in "The Street Scene: A Basic Model for an Epic Theatre"[19] – the dialogue that just took place. Their merriment is ended only when Shui Ta's virtuoso performance is turned on them: he tells them to get out. What happens in their little imitation is complicated. We see a performance re-enacted with a particular attitude – gloating amusement, like the attitude of fans recounting how their team routed another in a ball game. This action drives home the freeloaders' smug selfishness at the same time that it reminds us that Shui Ta is a performance, one that could be presented from various points of view. In this moment, of course, like Walter Kerr, we have to side with Shui

Ta, cheering his rejection of the freeloaders. But part of the reason we cheer him is that we see Shen Teh within Shui Ta, and recognize that she is standing up for herself. More important, our recognition of Shen Teh behind the mask of Shui Ta (and of an actor behind Shen Teh), encourages us to consider *other* points of view from which Shui Ta (and Shen Teh) might be presented. At the same time, if we feel like satisfied backers of a winning team when Shui Ta throws the freeloaders out, it's because it looks like justice is prevailing, like Shui Ta will temper Shen Teh's mercy, enabling her to live and do good.

But of course, we can't hold on to this hope uncritically. The contradiction has already been set forth: Shen Teh can't do good unless Shui Ta does well. And if cheating the Carpenter is what enables Shui Ta to do well – no matter how much it entertains the freeloaders – we see at once its dubious merit. The "Street Scene"-style performance by the freeloaders sharpens our awareness of this bind by placing before us our own emotional reactions to Shui Ta. Will we, like the freeloaders, have a laugh over Shui Ta's cold treatment of others? And if so, what does that laugh show us? That we judge the freeloaders harshly (no sentimental portrait of the poor and downtrodden for Brecht!), that we appreciate the comic device of reversal, that we grasp the central contradiction to be expanded upon in the play – that one can't be good without having means, and acquiring means prevents one from being good.

Other ironic reminders of Shen Teh's performance of Shui Ta function in similar ways. In Scene Three, Shen Teh responds to Yang Sun's challenge, "You're not much of an entertainer," with the line, "I can play the zither a little and imitate people." Then, the stage directions instruct, "She speaks in a deep voice, imitating a dignified gentleman," saying, " 'Good Lord, I must have forgotten my pocketbook!' But then I got the shop. The first thing I did was give away my zither. I said to myself, now I can be a deadhead, and it won't matter." Here, Shen Teh switches to verse: "I'm rich, I said to myself. / I walk alone. I sleep alone. / For a whole year, I said to myself / I'll have nothing to do with a man."

At one level, of course, this is so much flirtatious banter. But again, even at this curiously romantic moment, Brecht reminds us of the cousin not merely waiting in the wings, but lurking within the performer we see speaking "in a deep voice." What's more, Shen Teh can mention getting rid of her zither as a humorous throw-away; to say that she will have nothing to do with a man requires heightened speech because, not only is her evident attraction for Yang Sun contradicting this pronouncement, but her impersonation of Shui Ta suggests that being rich necessitates having *everything* to do with a man, even if it's one she embodies herself.

Similarly, in Scene Five, right after the "Song of Defenselessness," Shui Ta sits in the tobacco shop reading the paper. When he hears Yang Sun's voice from outside, the stage directions command, "Shui Ta runs to the mirror with the light steps of Shen Teh and is about to arrange his hair when he sees his mistake in the mirror. He turns away with a soft laugh." This is the only occasion in the play when Shen Teh's character so boldly peeps through the Shui Ta disguise, where we see Shen Teh acknowledge her performance by momentarily forgetting it. (Still, the stage directions refer to *his* hair, *his* mistake.) Several things are accomplished by this self-conscious action. First, Brecht increases the disdain with which we react to Yang Sun's coarse treatment of Shen Teh by reminding us of her romantic enthusiasm, and showing how thoroughly love has swept her away. At the same time, it asks us to prick up our double vision, increasing our ironic pleasure in registering how wrong Yang Sun is to think he is shooting the breeze with one of the guys. Once again, the double character ignites our dialectical attention, making us at once more empathetic and more critical. All this raises the stakes for the moment later in the scene when Yang Sun reveals that he has no intention of taking Shen Teh to Peking with him.

Yang Sun assumes a macho stance when Shui Ta says that Shen Teh will not go along with his decision: "You're going to appeal to her reason? She hasn't got any reason." Some critics point to this line as an indication that Brecht is reinforcing a misogynistic stereotype of femininity. But that is to disregard the play's theatrical dynamics. Yang Sun's remark is not endorsed; its appalling nature is pointed to by our recognition of Shen Teh's hidden presence. Yang Sun is unmistakably an ambitious lout, not a sanctioned mouthpiece for what Gay Gibson Cima calls Brecht's "profound ambivalence toward women."[20] That it turns out to be true, in terms of the plot, that Shen Teh pays little mind to her reason – she runs off with Yang Sun after all, because, as he puts it, "I've got my hand on her bosom" – does not mean that the play is doubting the intelligence of women. Rather, Brecht calls forth a familiar (and derogatory) image of women in order to make it strange because, after all, the familiar cannot be rendered strange without first being established *as familiar*. By means of the *Verfremdungseffekt* – the central mechanism of which is the Shui Ta disguise – Brecht lets us take a look at the conditions that give rise to this image of love and the commodified, irrational woman. (In addition, that Shen Teh so abandons herself to this lust contradicts several critics who complain that Brecht denies this female character her "desire."[21])

Shen Teh next refers to herself as Shui Ta in Scene Six, the wedding scene. Her marriage to Yang Sun is delayed – pathetically in terms of

our feeling for Shen Teh; comically in terms of the gag of making the
flow of wine the celebration's hourglass – because Yang Sun and his
mother await Shui Ta, who, they hope, will bring money. Shen Teh
asserts: "My cousin cannot be where I am." Why is this line here? We in
the audience already know this; Yang Sun and his mother aren't meant
to – and don't – understand what she means. Like Benedick's stating-
the-obvious remark, "This looks not like a nuptial," in *Much Ado About
Nothing*, Shen Teh's line pulls the scene away from the precipice of
melodrama. It signals us: Don't get so carried away by this bittersweet
episode that you forget to employ your complex seeing; the double
character once more forces an epic interruption, refocusing our attention.

The wedding ends, of course, without Shui Ta's arrival; like St
Neverkin's day described in Yang Sun's song – "when the poor woman's
son will ascend the king's throne" and "life on earth will become a
sweet dream" – Shui Ta will never, *can* never, come, at least not until a
vexing contradiction can be resolved. In this scene, waiting is the central
gestus: for the wedding, for Shui Ta, for the good times. The ending
stage direction has Shen Teh, Yang Sun and Mrs Yang sitting together,
"two of them looking toward the door."

But of course, Shui Ta does come, in Scene Seven. In fact, Shui Ta
dominates the last portion of the play, the "tobacco king" replacing the
"angel of the slums" almost as thoroughly as Jeriah Jip overtakes Galy
Gay in *Man Is Man*. The mechanism that both retrieves and eventually
undoes Shui Ta is Shen Teh's pregnancy; it instigates Shen Teh's most
thorough – and least sustainable – transformation. Significantly, in a
working outline for the Santa Monica version, Brecht uses this same
word to describe Shen Teh's reaction to seeing a child forage for food in
the garbage: "The sight brings about a complete transformation in her.
She makes a big speech to the audience proclaiming her determination
to turn herself into a tigress for the sake of the child in her womb."[22]
The one transformation brings forth the other; they become one and the
same.

Even though Brecht's image of motherhood here is not exactly sweet
and touching – Shen Teh's says she'll treat others like a "tiger and a wild
beast" – and even though the image is distanced by an ironic reversal –
becoming a bad man enables her to be a good mother – some critics
point especially at this scene to nail Brecht with their charge of misogyny. In a much-quoted essay, Sarah Lennox asserts, "a major virtue of
[Brecht's] mother figure is her willingness to be instrumentalized, serving others while ignoring her own subjective needs."[23] Anne Herrmann
goes further:

By placing mothers in the female subject position, Brecht not only desexualizes her, but also insists on biological differences as they were used and misused by both the sex reformers of the Weimar Republic (1918–1933) and the Nazis of the Third Reich (1933–1945).[24]

Of course Shen Teh occupies this "subject position" for seven-eighths of the play before she becomes pregnant. And while Brecht may use as a plot device the unavoidable biological fact that women can get pregnant, its epic presentation reveals rather than reinforces essentialist propaganda about a woman's proper role. The formal verse of Shen Teh's "big speech" is one clue that the scene must be played for distance. And the about-to-be-enacted costume change is a further reminder that Shen Teh's gender is as provisional as it is providential.

Shen Teh's pregnancy brings about another transformation. It marks the pivotal point where one expectation is exchanged for another. Up until then, we wait for Shui Ta, knowing just when he'll appear to bail Shen Teh out; after, we wait for Shen Teh, hoping (though knowing better) that she'll come back and set things right. Like the freeloaders, we undergo a change. They transform from exploiting loafers to exploited workers; we change the direction in which we yearn for a resolution.

This action of transformation is essential to the play, in terms of both the parable's story and its procedure – and essential, too, to the very purpose of epic theater. The central transformation of Shen Teh into Shui Ta provides a standard against which other transformations can be regarded: of the exploiting into the exploited, of the tobacco shop into a factory, of unemployed flier into unrelenting foreman (that is, labor into management), of the gods into judges – and most of all, the transformation theater enacts, of actor into character, stage into setting. By making the act of theater viewing strange, Brecht subjects all the transformations in the story to a parallel interrogation: do they have to happen? In that way? How do I, as a spectator taking part through a kind of imaginative complicity, enable these events to take place?

This dramatic motif, echoed by the theatrical process, is not just a game of self-referentiality. Brecht's metatheatrical pointings direct our attention to the possibility of change and to our role in effecting it. Herein lies the revolutionary nature of Brecht's dramaturgy. His intention was not to provide a recipe for socialism, as so many detractors have summarily suggested, but to offer spectators the pleasurable experience of practicing and honing their critical attitude in the epic theater, so it could be applied more successfully in the world.

The whetstone in *Good Person* is what Brecht called "the continual fusion and dissolution of the two characters,"[25] Shen Teh and Shui Ta. Brecht sought to achieve the same ebb and flow of sympathy and antipathy with many of his protagonists – Mother Courage as victim and villain, Galileo as scholar and cheat, Puntila as humanist and misanthrope, Azdak as wiseman and bum. Walter Sokel calls these "split characters",[26] but they are more double than split, as we always experience one side of the character through the memory and expectation of the other. Brecht was drawn to this device, no doubt, because it steadfastly requires complex seeing; the double character serves as a focal point for the heightened, self-conscious perception we must engage in the epic theater. In turn, this double character reinforces the way in which we perceive everyone on stage – as characters *and* as actors showing them to us. Shen Te/Shui Ta is not only Brecht's most literal use of this division, but also the one that most effectively and evocatively attaches the dialectic of theater to the dialectic of moral life.

Examining the theatrical activity of the "Song of Defenselessness" – costuming and epic singing – has already shown how the theatrical dialectic is laid out and twined into a provocative paradox. Seeing how this activity raises particular social questions requires an examination of the song itself. Each of the song's three stanzas is preceded by another step in Shen Teh's transformation to Shui Ta; similarly, each stanza offers a more extreme description of human relations in "our country." It bears quoting in its entirety:

In our country
A useful man needs luck. Only
If he has influential helpers
Can he make himself useful.
The good
Cannot help themselves and the gods are powerless.
    So why can't the gods have bazookas and gunboats
    Dreadnoughts and machine-guns, bombers and mortars
    To shatter the wicked and succor the good folk?
    What's good for the good can't hurt the immortals!

The good
Cannot stay good for long in our country.
Where plates are empty, the diners are soon at each other's throats.
Ah, the divine commandments
Are little help against penury.
    So why can't the gods come down in the markets
    And hand out their bounty to each and his brother

And let us, once hunger and thirst have been sated
Be friendly and kindly toward one another?

Merely to get your dinner
Requires the ruthlessness of an empire builder.
Without trampling on twelve others
No one can help a wretched man.
So why can't the gods decide in the heavens
To make the world good for the good people in it?
Why can't they come down with tanks and with cannon
Make merciless war upon evil and win it?

Each verse is made up of a statement followed by a rhetorical question. These follow two different paths of development. The statements describe conditions that make it difficult for one to be useful, to be good, or to help others, tracing a trajectory of increasing levels of kindness, which are then coupled with increasingly unsurmountable obstacles – lucklessness, poverty, inherent contradiction. Each of these plaintive statements provides one half of a syllogism: this is how things are. The second series of verses provide the other half, the *then* that follows the first statement's implied *if*. So why don't the gods do something? Why don't they obliterate the bad and reward the good? Why don't they create a charitable world? Why don't they have weapons to enforce charity? This progression is offered as the logical response to all three conditional statements.

But, of course, the logic is faulty. As the first stanza tells us "the gods are powerless," suffering from "Defenselessness" – or in a more literal translation of *Wehrlosigkeit*, weaponless-ness. And we know from the prologue that the gods are disheveled and incompetent; even if they had weapons, they couldn't effect the transformation the song calls for any more than they can produce a *denouement* at the end of the play. The implication is that *people* have to accomplish what all-powerful gods are incapable of. That, in a way, is what Shen Teh tries to do by taking on the guise of Shui Ta. (It is also the "Good People" who lack weapons.) His mask and costume, then, are her armor, his manner – the ruthlessness of an empire builder – her weapon. Yet the inherent contradiction of the song – combined with the complex seeing demanded by the costume change – indicate that Shen Te's effort is doomed to fail. Thus, at the very moment when the plot promises the transformation as the solution to Shen Teh's predicament, the song declares that it will not work. Bringing about a climate in which goodness can thrive requires a more fundamental change than acting can accomplish.

The song, then, has a complicated *gestus*. Primarily it is a song of justification, much like Macheath's summing-up anthem at the end of *Threepenny Opera*. Shen Teh *must* do this in order, merely, to survive. (Indeed, the recapitulation of Shui Ta's action in the trial scene at the end of the play provides rationales for his cruel behavior that are difficult to refute.) But this *gestus* provokes a sense of lament and refusal because the song contains – and displays – the inadequacies of its own argument.

The more the song ratchets up the need for the disguise, the more Shui Ta is brought to life – both in the completion of his costuming, and in the way the song's point of view comes to express one we would associate more with his character than with Shen Teh's. As she takes on his appearance, she takes on his mentality. Thus, the transformation reflects the Marxist imperative so central to Brecht's epic theater – that social being determines thought. This principle, of course, is an underpinning of epic acting, which reverses the Stanislavskian process by which an actor builds action from character, proposing instead that the actor derive character from action – especially so that character can be shown to be a product of social forces.

Any critique of Brecht's use of gender in *Good Person* must begin with this principle – but few of them do. Most feminist readings of the play call for a materialist feminist assessment, but pay no attention to the most significant materialist fact: that the play is meant to be performed, in epic style, on a stage before an audience. (One might think that Brecht's inability to stage *Good Person* in his lifetime, and thus to complete the work through the all-important production process, contributes to this tendency to neglect the idea of the play in performance. But these same critics, despite Brecht's extensive revisions, clarifying notes, and *Modelbuch*, write in the same abstract manner about *Mother Courage and Her Children*.) John Fuegi, for example, is right that Shen Teh as a woman is "virtually a personification of feeling, while Shui Ta as a man is made virtually a personification of reason or calculation."[27] But he's right only up to a point because he doesn't credit the play with pointing out and using that critical conclusion. Fuegi adds, "The poetic metaphor achieves its full force only by the complete exploitation of societal pre-judgements (whether Chinese or Western) of the 'nature' of men and women. Only by 'masking' Shen Teh are relations between the sexes in Setzuan literally unmasked."[28] Leaving aside the point that the society of Szechwan is not "Chinese" in any realistic historical or cultural sense (Brecht likened it to such "poetic conceptions" as the imaginary Kilkoa of *Man Is Man* and London of *Threepenny*[29]), Fuegi, like many who have followed him, fails to consider how epic theater practice highlights precisely the assumptions he claims the play rests on.

Good Person not only *exploits* pre-judgments about the "nature" of men and women, it forces us to confront those pre-judgments for what they are. How can we hold onto the belief that Shen Teh is kind and emotional *because* she is female when we are repeatedly reminded that she is Shui Ta? And how can we maintain that Shui Ta is hard and self-serving *because* he is male, when we are repeatedly reminded that he is Shen Teh? Besides, the meanness of Mrs Mi Tzu and the decency of Wang – among others – make it difficult to maintain that the play is awash in moral sexual stereotyping.

To insist that Shen Teh represents a misogynistic stereotype is also to overlook that the play is a parable. Shen Teh is good not because she is female, but because it is her function in the parable to be good. It's astonishing how frequently critics lend Shen Teh psychological depth more fitting to an entirely different genre. To name just a few examples, Fuegi writes that she suffers from a "schizoid personality";[30] Cima worries that the impossibility of meeting the gods' commandments to be good "dictat[es] within Shen Teh a feeling of failure";[31] Sue-Ellen Case diagnoses "an internal crisis of gender behavior."[32] But the parable designation can be oversimplified, too, leading to such groundless accusations as Herrmann's – that "Brecht used his woman figures to embody Communist Party policy at a particular historical moment."[33]

Good Person was written over a long period, primarily during Brecht's exile in Scandinavia. But the idea first surfaces in his journals in the late 1920s, and he attends to it on and off for some twenty years, announcing the play's completion in 1941 – though complains that it will never be finished if he doesn't direct a production. (And in 1943, while living in Santa Monica, he abridges and adapts the play for an American production that never materializes.) During the early years of the play's development, Brecht was experimenting feverishly with the nature of dramatic character in the epic theater and with its relation to epic structure. In the *Lehrstücke*, for example (1928–1933), which many critics mistakenly dismiss as Brecht preaching Marxism directly through the mouths of his characters, he tried out various ways of creating and representing character – by report from various points of view, by re-enactment of a past event by observers, by having different actors exchange roles periodically throughout the play.[34] Emphasizing that these learning plays taught something by being played – not by being read or watched – Brecht suggested that their intended pupil was the performer: Like Scarlatti compositions that limbered and strengthened the pianist for more elaborate pieces, the *Lehrstücke* were exercises in epic acting and its cousin, dialectical thinking. And they were exercises for Brecht in the development of character and dramatic action that would in turn demand dialectical thinking of the audience.

Brecht's notes on *Good Person* are often sketchy, but in the movement from European to Chinese setting, from the story of a prostitute disguising herself as a man "in order to help her sisters," to one who "dresses as a man in order to pose as [a cigar store's] proprietor, meanwhile continuing to practice as a prostitute,"[35] to the nuanced structure he finally settled on, one can trace Brecht's movement toward his dialectical theater. In some sense, he practiced the association of a double character with the paradox of goodness in his satire on bourgeois morality, *The Seven Deadly Sins of the Petit-Bourgeoisie* (1933), a collaboration with Kurt Weill. Its protagonists, the sisters Anna I and Anna II, travel the world trying to raise money for their family to buy a house. One, the salesperson, conveys their travails in words; the other, the goods being sold, through dance. Each scene illustrates a sin which must be avoided if one is to make a buck – but each of these, of course, is really a virtue. Scene by scene, the house takes shape on stage, walls rising as each sin is debated and avoided. Meanwhile a quartet of men representing the family – father, mother, two brothers – offers comments from a platform to the side. (The mother pronounces pieties in basso profundo.)

In the same year, Brecht worked with some of the *Good Person* themes in a short story called "The Job, or In the sweat of thy brow shalt thou fail to earn thy bread." The story is based on a true account of a woman who posed as her husband after he died in order take a job promised to him. The story's opening lines announce that it shows "the barbaric condition to which the great European countries had been reduced by their inability to keep their economies going except by force and exploitation"[36] after the First World War. The barbarity turns out to be not that the woman so masquerades, but that when discovered, she is fired, even arrested, and her job given to "one whose legs chanced to have between them the organ recorded on his birth certificate."[37] The protagonist in the end

> is thought to have worked as a waitress in a suburban bar, amid photographs (some of which she had posed for *after* being found out) showing her in shirtsleeves playing cards and drinking beer as a nightwatchman and to have been regarded as resident freak by the skittle players. Thereafter she probably sank without trace into the ranks of that army of millions who are forced to earn their modest bread by selling themselves, wholly, in part, or to one another, shedding in a few days century-old habits which had almost seemed

eternal and, as we have seen even changing sex, generally without success – who are in short lost and, if we are to believe the prevailing view, lost forever.

The original news account also intrigued Brecht's collaborators, Margarete Steffin and Elisabeth Hauptmann (and was used as a basis for two stories by Anna Seghers); in 1934 Hauptmann wrote to Brecht from the US saying that if he hadn't used the material, she'd like to rework her version. She referred to her "notes on the real case and about the transitory nature of sex distinctions."[38]

Brecht's story is little concerned with that transitory nature, but still treats gender as an artificial construction that serves male dominance, which he seems to regard as an auxiliary to capitalism. The night-watchman's job, the story says, "calls for reliability and courage, qualities that have from time immemorial been called *manly*." The woman's success in the post

> proves that courage, physical strength and presence of mind can be shown by anybody, man or woman, who really needs a job. In a few days the woman became a man, in the same way as men have become men over the millennia: through the production process.[39]

Like Marx, though, Brecht doesn't much factor women's unpaid labor into his definition of production; his protagonist sets up house with a woman who cares for the watchman's two children and looks after their home. Nonetheless, Brecht's story wryly challenges capitalism's enforcement of gender distinctions.

Good Person, to a large extent, amalgamates these two 1933 works, combining a critical use of the cross-dressing "progress narrative"[40] (one that doubts the nature of progress) with a comparison of the dialectics of capitalist ethics to the dialectics of a divided character. Drawing on the lessons of the *Lehrstücke*, and on increasingly sophisticated – and theatrically tested – epic theory, Brecht briefly picks up the 1934 sketch of *Die Ware Liebe* in Denmark in 1939, consigning it to the desk drawer, but figuring he "can use it to develop the epic technique and get back up to standard again."[41] He pokes at it again in Sweden, and then turns fuller attention to the play once he's settled in Finland. What enables him to move ahead on the play that "caused me more trouble than any other play ever did"[42] is his working out the form that could bring his parallel concerns together: the parable. *Good Person* was the first play to which Brecht assigned this label.

Brecht once described the parable as "far more artful than other forms. Lenin used the parable, not as an idealist, but as a materialist.

The parable allowed him to unravel complicated things. To the dramatist it offers the perfect solution, because it is concrete in abstraction: it makes the essential obvious."[43] Brecht's reference to Lenin is aesthetically telling: the parable is not a traditional dramatic form or genre, but is taken from a kind of didactic literature. The label has New Testament overtones as well. Thus, the parable is distinguished from its theatrical cousins, allegory and symbolist drama, in which what is presented to the audience is meant to stand for something else (and which can easily slide into dreaded expressionism). For Brecht, the parable is a condensed, intensified poetic form, at once concrete and indirect, that enables him to evoke familiar characters and situations quickly, so that he can then go about the epic task of making them strange.

G.W. Brandt has suggested that Brecht created "negative parables" that "illustrate a *wrong* state of affairs." He adds, "The negative parable . . . does not imply there is no such thing as right conduct, but the audience are not spoon-fed with a readily digestible moral."[44] This is an important corrective to those who add Brecht's Marxism to his invocation of the parable to conclude that his plays are ideological vehicles, Communist object lessons. Rather, the parable form enables Brecht to subject such doctrines to pleasurable critique. *Good Person* doesn't merely declare that a moral life is incompatible with capitalism; it lets us look at this tenet from a variety of angles, and asks us to consider its accuracy, cause, meaning, value.

To this end, Brecht labored to avoid what he called "dramatic taylorism,"[45] in *Good Person*, where "everything is much too rationalised." About a year later, when his journal records his "more or less" completion of the play, he reflects:

> the main danger was of being over-schematic. li gung [Shen Teh] had to be a person if she was to become a good person. as a result her goodness is not of a conventional kind; she is not wholly and invariably good, not even when she is being li gung. nor is lao go [Shui Ta] conventionally bad.[46]

This is one reason Brecht called for a "big, powerful person" in the role.[47]

Brecht's use of parable, then, was neither simple nor symbolic. It used recognizable figures, but gave them texture; it sought to teach something, but something more lively and demanding than a slogan that could be baked into a fortune cookie; its structure was unadornedly episodic, but it proceeded in zig-zags, buffeted by repeated epic interruptions.

Of course it's true that, through Shen Teh and Shui Ta, goodness is matched with femininity and nastiness with masculinity, but to suggest that Brecht represents these associations as fixed, natural absolutes is to assume that we experience theater as an unmediated re-creation of life, as a given to be passively absorbed and approved. That's rarely the case even in naturalistic theater; we always know we're watching a play. That fact of complex seeing, inherent in virtually all theater experience, frames what's represented, making it available for critique. Brecht seizes on this theatrical paradox – that engagement includes distance – and shines stage lights upon it. By doing so, he hoped to provoke the critique, to make our own experience of watching events enacted on stage a self-conscious part of the story. This process asserts that theater is the best-suited form for considering the world's contradictions, because viewing theater depends on a contradiction that, once exposed, can reveal the complexities and injustices of life.

It's foolhardy, then, to look for Brecht's radicalism, and his potentially feminist deconstructions of gender, on the surface of the story of a play, as, for instance David Z. Mairowitz does when he complains, "There is no challenge in Brecht to the arrangement of traditional sex roles."[48] Perhaps it would be easier to claim Brecht for our side if he'd written some plays with stories directly demonstrating how the social hierarchy relegates women to second-class status (and if he hadn't treated women so execrably himself). It might have been nice if he'd had Shen Teh imagine a little daughter, instead of a little son. But Brecht's challenges to social arrangements come through epic process, not through traditional dramatic show-and-tell. Indeed, if one considers Brecht's attitude toward identification and heroes, it seems downright ludicrous to look to him, as Iris Smith describes some feminists as doing, for "desiring and desirable behaviors modeled on stage . . . so that the feminist spectator could find herself there and project herself into the future."[49]

Brecht was more of a realist, but one whose realism, suggests Ferran, is optimistic because it "disposes us toward a critical observation of 'that which is.'"[50] The 'that which is' that most interested Brecht was, of course, the economic organization of modern life. But other aspects of social relations do not escape the glare of epic practice – especially, those that, in their own way, are like theater. Gender, quite plainly, is one of these. Thus Ekkehard Schall, the longtime Berliner Ensemble lead actor (and Brecht's son-in-law) could claim that one of the best examples of epic acting he'd ever seen was Marilyn Monroe's self-conscious performance in *How to Marry a Millionaire*.[51]

Brecht sensed this, even if he did not make much of it. In one telling comment, recommending rehearsal exercises that would help epic actors build their parts, Brecht suggests, "it is also good for the actors when they see their characters copied or portrayed in another form. If the part is played by somebody of the opposite sex the sex of the character will be more clearly brought out."[52] In watching a female actor play a male role, for example, the male actor observes gestures, stances, movement, vocal intonation – all the attributes that typically compose a conventional idea of male-ness. By separating them from the body to which these characteristics are thought to be fused the actor reveals how gender behavior is constituted. In this exercise, then, the male actor learns how to act male, how to detach his character's gender from the assumption that it naturally resides in and issues from his body.

It's no doubt possible that such an exercise could be used to reinforce notions of naturalized gender behavior – one can imagine, for example, an actor drawing the conclusion that his female colleague observes masculinity better than he does because it is so completely alien to her. But that's not the case with epic acting, which demands that all aspects of character be shown "like a quotation."[53] For as Janelle Reinelt has argued, "The Alienation effect hollows out and denaturalizes behaviors which are actually socially constructed, enforced through power relations and the myopia which results from habitual positioning within them."[54] Applying this process specifically to gender, Elin Diamond points out, "by alienating (not simply rejecting) iconicity [the semiotic observation that the actor's body resembles the character to which it refers], by foregrounding the expectation of resemblance, the ideology of gender is exposed and thrown back to the spectator."[55] As a result, "gender is exposed as a sexual costume, a sign of a role, not evidence of identity" and "the spectator is enabled to see a sign system *as* a sign system." In sum, Diamond asserts,

> Understanding gender as ideology – as a system of beliefs and behavior mapped across the bodies of females and males, which reinforces a social status quo – is to appreciate the continued timeliness of the *Verfremdungseffekt*, the purpose of which is to denaturalize and defamiliarize what ideology makes seem normal, acceptable, inescapable.[56]

Diamond offers the most sophisticated feminist reading of Brecht to date, but even she stops short of locating the gender-revealing *V-effekt* in Brecht's plays. Her failure to do this leads her to call for nuances of epic performance that Brecht had in fact developed. Diamond imagines a Brechtian–feminist practice that would build on epic acting, fashioning a performer who, "unlike her film counterpart, connotes not 'to-be-looked-at-ness' [a quality of fetishized female presence elaborated by

Laura Mulvey] . . . but rather 'looking-at-being-looked-at-ness.'"[57] Brecht had a name for this: the *gestus* of showing, the performer acknowledging that she is being watched and enjoyed. In addition, Diamond's performer would be "paradoxically available for *both* analysis and identification, paradoxically within representation while refusing its fixity." This, too, is precisely what already occurs in Brecht's epic theater – and no more clearly than in the character of Shen Teh/Shui Ta. As already noted the *V-effekt* depends on first establishing the familiar to make it strange; similarly, Brecht throws events into critical relief *after* drawing us into them. There's no smug anti-Brechtian point to score by saying that Shen Teh (or Brecht's other characters) inspires a wide range of feelings in us. That's a given; what matters is that we notice ourselves having them – and question why.

Shen Teh herself serves as a counter-model of this process: she runs off with Yang Sun, because, by her own reckoning, she is carried away "in a surge of feeling" (much like Filch in *Threepenny Opera*, when he falls for the phony beggars). This is just what spectators of the lulling "Aristotelian" theater do, abandoning reason to the heedless, easily manipulated, stirrings of the heart. We can't follow suit by getting caught up in Shen Te's predicament; the Shui Ta disguise and the epic pointing to the familiar, socially bound nature of that predicament serve as guardrail over the brink of sentimentality.

The play, then, offers a more profound lesson than the moral to which it's usually reduced – in John Willett's words, for instance, "in a competitive society goodness is often suicidal."[58] Beyond that, *Good Person* teaches the spectator about what kind of engagement is required for considering this simple-sounding dilemma. It demands nothing less than a new way of perceiving.

This, no doubt, is the reason Brecht first appealed to feminist theater makers in America, though many of his champions took inspiration from the spreading myth that Brecht was the great genius of agit-prop. Indeed, the more Brecht was reduced to being bearer of Marxist messages, the more he could serve as avatar for the feminist theaters that mushroomed across America in the 1970s; the more incompletely or imprecisely Brecht was understood, the more easily he could be latched onto as an icon of radical theater practice. Thus, theaters as different as At the Foot of the Mountain in Minneapolis and the Women's Experimental Theater in New York could be described as "Brechtian" simply because they promoted a political agenda and produced non-naturalistic plays. To take just one example, in her essay "Brecht and American Feminist Theatre," Karen Laughlin makes the case that Martha Boesing's *River Journal* recalls *Good Person* because the protagonist, a new bride, wears two different masks – that of an "earth mother" and that of a "coquette" – in order to perform her wifely duties and cope with her husband. Like Shen Teh's disguise as Shui Ta, this device, Laughlin argues:

> distances the actor-character from the role he or she adopts in order to survive in the given society. The audience, then, is invited not only to recognize these roles as pure inventions (though of undeniable power) but also to examine the social conditions which have caused the characters to take on these alternative identities. For both Brecht's Shen Teh and Boesing's Ann, the masks are necessary for survival within the dominant social systems (of either capitalism or patriarchal marriage) presented in each play.[59]

In terms of an extractable political message, Laughlin is right – up to a point. Boesing demonstrates the limitations to which women were subject, but Brecht is interested in more ethically complicated questions about social role and social organization. Dramatically speaking, Ann's masks function much more simply than Shen Teh's. In pointing out the confining and servile roles to which women were relegated in traditional marriages, Ann's masks obscure and oppress the "real" Ann, who struggles, finally, to break free. As Laughlin writes, "Boesing shows her heroine discarding the roles patriarchy has imposed on her as she moves away from her husband and towards the strongly feminine river of her play's title."[60] As we know, there is no such essentialist recourse in *Good Person*. Epic theater reveals *both* of Shen Teh's roles as inventions. What's more, the expressionistic tendencies of cultural feminism here and in much other feminist theater – "strongly feminine river," indeed! – might move Brecht to dismiss them, more or less as he sneered at Johst's *Der Einsame*, as so much "O Womyn" whining. (Of course Brecht's *Baal* imitates as it parodies *Der Einsame*, but Brecht avoids what he called the "O Man" moaning of Johst's tragic artist-hero, who claims, "I am the cosmos!")

Still, if such theaters – or their critics – overlooked certain complexities of epic theater in claiming Brecht, they were right to find an affinity between the *V-effekt* and the great "aha" mechanism of their own work, consciousness-raising, or C-R. In both, as Brecht said of epic theater, "What is 'natural' must have the force of what is startling."[61] Such devices as putting a pregnant man desperate for an abortion at the center of a drama, as Myrna Lamb did in *But What Have You Done for Me Lately?*, or telling the story of the *Oresteia* from the point of view of the women involved in the myth, as the Women's Experimental Theater did, certainly provoked a reassessment of the old way of looking at things. Nonetheless, Lamb's play probably owes more to *commedia dell'arte* than to Brecht; WET's probably has more in common with symbolist drama than with epic theater.

One reason, of course, is stylistic. Another is tone. For C-R not only afforded the famous "click" experience, after which nothing looks the same again, it also was a means of affirming solidarity and welcoming a recruit into the fold. As an essay by Kathie Sarachild in an early feminist pamphlet points out, "Consciousness-raising was seen as both a method for arriving at the truth and as a means for action and organizing."[62] The sentimental assumption of a single truth, and the famous ground rules of C-R, encouraging empathy and forbidding judgment, are completely at odds with the analytical purposes of the *V-effekt*.

More recently, as feminist theater (and, to a large degree, feminism itself) has moved into the academy, Brecht has been subjected to psychoanalytic, post-structuralist, and deconstructionist readings. It's impossible to characterize all of these assessments with a few broad strokes, but it's fair to say generally, I think, that the more Brecht has been scrutinized through these postmodern lenses, the more epic theater practice has gone out of focus. These are the sorts of delvings that come up with appraisals like:

> With the suppression of sexuality and the dynamics of desire, comes the rise of the asexual mother figure and the Epic style, with its material cleanliness, ascetic streamlining of thought and action, extreme assiduity of language, and the promise of concrete recompense for the absence of sensuality.[63]

None of those descriptions – ascetic thought, assiduity of language, material cleanliness, rewarded asensuality – belongs to *Good Person* (nor to other major epic plays), which often uses rich poetic language, has an action that is frequently interrupted, narratively described, or recapitulated, and puts a sensual romance at its center.

Now, feminist Brecht scholarship seems totally taken up with John Fuegi's inexplicable obsession: proving that Brecht was even more of a lout than we thought. Cima's chapter on Brecht in her book *Performing Women* refers to the author of *Good Person* and other plays as the Brecht Collective. It's indisputable that Hauptmann, Berlau, Steffin, and others were badly treated, exploited, and not accorded due credit – or royalties – for their substantial contributions to Brecht's work. But once this fact is acknowledged, it seems fruitless to focus on it at the expense of his (or their) plays. Now that capitalism – as they say – has won the cold war, and communism no longer serves as the great clobbering epithet for conveniently dismissing Brecht, his unscrupulous sexual and creative practices are forming themselves into a new club. The result is the same: the work gets read merely as an illustration of the accusation.

This process is quite different from Brecht's recent fate in Europe, where, Franz Xaver Kroetz once remarked, "You can perform Brecht like *My Fair Lady*. Tell an artistic director that you want to help society by directing Brecht in his theater and he'll fall over laughing."[64] There, to a large degree, Brecht became encased in the "inhibiting factor of classical status"[65] he once railed against, mummified at the Berliner Ensemble in productions that, contrary to Brecht's explicit instructions, followed the *Modelbücher*; enthroned by radical writers who would inevitably seek his overthrow; and so closely guarded by the Brecht estate, that young directors could hardly approach his work with the forward-looking spirit that Brecht exemplified. Nevertheless, Brecht remains a figure against whom other socially conscious playwrights are defined; there would be no tension in Europe over Brecht's work if he did not continue to hold it taut from one end. There's little chance that his plays will disappear from the repertoire. This is the context in which the German (then East German) novelist Karin Struck could assert, "If the guy were still alive I would grab and shake him and ask him: 'Why are you such a goddamned capitalist imperialist?'"[66]

Such a question has a different, desperate ring to it in America, where we have yet to reckon with Brecht. Perhaps now more than ever, in this post-communist era, we can come to appreciate the dramatic poetry of Brecht's plays, and the profound radical and feminist impact they promise – if only we would learn to recognize them.

4   Queering the canon

Azoi toot a Yid

"Praised are You, Adonai our God, who has not made me a woman."
"I thank You, Adonai our God, that I spend my time in houses of worship instead of in theaters."

– Orthodox prayers

"THOSE REVOLTING MIMICS"

There's a joke often told in my family about a certain Mr Goldberg who wants to audition for a renowned classical director preparing a production of *Hamlet*. Goldberg, stooped and wizened, shows up for the try-out, approaches the director, and greets him: "Gut mornink mister direktor. I am never forget your plays already I've seen. Your virk, if you don't mind my sayink so, is foist cless. Sech an honor to meet mit you, iz dis." The director squirms, glances at his watch, tells his assistants to get rid of this useless maniac. But the assistants suggest that just letting the fellow perform his monologue will be easier than trying to throw him out. Besides, they add, with a roll of the eyes, they don't want to be accused of anti-Semitism. So, checking his watch again and heaving an aggravated sigh, the director invites Mr Goldberg to take the stage.

Mr Goldberg feebly inches up the steps and into the spotlight. He straightens up, seeming all at once to grow two feet taller and thirty years younger. In clarion English, he recites "To be or not to be" with Gielgud's sensitivity, Scofield's passion, Olivier's charm. The director is riveted. No sooner have the words ". . . and lose the name of action" passed like music from his lips, than Mr Goldberg steps out of the spotlight and shrinks back to his original state. "Mr Goldberg," exclaims the director, "that was just amazing. I have to confess, I never would have expected such a performance from you. Such beautiful pronunciation, such feel for the poetry, such understanding, such depth. How did you do it?"

"Vaddaya mean?" Mr Goldberg replies with a shrug. "Dat's ektink."[1]

Like all good jokes, this one plays on several levels, offering pleasure in the reversal by which the outsider excels at the most inside of arts, not only claiming what is said not to belong to him, but surpassing those who assert sole ownership. The despised triumphs over despisers, outclasses the classy, and, in his naiveté, outsmarts the cognoscenti, even going so far as to shrug off the exceptional as no big deal. His chutzpah all the more chutzpadik because it is so innocent, the untutored instructs the maestro in the fundamentals of theater.

It's no accident that the play in question is *Hamlet* rather than, say, *Macbeth* or *Julius Caesar*. For inasmuch as modern Europe constructed the Jewish man as effeminate – even going so far as to charge that Jewish males menstruated[2] – it also regarded Hamlet as the most effeminate of tragic heroes. Edmund Vining, the late nineteenth-century scholar, even argued in *The Mystery of Hamlet* that the melancholy Dane was actually a princess disguised as a boy. Why else, he reasoned, would the hero be so languorous, weak, and lacking in "the readiness for action that adhere[s] in the perfect manly character"?[3] So there's another sharp irony at play in the joke: By embodying a tragic hero who, despite his femininity, stands for Shakespeare, himself the icon of Western civilization, Mr Goldberg rejects and ridicules the accusation that he is foreign and feminine. What's more, Mr Goldberg both overcomes and sustains a reviled image of Jewish masculinity, thereby denaturalizing it: at will, he can drop his wimpiness, his accent, his smallness, but he reverts triumphantly to this stereotypical guise, retaining it in his off-stage life.

Hamlet is also the great faker, the antic actor, and this association underlines more disturbing ways in which Mr Goldberg mocks and troubles Western ideals of art and manhood. For the more subtle, but more monumental, reversal in the joke is that Mr Goldberg turns on its head the long-standing anti-Semitic[4] accusation that Jews pass in dominant Western cultures, appearing to be like everyone else while cloaking their unshakable depravity beneath a veneer of normality. They can dress, speak, and behave like ordinary folks, the rhetoric goes, but beware: underneath there lurks – as the notorious Nazi propaganda film title says – "The Eternal Jew."

As Jews assimilated into Western Europe, anti-Semitic rhetoric became more and more obsessed with the "hiddenness" of their differences. Assimilation was, accordingly, *dis*simulation. And thus, as Sander Gilman has argued, the process of self-transformation came to be regarded as "inherently Jewish," and the capacity for mimicry as "a sign of Jewishness."[5] Emancipation provided the historical circumstances in which an overdetermined syllogism could play itself out: if within the Western tradition mimesis was bound up with femininity (as I suggested in the introduction), it's axiomatic that a tradition that defined the Jewish male as feminine would soon define him as masquerading as well – and extend that accusation to Jewish women. Dissembler, conniver, dishonest self-representer: Jews were hatching their conspiracies right under Christian noses. "An essential trait of the Jew is that he always tries to hide his origin when among non-Jews," states the narrator of *The Eternal Jew* in the cool, reasoning voice of an avuncular scientist. Over footage of "a bunch of Polish Jews still wearing caftans," and then of Jews in Berlin "more adept" at moving in "their clean European clothes," he issues the film's most urgent warning: "Outwardly, they try to act just like the host peoples. People without good instincts let themselves be deceived by this mimicry and consider Jews the same as they are. Therein lies the danger."

In this paradigm, the Jew is always already acting – or, more precisely, always already *ektink*, for the performance of the Jew on the stage of the modern West always plays on the tension between disappearance and difference. What happens, then, when Jews stage themselves within the formal artifice of theater?

Despite religious prohibitions against theater that went uncracked for centuries (except during the topsy-turvy carnival-like holiday of Purim), an Eastern European Jewish theater exploded into being at the turn of the century and flourished throughout the Yiddish-speaking diaspora for decades, flashing with brilliance at its peak in the 1920s and 1930s, then flickering into nostalgic entertainments as its audience was diminished by assimilation and migration restrictions, and then extinguished by the Nazi genocide.[6] This burst of theatrical invention – which more than one critic has likened to that of early modern England[7] – was in many respects a product of the Enlightenment, both the European Enlightenment and the corollary Emancipation that granted Jews access to dominant cultural expressions, and the Jewish Enlightenment, or *Haskalah*, which, beginning in the late eighteenth century, sought to bring into Jewish communities secular thought and writing, to nudge Jews out of their religion-bound traditions, and join them in the universalizing venture of modernity. To that end, the *Haskalah* leader Moses Mendelsohn and his followers argued that Jewish identity could be isolated as a private matter of religious belief and practice, and that otherwise, the Jew would be just like every other person, indeed, like every other *citizen*.

The irony, of course, is that it was just this move toward enfranchisement that left the Jew vulnerable to the emergent discourse of race. As Alain Finkielkraut puts it in *The Imaginary Jew*:

> Anti-Semitism turned racist only on the fateful day, when, as a consequence of Emancipation, you could no longer pick Jews out of a crowd at first glance. . . . Since the Jews – those revolting mimics – were no longer distinguishable by any particular trait, they were graced with a distinct mentality. Science was charged with succeeding where the gaze had failed, asked to make sure that the adversary remained foreign. . . . Racial hatred and its blind rage were essentially the Jews' punishment for no longer placing their difference on display.[8]

As the Jew comes out of the *shtetl* and into the streets with the Enlightenment, and the Enlightenment comes out of the West and into the *shtetl* in the form of the *Haskalah*, the newly racialized body of the Jew is etched into Western Europe's discourses of medicine, literature, and popular culture. Meanwhile, the *Maskilim*, the activists of the *Haskalah* movement, project these discourses eastward as they try to liberate their brothers and sisters – or at least separate themselves from them – by forging a new Judaism, a new culture, a new identity. Remarkably, at the historical moment when, as Linda Nochlin writes, "Jewish identity and the Jew of anti-Semitism are brought into being by the same representational trajectory,"[9] Jews brashly – even ecstatically – put their difference on display in the theater. How this difference was received depended, of course, on who the audience was and what strategies the production in question deployed. Still, when the Jew took the stage, the theater's long-standing symbiosis between femininity and the mimetic latched onto a third term – one already coded as dissembling and gender dysfunctional.

As modernity strained to define nations, races, genders, cultures, the Jew became a figure of excess, spilling out of categories even as their contours were drawn. For what were these people, after all? An ethnicity, a race, a religion, a nationality? Even they couldn't say. Internally, Bundists, Hasidim, Zionists, and others competed vigorously to determine Jewish identity and meaning. So whether playing for Jewish audiences or for gentiles, when Jews gallivanted across such boundaries in Western theaters or in their own theater of the early twentieth century they performed an overdetermined dance on the fraying demarcation of difference.

Sarah Bernhardt strutting her outrageousness on and off stage across Western Europe and America; Yiddish theater artists appropriating

Shakespeare in a move that at once drew them to and drove them from the Western canon; the early Yiddish *shund*, or trashy, theater overstepping all proprieties of dramatic art; high-minded, self-described "universal" Yiddish playwrights like Sholem Asch scandalizing religious Jews and non-Jewish Americans with his frank depiction of homosexuality: Jews in the early twentieth-century theater magnified, manipulated, mobilized, made merriment of the Jew's marginality. *Azoi toot a Yid*: It's the way of the Jew.

ANOTHER JEWISH HAMLET

A product of the Emancipation in the West, Sarah Bernhardt, as several scholars have recently suggested, was a lightning rod for emergent stereotypes that conflated voracious femininity, Jewishness, self-dramatization, and all the attendant attributes of depravity, disease, and greed. For admirers and detractors alike, Bernhardt's "race" explained her success in her profession, and then it collapsed with her profession to explain her every deviation from acceptable norms: her indeterminant nationality (Dutch or French, no one could quite say; touring the world to play not only across Europe, but also in Australia, America, and Russia she was an internationalist, the quintessential wandering Jew); erotic excesses (promiscuity and much-discussed bisexuality); gender insubordination (her bossiness, position as theater manager, and celebrated cross-dressing).[10]

Sander Gilman argues that Bernhardt popularly came to epitomize the stereotype, so prevalent in her time, of the destructive *belle juive*, especially as she became identified as Wilde's original Salome (though she never performed the role). Gilman writes:

> The Jewishness of Bernhardt provides an ambiguous masculinity – making her a "third sex." And this is associated in a direct manner with her "modern" image as Salome, the Jewish princess whose visibly yellow skin reveals her diseased, corrupt nature as a Jew . . . the Jewish female becomes the destructive seducer – the parallel image of the Jewish male. . . . Imagining Bernhardt playing Salome on the London stage was the perfect meshing of the role and the performer. For in this match of the emancipated Jewish actress and the destructive Biblical Jewess, the nature of the Jew as the corrupter of the non-Jewish world was embodied. [11]

If Salome provided "the perfect meshing of the role and performer" across the axis of "race," then Bernhardt's performance as Hamlet did so just as powerfully across the intersecting access of gender.[12] Though it was hardly scandalous for a woman to take on the role by the time Bernhardt tried her hand at it in 1899, and though Bernhardt had already performed other male roles, reviewers received her Hamlet so reproachfully that she seems to have surpassed even her own capacity to go too far. What was it that placed the production beyond the pale? Few reviewers actually say. Instead, they ridicule and reprimand. Max Beerbohm, for one, "cannot imagine any one capable of more than a hollow pretence at taking it seriously."[13] Out of respect for Bernhardt, Beerbohm notes, he joined the rest of the audience in refraining from laughing in the theater, waiting until he was on the way home "and well out of earshot of the Adelphi, before I unsealed the accumulations of my merriment." Beerbohm rages against the "ruinous" French translation; he also rejects, on principle, Bernhardt's "absurd" decision to take the role, for he is concerned that she might "create a precedent among women." Never mind that in the 1890s Millicent Brandmann-Palmer had played a thousand performances of Hamlet across England (and that since Sarah Siddons in 1776, countless other women had done the Dane, too). There was something particularly dangerous and disturbing in Bernhardt's uppity take on the stage classic.

New York critics agreed. When Bernhardt played there some months later, William Winter called it "a performance well calculated to commend itself to persons interested in freaks."[14] Others dismissed the production as a farce.[15]

The great breach, it seems, was that Bernhardt's Hamlet was too butch – more aggressive, more active, more masculine than *male* actors had ever dared make him. Portraying a Hamlet who was aggressively antic, Bernhardt knocked together the heads of Rosencrantz and Guildenstern, kicked Polonius in the shins and caught a fly off his nose, peered through Ophelia's hair to watch the mousetrap play, fell dying into Horatio's arms and was borne away on a pair of shields. What's more, she fenced masterfully in the final act. In sum, chided the reviewer in the *Birmingham Gazette*, "she makes [Hamlet] too short a time the philosopher and too much the man of vengeance."[16]

In making Hamlet more "manly" than any man had ever done, Bernhardt doubly crossed the canonical text, from which she was already doubly distanced as a French-speaker and a Jew. It was bad enough that she would play the part, but to do more than imitate what male actors had long been doing and venture her own interpretation was to overstep all the female Hamlets who had come before. As one contemporary critic described it, Bernhardt offered a Hamlet "never before imagined."[17] And it was this excessive assumption of entitlement that offended even her most admiring critics.

Bernhardt boasted to a male journalist that women could understand Hamlet better than men. "[Playing the role] takes the brains of a man and the intuitive almost psychic power of a woman to give a true rendering of it," she said.[18] It went without saying that this Jewess possessed both.

It's impossible to know whether Bernhardt thought as self-consciously about her transgressiveness as a Jew because she didn't so flamboyantly display that identity (though she was an outspoken Dreyfusard). But then she didn't have to because others did that for her: turn-of-the-century cartoons and advertisements featuring Bernhardt often exaggerated her nose, emphasized her thick, unruly hair, and surrounded her with six-pointed stars – all frequent (and often derisive) signifiers for the Jew.[19] Carol Ockman points out how contemporary images of Bernhardt not only displayed her as mannish, but then called upon that mannishness to assert Bernhardt's "putative lust for money":[20] stereotypes of the *belle juive*'s masculine power, disguised by her seductive charms, converged with stereotypes of the Jew's avarice – and vice versa.

Nowhere was this more evident, perhaps, than in Marie Colombier's thinly veiled, vicious biography of Bernhardt, *Memoirs of Sarah Barnum*, which makes much of Bernhardt's insatiable sexual appetites and "the commercial intelligence inherent to her race."[21] Ockman writes,

> All these images are informed, at least in part, by the subtext of womanhood gone awry, either in the sexual arena through promiscuity or in the creative one through mannishness. Jewishness frequently intersects with stereotypes of unnatural femininity in both these realms.[22]

The idea of Bernhardt as Salome underlined the connection in the sexual arena; her innovative Hamlet did so in the creative one.

Bernhardt was marked as a Jew on the stage(s) of Western Europe, her own deliberate cultivation of her public image no match for the prevailing caricatures of her as the spectacular Jewess. Indeed, Bernhardt's Hamlet-like self-displays only confirmed the stereotype for those who would invoke it. For them, her acting, no matter the role, was never severed from her projection of self. She gobbled up protagonists like the *belle juive* devoured men. As George Bernard Shaw disparagingly summed up, "The dress, the title of the play, the order of the words may vary; but the woman is always the same. She does not enter into the leading character: she substitutes herself for it."[23]

So capacious was Bernhardt that a London obituary called her "the

Plate 4 Sarah Bernhardt. Photo courtesy of the Archives of the YIVO
Institute for Jewish Research.

embodiment of Oriental exoticism: the strange, chimaeric idol-woman; something not in nature, a nightmarish exaggeration, the supreme of artifice."[24] Certainly that exoticism was imagined to have originated in a constructed Orientalist East – perhaps the East of Salome, but more particularly, the *shtetl* world of Eastern Europe, the breeding-ground of the Jew who was invading the cultural imagination of the West as its own nightmarish exaggeration.[25]

IBERGESETZ UN FARBESSERT

Bernhardt's Hamlet might tacitly have invoked the Jew through circulating associations among Jewishness, gender disruption, cultural appropriation, and histrionic self-display. At the same time, the Jew was invoking Hamlet through brazen assertion, at once colonizing Shakespeare toward Jews' own communal ends, and appealing to the Bard's standing as such for the legitimacy it might lend.

In the Yiddish *Hamlet*, which was presented on New York's Lower East Side about the same time Bernhardt played the prince uptown, there's no need to poison the old king. He dies of a broken heart when he learns that his queen has been wooed away by his brother. Hamlet comes to town for the wedding – returning from rabbinical school – and transforms it into a funeral. In scene after scene, he rants against rabbinic sects to whose mystical claims he objects. The uncle tries to get rid of Hamlet by spreading rumors that the youth is a Nihilist, but Hamlet turns the tables, and the uncle is packed off to Siberia instead. The final act takes place in a graveyard during a blizzard, and funeral follows wedding again. Ophelia is carried in on a bier, Hamlet marries her anyway and then dies, like his father, of a broken heart.

Though such adaptations were often billed in bold, bragging letters as "*ibergesetz un farbessert*" – translated and improved – audiences apparently still gave all the credit to Shakespeare. According to one infamous story, Yiddish audiences were so taken with *Hamlet* that, at the end, they called for the author.

It was hardly only Jews who seized and shuffled Shakespeare in those days, but their eagerness to lay claim to the newly-institutionalized emblem of Western cap-A Art, while also Yiddishizing him, illustrates the dialectical push-and-pull of Yiddish theater toward high culture, cosmopolitan savvy, and intellectual sophistication on the one hand, and mass appeal, sensational shtetlism, and garish sentimentality on the other. Often these oppositional elements were apparent in a single play, and often even in a single actor's performance.

As the Jews of Eastern Europe stuck one foot out of the *shtetl* and planted it in the Enlightenment, and then leapt headlong into the *gold-eneh medina* of America, Yiddish theater – and its audiences – straddled two worlds. Second only to the prolific Yiddish press, the Yiddish theater not only reflected, but helped produce the newly proletarianized American Jew. Inviting Jews simultaneously to remember an old life and to reshape themselves in and for a new one, the theater itself became a contested site of defining – of *engendering* – an ever-evasive Jewish identity.

Though the Yiddish theater began in Romania in 1876, and caught fire throughout Eastern Europe, it blazed most ferociously in immigrant communities, forging the culture of a doubled diaspora. New York's Second Avenue was its epicenter, but Yiddish theater remained international throughout its short life, its stars touring from, say, Budapest to Vilna to London to Buenos Aires to Chicago and then back to New York. The huge wave of Jewish immigration from Eastern Europe to New York after the pogroms of the 1880s brought over its first hungry audience; the 1883 ukase outlawing Yiddish-language performance throughout the Pale sent eager actors with them. The second wave in the early 1900s (spurred by the infamous Kishinev pogrom and the failure of the 1905 Russian revolution) carried a new generation that had been exposed to a developing secular (and leftist) Yiddish culture; among them came an energetic population of young intellectuals dedicated to carrying Yiddish culture to majestic heights.

Originating in music-hall-like, improvisational forms, Yiddish theater sprang to life as a thoroughly popular art. Its earliest, prolific, and rival writers, such as Lateiner and Hurwitz, "baked" plays by the dozen, as the contemptuous phrase had it, stealing from whatever mass-pleasing melodramas they could find in other languages, twisting them just so to make the hero a persecuted Jew, and leaving room for the actors to improvise – which they did, even when there wasn't room. Like Yiddish itself, which picked up its syntax from German, alphabet from Hebrew, phrases from Russian, Slovenian, and anything else to hand, the Yiddish theater was an eclectic, thoroughly internationalist form. Yet it was not a hybrid, amalgam, nor senseless mish-mosh (as more than one critic accused both the language and its theater of being), but a new thing in its own right. Properly contradictory, it borrowed from every place Jews had wandered, but remained absolutely *sui generis*. The plays were formulaic but arbitrary, episodic but drawn out, secular but peppered with scenes of Jewish ceremonies and rituals.

Certainly there never would have been a Yiddish theater without the *Haskalah*, but the movement's intellectual activists were not at all pleased with what they took to be a degrading use of an art form that should, instead, have been elevating the masses. They derided this vital, raucous people's theater as *shund* – trash. An 1888 editorial from *Der Folks Advokat* pungently captures the intelligentsia's disdain:

> The theatre has fallen into dirty hands with people who have no understanding of dramatic art and of real life. It is in the hands of people who consider the Jewish public as stupid fools. . . . They dirty up the stage with such horrors and with such dumb effects that Moyshe sits in the theatre and hardly knows what is happening to him. . . . These dramatists take away hard-earned money from the poor Jewish workers. Instead of theatre they give a circus. They profane dramatic art and do not allow real authors to approach the stage.[26]

It's telling that this diatribe invents a glorious past that never existed – the Yiddish theater had never been in any other hands. And more telling that the theater-going rube was monikered Moyshe. Not only had he not yet become Mark or Mike, he wasn't Malka or Mirele, either. For one of the most denigrated qualities of *shund*, from the point of view of the self-appointed saviors of Yiddish culture, anyway, was that it belonged to the lowly order of feminine literature, a domestic Yiddish melodrama with little regard for high principles of Western dramaturgy. Poor Moyshe got caught up in this coarse, tear-jerking theater instead of developing a cultivated taste for art. The gravest sin of *shund*, in other words, was that it re-feminized the Jewish male, fixing him in a stereotype he had expected to leave behind in the *shtetl* when he emigrated (internally) to the Enlightenment or (externally) to America.

From the beginning, the effort to create a serious, secular Yiddish literature involved a conscious move to masculinize the language. The aptly-named *mameloshen*, the mother tongue of Eastern European Jewry, stood dialectically against the *loshen-kodesh*, the holy tongue, the Hebrew in which educated men read scripture and commentary. Early Yiddish literature was aimed, logically enough, at the female reader, for, as Shmuel Niger points out in a pioneering 1919 essay, educated men were immersed in religious books, and wouldn't have wasted their time on secular stories. Though Sheva Zucker notes that the split wasn't absolute – besides speaking Yiddish in home and secular affairs, men participated in the Old Yiddish literature, too, by singing Yiddish folksongs and some women learned Hebrew[27] – the languages were decidedly gendered. Niger writes, for example, that "Even in wills, the part pertaining to the daughters or to other women was in Yiddish while the rest was in Hebrew."[28]

Women even prayed in Yiddish. Indeed, they produced – and some men produced for them – a vast literature of *tkhines*, a sort of domestic liturgy in which, Niger writes, "The woman does not pray to God, rather she spends time with Him, arguing with Him and complaining as if He were a close friend. She even addresses him with *du*, the familiar form in Yiddish of 'you'." What's more, adds Niger, "For the Jewish woman, God is not a God of vengeance, but a compassionate, kind, and gracious God. . . . He has become, as it were, feminized."[29]

It was reluctantly, then, that the Maskilim conceded that if they wanted to reach the uneducated masses of Eastern European Jewry, they'd have to speak to them in the crude, impure "jargon" that everyone understood. When they marshalled the *mameloshen* into the service of serious secular literature, they consciously sought to recast it as a language fit for the profound prose of men. Ironically, they were aided in this reclamation of Yiddish by their ideological enemies, the Hasidim, the mystical Jews who argued that men could have unmediated relationships with God, without being learned in Hebrew. In both cases, men were "elevating" Yiddish by shaping it to their grand concerns.[30] Masculinizing Yiddish, they thought, was the means by which Jewish life itself was going to be *ibergesetz un farbessert*.

In the theater, Shakespeare would be an agent of this transformation – or so its first redeemer, Jacob Gordin, believed. Gordin was a Russian-Jewish immigré who came to the US in 1891 hoping to start a communal agricultural colony, but he settled for trying to free the theater from the clutches of those dirty hands. High-minded actors, such as Jacob Adler, welcomed Gordin as a savior who could help build the Yiddish theater he called for in an 1892 manifesto in the *Arbeiter Zeitung*, one "playing only serious and interesting dramas, beautiful musical operas, giving true portrayals of life."[31] On the other hand, the great *shund* comedian, Zelig Mogulesko, almost came to blows with Gordin during rehearsals of his first play, *Siberia*, when Gordin tried to prevent the actor from inserting a *kuplet*, a comic patter song, into the second act. For even considering such an infraction against a Yiddish theatrical tradition, Mogulesko called Gordin an anti-Semite and threw him out of the rehearsal. Gordin finally won the day – but not without Adler making an intermission speech at the premiere of *Siberia* in which he chastised the snack-munching *shund* crowd for not appreciating Gordin's masterpiece. "Friends, friends," he implored, "If you only understood what a great work we are playing for you today, you wouldn't laugh and you wouldn't jeer." Adler wept.[32] The show was a hit. But the *shund* continued to thrive, and Gordin himself relied on many of its tricks. The "father" of Yiddish literature, I.L. Peretz, called Gordin's plays "partway between art and *shund*."[33]

Gordin wrote many of them, but his most popular was *The Jewish King Lear*, which premiered in New York in 1892 starring Jacob Adler, and was much revived for the next fifty years. Gordin reconstituted Shakespeare's tragedy as a domestic melodrama set in Vilna. On the eve of Purim, David Masheles, planning to retire to Jerusalem, turns his wealth over to his three daughters even though his youngest, Teibele, implores him not to. Her tutor (and suitor), Jaffe, underlines her advice by telling David the tragic story of old King Lear, noting, by the way, that Teibele rather resembles Cordelia.

The play pits competing Jewish sects against each other – David's sons-in-law are a cold, rationalistic Mitnagid, and a mystical, drunken Hasid. Together they are pitted against enlightened Teibele (so enlightened, in fact, that she not only marries a doctor, but also becomes one). The other two daughters – prefiguring, perhaps, the vicious, post-war stereotype of the Jewish American Princess – become monstrously materialistic housewives who connive with their husbands to swindle David.

Despite some song-and-dance interludes, the play presents scenes of mounting cruelty: the daughters and their husbands humiliate, insult, and starve David, who has returned from Palestine disappointed in the religious rigidity there. Worse, David has gone blind – opening the way for some shameless schtick as his tormentors lead him into a wall. In the end, though, the *mishpocheh* is united for Teibele and Jaffe's wedding. David forgives each and every one, extolling the power of familial love and resuming the proper, presiding place of the self-sacrificing patriarch.

This hit was quickly followed by Gordin's *Jewish Queen Lear*, later retitled after its matriarchal protagonist as *Mirele Efros*. The plot spirals downward as Mirele's new daughter-in-law deposes Mirele as head of the household and of the family business. Scenes of petty nastiness abound, at last driving Mirele from her home. Thirteen years later, all come back together to celebrate Mirele's grandson's bar mitzvah. (Though first there's much suspense and handwringing over whether Mirele will, in fact, attend.)

As these summaries suggest, Gordin's Yiddishized Shakespeare brought topical issues onto the Yiddish stage by taking up conflicts raging within the Jewish community – between one religious sect and another, secularists and observant Jews, Zionists and Bundists, assimilationists and traditionalists, greenhorns and their American kids. Often, the audience got to have it both ways. David Masheles can rage against religious hypocrisy and backward customs, but the play's reconciliation is played under the comforting image of the traditional wedding canopy. Despite David's embrace of secularism and the modern world, the play resolves with the reassurance that the all-important family will remain – *must* remain – intact. Such plays milked familiar, nostalgic images of Jewish festival and lifecycle celebrations – Mirele Efros lighting Sabbath candles, her grandson studying for his bar mitzvah – to bind community even as they rent melodrama from that community's sharp-edged splinters. Mawkish, mechanical, even manipulative, *Mirele Efros*, and other plays like it, writes Irving Howe:

> spoke to the common Jewish perception, grounded in a sufficiency of historical experience, that the survival of a persecuted minority required an iron adherence to traditional patterns of family life. Mirele represents the conserving strength of the past, which alone enabled the Jews to hold together in time. And audiences grasped this intuitively, just as Gordin had projected it intuitively.[34]

That specter of hostility toward Jews from the surrounding world was never far from the surface. In *The Jewish King Lear* Teibele announces that Jaffe was offered a professorship – but only on the condition that he convert to Christianity. Indeed, it didn't take much in plays set in the *shtetl* – a glance at the door, an "oy" grunted out as if a weight were crushing onto the speaker's shoulders – to evoke pogroms massing in the wings.

There was a sense, then, in which Gordin injected a new seriousness into the Yiddish theater as he had promised, but he did not change its essential form. Gordin's dramaturgy didn't alter the vital exchange between actor and audience that throbbed at the heart of *shund*. When Adler cried out, "*Shenkt a neduve der Yiddisher Kenig Lear*" ("alms for the Jewish King Lear"), spectators tossed him coins. If a play featured a character who was sick, the actors weren't surprised to find fans at the stage door after the show, offering jars of home-made chicken soup.

Even more than speaking "to the common Jewish perception," the power of this indigenous theater was its capacity to collapse the boundary between actor and character, and between audience and stage. Performers were known to interrupt the action of a play not only to sing a favorite tune, recite a stunning (though irrelevant) monologue, or deliver a speech on, maybe, Maimonides, but to complain about real troubles at home, or even to invite spectators to their upcoming weddings. Fearful of losing the audience's adoration, actors would often refuse to take the part of a villain. Those who achieved monumental stature acquired devoted fans, or *patriotn*, who followed them around, brawled with *patriotn* of other stars, even sabotaged performances of their hero's rivals. In this hyperbolic space, whether seeing melodramas

Plate 5 Jacob Adler as the *Yiddish King Lear*, New York, 1892. Illustration courtesy of the Archives of the YIVO Institute for Jewish Research.

set in sweatshops or sentimental comedies set in *shtetlach*, garment workers and other toiling immigrants didn't so much escape from their lives of drudgery as enrich, examine, and remake those lives by becoming full participants in the creation of new ones.

This relationship was so extraordinary that, in a 1919 article for *The Drama Magazine* classifying audiences into four types, the critic Rachel Crothers had to put Yiddish theater-goers into their own category. She easily explains the first three types of spectators: the ultra-critical, the high-brow, the "entertain-me" crowd. Then she writes, "separate and apart is the group that can only be described as the Yiddish theater audience."[35] It was this relationship that the intelligentsia would have to sever to Westernize, and masculinize, Yiddish theater.

Couldn't Moyshe grasp that what was staged was only a play? the intellectual vanguard demanded. Didn't audiences understand the difference between fiction and life? Irving Howe offers an important retort when he writes, "The central aesthetic question is this: to what extent is it profitable to think of Yiddish theatre in the terms commonly employed for sophisticated Western theatre?"[36]

The answer has to be: not much. For the Yiddish theater aggressively rejected that central principle of Western theater that posits a boundary between spectator and drama. Throughout the history of Western theater that boundary may have been enforced, transgressed, exaggerated, pointed to – but it has always remained a given. In the Yiddish theater, though, the division is never fully asserted, as if the very idea of such a border is irrelevant to a people – and a language – that thrived outside the terms of the nation state. If the fellow in the famous example runs onto the stage to save Desdemona from Othello because he is unable or refuses to enter the terms of imaginative exchange established by the production he's watching (as I argue in the introduction), the Yiddish spectator follows the instructions to the T – it's just that the instructions are different. Constantly interrupting the play's action, addressing the audience directly, crowing about their virtuosity, collapsing the fictive and the real, Yiddish actors encouraged their audience to cast themselves into the world of the play with as much abandon as they'd cast themselves into the new world. Spectators entered the dramatic fiction as if the border between stage and audience were as arbitrary – and effectual – as that between, say, Poland and Lithuania. And with the same ease, the dramatic fiction entered the lives of Jewish immigrants, who would continue talking and arguing for days about the plight of characters they'd seen.

Those who wanted to see Jews as full participants in and as producers of Western culture would dismantle the barriers between

Yiddish and the dominant culture by erecting a fourth wall. One way the art-theater movement did so was by bringing Ibsen, Chekhov, and other innovative Western dramatists to the Yiddish stage (often before they were played in America's English-speaking theaters). As for original Yiddish plays with weighty ambitions, their fourth walls would contain the audience, only to make the fluidity of other divisions ever more apparent. As the form of Yiddish theater was "normalized," the excesses and instabilities that gushed out of *shund* were displaced into the metaphoric tropes of the new work. Indeed, the lasting plays in the canon of Yiddish drama often thread issues of sexuality and gender around their existential investigations of what it means to be a Jew.

TREYF

A case in point is one of the most well-known works of the Yiddish theater, Sholem Asch's *God of Vengeance* (*Got fun Nekome*), a cross-over play in several respects. Written in 1906 and first produced in German by Max Reinhardt at the Deutsches Theater in 1910, it forged one of the links between the growing Yiddish art-theater movement and its European models. Presented to Yiddish audiences in the US, it introduced a gritty European realism into Yiddish theater's domestic melodrama. Finally, it was one of the first serious, original Yiddish plays to be presented, in English, on Broadway.

Born in Kutno and nurtured in Warsaw by I.L. Peretz (who persuaded Asch to write in Yiddish instead of Hebrew), Asch particularly admired the work of Maxim Gorki and Mikhail Artzybashev and wanted to apply their innovations to Yiddish literature by casting an unblinking eye on the whole of Jewish life. Though his early *shtetl* fiction echoes the idyllic tone of Sholom Aleichem and others, his stories in urban settings, such as his early novel *Motke the Thief*, depict the Yiddish world's own lower depths.

The strength of Asch's fiction is its descriptive force – what Howe calls "painterly verbal effects, remembered scenes drawn with slapdash primary colors."[37] Often his candid, nonjudgmental detailing of sexual, family-disrupting, or even criminal behavior takes place beneath an overarching sense of pathos. More interested in setting than character, collective than individual, Asch, writes the critic Ben Siegel, often "traced the steady ossifying of once-vital group responses to life and faith into cold ritual and custom."[38] Asch translated these qualities to the stage in the literal-minded way of the novelist. Though dramaturgically mundane, even clumsy, Asch's plays share his fiction's eagerness to bring the world to light in all its teeming misery, and to cast its moral predicaments in clear, if unorthodox, terms.

More than for its subtlety or dramatic style, then, *God of Vengeance* stands as a study in Jewish dislocation, both in terms of the themes the play addresses, and in terms of the disparate controversies it stirred when presented to different audiences. The play challenged the bounds of Jewish normativity both internally – when it was produced in Yiddish – and externally – when it premiered on Broadway.

The play concerns the efforts of a brothel keeper named Yankl Tshaptshovitsh to keep his marriage-aged daughter, Rivkele, free from the taint of the business he shares with his wife Sorre, a former prostitute. The compressed, mechanical action unwinds over less than 24 hours, as Yankl's grand hopes for redemption come crashing down in an act of divine retribution. Or at least that's Yankl's point of view on what happens when he commissions a Torah scroll to gain a stamp of respectability from the religious community, and to use as a dowry for a scholarly son-in-law, only to find that Rivkele has run off in the night with Manke, one of the women in his employ.

On its home turf, *Got fun Nekome* was enthusiastically received by popular audiences, and remained in the repertoire for years. Though set in "a large provincial town in Russian Poland,"[39] Yiddish-American audiences would have recognized the blocks of their neighborhoods where prostitutes plied their trade; on Allen Street, historian Jenna Weissman Joselit writes, there seemed to be "one hundred women on every street corner."[40] Indeed, *Got fun Nekome* sparked a spate of melodramatic prostitution plays – and even a Yiddish version of *Mrs Warren's Profession*.

Jewish objections did come, however, from religious Jews (who typically didn't go to the theater) as well as from some intellectuals sputtering in the Yiddish press against the play for bringing this underworld to light. But the more radical impact of *God of Vengeance* came from the complex, challenging ways in which the play satirized piety, exposed domestic violence, revealed the constraining options available to women within a traditional Jewish world, and, most insolently of all, philosophically rhymed whoring with Torah.

Writing within a schematic, symbolic realism of the period, Asch invokes and inverts religious phrases and images that would have resonated with Yiddish-speaking audiences. The setting of an old wooden house, whose main floor serves as the apartment of Yankl and his family, and whose basement contains the brothel, was ridiculed by American critics who complained that this residential arrangement strained credibility; but Yiddish audiences would have grasped the

emblematic staging of Judaism's diurnal dialectics. As the laws of
kashrut demand the separation of meat and milk, as the *mehitzah* in a
synagogue divides men from women, as the prayer marking the end of
the Sabbath praises God for making distinctions between the holy and
the profane, the people Israel and the other nations, the Sabbath and the
every-day, so Yankl insists on segregating his household from his
whorehouse. "I don't want any mixing between my home and the basement," he insists. When that turns out to be impossible, it's not just
because – as Ibsen-exposed critics of the English-language production
gathered – the sins of the parents are visited upon the children. More
than that, Asch is questioning the results of division itself: he is attack-
ing the antimonies of Jewish life as its religion became fixed and its
secular culture became unmoored – and both became enmeshed in commerce.

Asch marks these contradictions most clearly by making the Torah,
the sacred scroll containing the Five Books of Moses, the central token
of exchange in *God of Vengeance*. "Torah" (or "Toyre" in its Yiddish
pronunciation) can be used colloquially to mean "learning" – specifically Torah-study, but generically, too, as the translator Joachim
Neugroschel points out.[41] Yiddish audiences, he says, would have been
familiar with a common proverb that employed this word in its most
secular sense: "*Toyre iz di beste skhoyre*" ("Knowledge is the best merchandise"). Asch audaciously draws a direct correspondence between
this generic use of the term and the actual holy book, by having Yankl
use the commission to buy reputability for his family, and a bridegroom
for his daughter. Going further, Asch equates the Torah scroll itself
with Rivkele, and, through her, with prostitution.

While this may have seemed sacrilegious enough to the pious, Asch's
worse offense is that he draws these correspondences according to
Judaism's own traditional terms. When, for instance, Yankl conflates
Rivkele with the Torah scroll – "The Torah has been defiled," he cries
upon learning that Rivkele has run away with Manke – he is merely
extending a common trope to its logical conclusion. "Torah" is a feminine noun in Hebrew, and much liturgy refers to the scroll as "she." It is
draped in embroidered velvet and adorned in silver and jewels. In synagogue men cradle the dressed-up Torah in their arms and, on festivals,
even dance with it; they press their lips to their prayershawls and then
pass the kiss to the Torah by brushing the *tallis*'s fringes against it.
Pious men dare not touch the Torah's parchment when they read from
the scroll, but use a pointer to keep their place, just as they are forbidden to touch any woman other than their own wives. The Talmudic
scholar Daniel Boyarin goes so far as to figure the Torah for the Rabbis

as "the Other Woman."[42] For all Asch insisted "I am not a Jewish artist, I am a universal artist,"[43] his schema assumes saturated knowledge of these tenets and practices.

Over and over Asch calls forth familiar Jewish custom, only to violate it. But typically, he violates it in several directions, suggesting at once that such transgression can be corrupting – or liberating. Asch makes activity around women's hair a key phrase of this leitmotif. Frequently, for instance, stage directions instruct Sorre to tuck her "coquettish curls" into her *shaytl* – the wig married women wore (over a shorn head) to observe the religious commandment that their own alluring tresses be covered. That Sorre's locks peep out uncontrollably suggests that, like Yankl, her attempt to appear devout is so much hypocritical posing. At the same time, young women's hair – in particular, Rivkele's – represents a healthy, sensuous vitality. Asch lends the women in the brothel an almost raw, bucolic innocence when he has them run out into the night to wash their hair in rain. Most of all, hair binds Rivkele to Manke, haunting all their scenes together with the unstated, but well-known custom of cutting off a Jewish woman's hair after her wedding.

In the first scene, Rivkele horrifies her mother by suggesting that Manke come up "and do my hair. I love it when she combs my hair. She does it so beautifully." And the scene ends with Sorre speaking from off stage about Rivkele's imminent marriage, while on stage, Rivkele is cradled in Manke's arms. When Rivkele sneaks fatefully down to the whorehouse in Act Two, she first "Sticks her head with its black hair through the small window." Manke eggs her on: "Don't be scared of your father, he won't wake up that soon. C'mon, let's stand out in the rain. I'll loosen your hair. (She undoes Rivkele's black braids.) There, and now I'll wash your hair in the rain." The blunt, beautiful seduction is completed when Manke and Rivkele have come in from romping outside; "their hair, washed in the rain, is disheveled." Manke speaks "with restrained love and passion":

I uncovered your breasts and I washed them in rainwater that ran over my hands. . . . Your breasts are so white and firm. . . . And the blood in your breasts becomes cool under my hand, like white snow . . . like frozen water. . . . And they smell like grass in the meadows. . . . And I loosened your hair. . . . Like this. . . . (Runs her fingers through Rivkele's hair.) I held your hair like this in the rain and I washed it. . . . And your hair smells so good . . . like the rain. (She buries her face in Rivkele's hair.) It smells so sweetly of May showers . . . so light, so soft . . . and so fresh . . . like the grass in the

meadow . . . like apples on a tree. . . . Cool me like this . . . No,
wait. . . . Let me comb your hair like a bride's hair, parted down the
middle with two long black braids. (Combs Rivkele's hair.) Do you
want to, Rivkele? Do you want to?

(Ellipses in original)

At first Manke's invitation is for Rivkele to "snuggle up close to me,"
then to "sleep with me all night," then to run away with her "where no
one will yell or hit." And to each, Rivkele answers breathless assent.

The scene's eroticism is unmistakable, irrepressible. (Before the play
had even been staged, enough steam had risen off the published script
to provoke a parody in a Yiddish theater journal in Warsaw in 1908. In
"God of Mercy" by David Frischman, Yankl is an upstanding, assimilated businessman who buys a whore for his son to try to lure him away
from the temptations of Talmud and the homosexual world of the
yeshiva. "Rest your nose in the hunch of my back. I'm embracing you
with my sidelocks," the seductive student coos to Yankl's son, urging
him to run away with him to the yeshiva.[44]) As tender as it is sexy,
Asch's scene offers one of the only moments in the play that is free from
violence.

Yankl beats Rivkele, drags his wife by the hair, kicks her so noisily
that the pimp downstairs remarks, "Does he have to tear up his boots
on account of his wife?" And the pimp makes this wisecrack only
moments after he is confronted by his own wife-to-be with the armful of
bruises she suffered from *him*. Even as the young prostitutes Basha and
Reyzl recall their *shtetl* backgrounds with nostalgia, they note the violence they escaped there. "The first sorrel must be coming in now, back
home," Basha rhapsodizes, cutting short her dream of returning there in
a new hat with terror of her father. "He'd kill me on the spot," she says,
going on to describe how once "he took a stick and he banged my arm
so hard here (Shows her arm.) that I still have a scar." She pauses, then
adds, "I come from a respectable home."

Thus, even as respectability is the prize Yankl values above all, Asch
reveals how untenable it is for women. He shows further sympathy for
their decision to become prostitutes by letting Basha go on to describe
the suffocation she'd have endured if she'd stayed home and married the
local butcher (whose nickname is "Medicine"): "Imagine getting
hitched with him and havin' a little 'Medicine' every year. Ughhh."
Rezyl asks, "And whattya got here?" Basha's answer is easy: "Why, here
I'm a free person."

Asch is careful not to romanticize the prostitutes' lives – they complain about their johns, cower before their pimp, are haunted in dreams

by their grief-stricken mothers – but he does suggest that for Rivkele, for any young woman, joining the realm of the respectable means enduring violence, or at best, being confined like a Torah scroll. Is it any wonder that Manke imagines the two of them "dress[ing] up like officers and rid[ing] around on horses"? That the only place they have to run is to another brothel only underscores these limitations – and provides the device on which the plot's moral crisis hinges.

The morning after Rivkele's flight, Sorre retrieves her, and Yankl, driven mad with rage, confronts her: "Are you still a chaste [kosher] Jewish girl? Tell me – right here and now!" Rivkele answers, "I don't know." Over the night, she has certainly gained the boldness to tell Yankl that she doesn't want to get married yet. And she sasses him when he sputters that "I don't know" is not a good enough answer, saying, "Oh, but it was all right for Mama? And it was all right for Papa? I know everything. Hit me, hit me!"

"I don't know" and "I know everything" are the contradictory exclamations that fuel Yankl's frenzy. But what is it that she knows? And what is it that she doesn't know? Asch, significantly, doesn't let on.

Most critics reacted like Yankl, accusing Rivkele of having joined the oldest profession. But what if she was, as Manke offered, "sleep[ing] with me all night . . . in one bed"? To say Rivkele "knows everything" after sleeping with Manke is not to collapse into a cozy essentialism about sexuality. But given the ugly portrait of barbarous men that Asch paints, Rivkele might have acquired an inchoate (if anachronistic) understanding of Jill Johnston's famous quip that feminism is the theory, lesbianism the practice. That is, without stripping the women of their desire, Asch suggests that their liaison is their only viable alternative to a life of victimhood and despair. He makes it plain enough that Rivkele's relationship with Manke is the only one where she is not for sale, neither as a whore, nor as the bride for a young Talmudist, whom Yankl has promised to support.

As for what Rivkele *doesn't* know, if she was sleeping with Manke, *is* she still a virgin? The Yiddish offers richer ambiguities: is she still *kosher*? Neugroschel notes that Asch "obsesses" on this adjective, always choosing it over Yiddish synonyms for "pure," "decent," "chaste," "innocent," "just," and so on.[45] And then Asch inverts it when he has Sorre talk about a "kosher" sum of cash. What defines something as holy, undefiled, honest, pure? That is, what keeps it from becoming *treyf*? *God of Vengeance* offers an impertinent answer: not Jewish law any more than the marketplace.

Yankl is right, of course, that the Torah has become *treyf*, but not because his daughter has fallen, rather because Yankl and the religious community would turn them both into merchandise. In the world of Asch's play, there's only one thing that's kosher: the illicit love between Rivkele and Manke.

Still, that love brought on criminal proceedings and scandal in 1923, when the English-language *God of Vengeance* presented Broadway with its first lesbian love scene. The cast and the show's producer were arrested following a performance, and some months later, in an unprecedented ruling, a jury convicted them of promulgating obscenity.

This history has been recuperated in recent years as scholars have begun to construct a narrative of lesbian and gay visibility on the American stage.[46] This has been important work to be sure, but in concentrating on puritanical objections to prostitution and homosexuality in *God of Vengeance*, these accounts have neglected the same critics' overlapping disgust for the Eastern European Jew. Echoing *God of Vengeance*'s own thematic conundrum, the judge in the case against the play's perpetrators said in his charge to the jury, "The people of the State of New York are anxious to have pure dramas."[47] But "obscenity" in drama was not the only *treyf* that the state wanted to eradicate.

This was the era of the Palmer Raids, an increasingly isolationist government, and tightened immigration laws, which deliberately choked off the influx of Jews from Eastern Europe. It was also a time, as the cultural critic Walter Benn Michaels has argued, that ideas of race in America were shifting from biological models toward a more slippery, nationalistic notion of "culture." Jews troubled this new paradigm.[48] In several ways, *God of Vengeance* played protagonist in an anxious drama of national definition, and played it primarily for two skittish audiences.

One was the already assimilated Jewish-American community, mostly German Jews who had preceded the Eastern Europeans into the Enlightenment, as well as across the ocean. Indeed, this generally well-heeled community deplored the Yiddish theater as an affront to their refined tastes and as an embarrassment to their people. After early protests, they generally left the Yiddish theater alone as long as it stayed in the ghetto, where, they insisted, it belonged. When *God of Vengeance* came to Broadway (after a generally unperturbed run at the Provincetown Theater in Greenwich Village), it was a Reform rabbi, Joseph Silverman, who first brought a complaint against the play, charging that it was anti-Semitic. "The play libels the Jewish religion," Silverman told Abe Cahan ("czar of the Yiddish press"[49]) in an interview in the *Jewish Daily Forward*. Cahan asked Silverman why he had never complained about the play during the dozen years it had been presented in the Yiddish theater. "[I]t matters nothing to me what goes on there," the rabbi replied.[50] What mattered was making a *shande far di goyim* – airing dirty laundry in public. This audience preferred more genteel (more gentile?) portrayals of Jews, such as on offer in the 1922–23 Broadway season in John Galsworthy's *Loyalties*. In this balanced issue-play, the class-climbing son of a Jewish carpet dealer demands entry into restricted echelons of high society. Learning to leave his garishness, if not his religious identity, behind, the hero, Ferdinand de Levis, remains proud, resolute, dignified.

This is a far cry from the image of Rudolf Schildkraut's Yankl Tshaptshovitsh, who, according to one review, "slaps his cheeks . . . pulls his hair and froth issues from his lips. He gurgles and mumbles, his eyes grow wet and glassy and he dies a dozen deaths."[51] Ironically, the production was in large measure meant as a vehicle to convey Rudolf Schildkraut into stardom on the American stage, where his *oysgegrint* (ungreened, acculturated) son Joseph was already a fetching romantic lead. In any case, it was not the alleged anti-Semitism that, in the end, was used to justify criminal charges. But the excessiveness of the performance, its Jewishness, was inextricably, if tacitly, tied to the indictment for obscenity. The connection is all too clear in contemporary reviews of the play.

While many of them praise Schildkraut's intense performance, most find fault with his abiding accent. Citing that accent, many critics slide into a denunciation of the play's "foreignness" and, through it, to a coded explanation of the play's unspeakable acts. No one invokes a term like "jewpervert," which had been coined a decade earlier by a commentator on the Leo Frank case,[52] but the sentiment toward such conflation seeps out. *God of Vengeance*, wrote Burns Mantle in the *Daily News*, is "an ugly story and hopelessly foreign to our Anglo-Saxon taste and understanding."[53] "The play was a somber affair on one of those sordid themes which do not appeal to American tastes," concurred the *Mail*.[54] To the *Globe* reviewer, "this is alien stuff, and, because alien, offensive."[55] "It has," added the *Call*, "an unmistakable Oriental quality in its religious and ethical mood, in its sexual standards, and in the lyric beauty that gleams now and again out of the muck and filth of debased human life."[56]

For the most part, both Jews and lesbians go unnamed in these reviews, but they inflect each other through their absence, the critics conjuring them by their mutual displacement onto prostitution and the alien. These writers could have been talking about either group in their discreet phrases. The play, said the *Telegraph*, "deals with a subject that taxes all one's supply of euphemisms to recount."[57] Thus the reviewers re-enact the very trope that produces so much of their anxiety in the first place: the ability of the Jew and of the homosexual to skulk among them. The play is punished for parading queerness and Jewishness on the Great White Way. As queers and Jews haunt the national imagination with their fearsome activities in the closet, they get conflated – queerness-as-Jewishness, Jewishness-as-queerness – in a public discussion that dares not speak their names.

Less than two decades later, when the association among these terms became violently explicit in Europe, when "jewpervert" became one of the propagandistic underpinnings of genocide, Asch banned performances of *God of Vengeance*.

In the US, the play wasn't revived until 1974 when New York's Jewish Repertory Company staged it with little fanfare and less reaction. But more recently, *God of Vengeance* has been swept up in a wave of renewed interest in Yiddish language and culture, whose crest is being ridden by countercultural, leftist, and queer American Jews.

SO, NU?

Two generations after the Shoah, several more after the first huge waves of Jewish immigration to the US, a growing number of young American Ashkenazi Jews is looking for a meaningful way to be Jewish – even a reason to *stay* Jewish. Feminists and gays and lesbians who feel little reason to battle the (arguably) hostile and intransigent religious texts; secular Jews who don't identify with the gung-ho Zionism that has become the religion of their parents; social-justice activists recognizing an empowering heritage in the Yiddish Labor Bund; those anxious to preserve a culture whose last survivors are dying out; queers looking for a model of how to live between two worlds, that is, how to participate fully in America without assimilating completely: these young Jews are flocking to Yiddish language classes and buying up klezmer CDs, in a giddy turn toward Yiddishkeit. And some Jewish theater artists are leading them there – two prominent playwrights, Donald Margulies and Tony Kushner, have even adapted Yiddish plays.

They're lured by this work for contemporary reasons. Jonathan Boyarin has discussed how the process of Jewish exclusion "was integral to the invention of Europe";[58] now queerness has become a central term against which the American nation defines itself. In that process, homophobic campaigns often import the rhetoric of European anti-Semitism for their queer-bashings.[59] In this climate, these artists are divining the connection, and critically reactivating "Jew" as an associated term of inquiry, insight, and ideological insurrection. Meanwhile, the electricity of "Jew" as a flickering term of

difference is being recharged in the daring work of feminist performance artists.

They face some challenging problems. When Jews have successfully
entered every level of American politics and culture, is there still juice in
Jewish difference? And can it be tapped in the American theater, where
Jews have been so well-integrated for so long that Tyrone Guthrie once
remarked, if Jews abandoned American theater, it "would collapse
about next Thursday"?[60] Can the Yiddish canon itself be queered?

One approach has been to queer what have become the comfortable
tropes of comfortable Jewish life in late twentieth-century America, as
Donald Margulies has been doing over the last decade or so, in mor-
dantly hilarious plays that skew traditional takes on the Holocaust, the
comedic (and theatrically commodified) Jewish family, and assimilation.
In *What's Wrong With This Picture?* a dead mother returns to her
family's Brooklyn apartment until her husband and son are prepared to
get along without her; in *Loman Family Picnic*, the protagonist runs off
with his son's bar mitzvah money; and in the manic, morbid drama, *The
Model Apartment*, a pair of aging Holocaust survivors try to find some
solace in retirement, but are set upon by their obese, schizophrenic
daughter. In all of these, Margulies shakes pieties with compassion,
shifting sentimentality into a dark humor and honest pain. These works
have twisted traditional dramatic structures into revealing distortions –
parodying Neil Simonesque comedy, inverting Arthur Miller, exploding
the domesticating Holocaust drama. Currently, Margulies is working
on an adaptation of *God of Vengeance* for production at the Long
Wharf Theater in New Haven, Connecticut in late 1997.[61]

It's no surprise that he should be drawn to Asch's unflinching examination of Jewish prostitutes and brutish men. In what director Gordon
Edelstein calls a "faithful but freewheeling"[62] adaptation, Margulies
transports the action from the turn-of-the-century Russian–Polish town
to the Lower East Side of 1920s New York, and thus draws its conflict
closer to home: Yankl's brothel is depicted as a function of his drive to
make a bundle and assimilate.

While Margulies' audience, a high proportion of them Jews, might
not appreciate the implications of this conflict for their own American
success – is assimilation always a kind of pimping? – they're not likely
to be shocked by Manke and Rivkele's passionate kisses. Even
American television sit-coms have lesbian characters nowadays. The
question is whether Manke and Rivkele will be understood as lesbians
in a contemporary, sit-commy sense. Will Rivkele inevitably be regarded
as having a lesbian "identity," and will that "identity" then *explain* her
predicament? In other words, would everything be okay if she could just

come out to her dad? Obviously that flattens out the play's layered moral complexities. On the other hand, if Rivkele innocently falls in love with the only person who shows her compassion and tenderness, is she "really a lesbian"; that is, does Manke become just another predator in this mercenary world (and in a long line of predatory stage lesbians)? Is there a way, in our heavily psychologized theater, to activate the old melodrama's antimonies? Perhaps not. But no doubt Margulies' version will set off some new ones. His less-than-romantic depiction of the "world of our fathers" may turn out to be a bigger transgression than representing erotic love in the world of our mothers.

The homoeroticism of S. Ansky's *The Dybbuk*, the story of a young scholar who dies when he learns his beloved is betrothed to another man, and then possesses her body as a restless spirit, is far more submerged. In his adaptation for the Hartford Stage in 1995, Tony Kushner levitated it to the surface, and provided a feminist perspective for ballast. In Kushner's version, the play's intensely homosocial world vibrates with erotic implication: the students' orgiastic dancing in the synagogue, the displaced marriage between the two fathers who have promised to betroth their children to each other, the son's sensual recitation of the "Song of Songs." Kushner interpolates a feminist point of view by letting the first act's layabout scholars debate women's exclusion from the synagogue floor as part of their Talmudic banter, and by having the trembling groom arranged for the lovelorn Leah declare how pleased he is to thank God, in daily morning prayers, that he was not born a woman. Thus the sin of Leah's father that provokes the Dybbuk's possession of her – the father's avaricious neglect of his vow that if he had a daughter she would marry his friend's son – extends to include a critique of treating women as chattel.

Ansky (pen name of Shloyme Zanvl Rappoport) wrote the mystical melodrama after collecting Hasidic tales and *shtetl* folklore as an ethnographer in the Ukraine from 1911 to 1914. Then he wove the material – superstitions and disputations, curses and prayers, parables and politics – into a muscular, metaphysical evocation of a communal life on the verge of vanishing. Ansky's alternative title was *Between Two Worlds*.

Between two worlds is, in essence, where the play takes place. Throughout *The Dybbuk* opposing ideas require and reproduce each other: death resides in life, male in female, the spiritual in the carnal, religious doubt in devotion, evil in goodness, social well-being in private acts, Hasidism in modernity, the holy in the profane. And, in each instance, vice versa. This unsettling play unites spiritual, political, social, romantic, and ethical investigations – the dialectical obsessions of Kushner's own writing.

If Margulies' work queers Jewish themes, Kushner's often "jews" queer ones. His most significant work to date, *Angels in America*, was hailed as an ingenious, radical gay play; it is also, inextricably, profoundly Jewish. A scene late in Part Two, "Perestroika," was actually written in Yiddish (though, unfortunately, it is usually cut in production). More generally in *Angels*, Kushner offers complicated, contradictory Jewish types – reactionary Roy Cohn, liberal Louis Ironson, dead radical Ethel Rosenberg – to examine the trajectory of the Jew in American politics and popular imagery. Then he transfers Leslie Fiedler's infamous 1949 claim that after the Holocaust "in this apocalyptic period of atomization and uprooting . . . the image of the Jew tends to become the image of everyone . . . the central symbol, the essential myth of the whole Western World"[63] onto his protagonist with AIDS, Prior Walter, the gay man who describes himself not just as a typical homosexual, but as *stereo*typical. In *Angels in America* the stereotypical queer becomes the metaphorical Jew.[64]

More than many of the theorists in the burgeoning field of Jewish cultural studies, Kushner and Margulies engage the valences of Jewishness and gender that cluster around women.[65] But it's Jewish feminist performance artists who still walk the dangerous edges of these imbrications. Working within a form that – as Shaw said of Bernhardt – the actor does not enter into a leading character but "substitutes herself for it," a form that is not only written on, but by means of, the performer's body, artists such as Rachel Rosenthal and Jennifer Miller are facing down the *belle juive* with their self-conscious, even aggressive performances of "womanhood gone awry." They do so within, and against, the context of particularly American stereotypes of Jewish "womanhood gone awry": the overbearing, husband-usurping Jewish mother (whose attributes match those of the stereotypical mother of a gay man) and the Jewish-American Princess, whose insatiable desire for material wealth ("the commercial intelligence inherent to her race"?) has been so conflated with her sexuality as to *become* it.[66] Indeed, the persistence and ubiquity of these stereotypes in American popular culture suggests that it's precisely female Jewishness that still pulses with foreboding difference.

Ann Pellegrini has noted that in discussions of how Western Europe constructed the male Jew as feminine, "the female Jewish body goes missing."[67] In discussions of how Rosenthal and Miller, through their presented bodies, deconstruct gender, the Jew goes missing. But guaranteed a long half-life by the compulsory Christianity of American culture, the disruptive figure of the Jew glimmers through their work. It's no accident that, by her looks and the sound of her name alone,

Rosenthal has been used as a poster girl for performativity. Her photograph graces the cover of several recent books on gender and performance, even though her work is not discussed within their pages.[68]

Rosenthal and Miller come from different generations, economic classes, countries of birth, regions of the US, and most important, divergent performance traditions; they don't have much in common in terms of style or strategy. Neither makes work with particular "Jewish content" (a phrase used by Jewish educators in the US to distinguish their secular curriculum from material explicitly linked to Jewish history and sacred texts). But both use autobiography and, especially, their own bodies, in work that is at once conventional and presentational, virtuosic and direct. And for both, hair – that unruly signifier of the Jewess in *fin-de-siècle* European caricatures, that marker of pre-marital purity and irresistible eroticism in Orthodox Judaism – helps them challenge cozy assumptions about gender categories and about the hierarchal structures such classifications breed.

Miller, founder of and performer with Circus Amok, a New York-based touring company of rabble-rousing acrobats, jugglers, stiltwalkers, and fire-eaters, has said that hair has made her life a full-time performance:[69] she has a beard. In several interviews and in the film "Juggling Gender,"[70] Miller has recounted how coming of age in the 1970s, she developed a lesbian-feminist ideology alongside her identification with the circus, meanwhile immersing herself in the East Village performance scene of New York City. She explains that together they allowed her to make the decision to let her beard grow, and as a result, to escape the "tyranny of gender." Having been raised in an assimilated Jewish family, Miller has more recently begun exploring that background; she has said that in a process similar to accepting her beard, she has made a deliberate choice to become the Jew that she already is.

Circus Amok brings its queer, urban circus to all kinds of neighborhoods in New York over the summer, especially to those usually cut off from contemporary performance. Presenting skillful, somewhat chaotic romps, with a loud band and louder costumes, the group takes on contemporary issues, building performances of traditional circus feats and punning, political texts. In a South Bronx performance in 1995, a sideshow-like sketch on "endangered species" presented "the unbelievable sight of a surviving gay man." In another skit about restrictive immigration policy, Miller cavorted on stilts as a tottering Statue of Liberty. One of her most celebrated tricks (in homage to that famous rabbi's son, Harry Houdini) is to break free of a straitjacket while

Plate 6 Jennifer Miller: The "tyranny of gender" going up in flames. Photo by Dona Ann McAdams.

pattering on the meaning of liberation. In my favorite schtick, she juggles machetes – pretending almost to drop them on the folks in the front row – while discoursing on the history of bearded ladies. Describing her own empowering choice to join their ranks by refusing to continue electrolysis treatments, she challenges the audience with machete-like sharpness to consider the parts of themselves that they hide in the closet. Inspiring awe at the sheer skill, laughter over the faux-stumbling, anxiety about the possibility of a dangerous error, and discomfort with her confrontational text, the piece reveals everyone's negotiation of social roles as a juggling act.

Miller's refusal to assimilate has been accepted, she says, in the Hasidic neighborhood of Brooklyn, where she happens to live. No one hassles her there, as she moves among women who cover their shorn heads with wigs, and men who let their own scraggly beards grow so long they blend into their long, dark coats. Like them, Miller puts her difference on display, performing in a rhetorical forcefield where Jewishness – and especially, gender-disrupting female Jewishness – remains one of the vital charges.

If Miller could pass in that neighborhood as a Hasidic *yeshiva bocher*, Rosenthal, with her shaved head, could pass as her mother – except that she always lets her bald pate shine forth. Born in Paris of Russian-Jewish parents, and reared there until her family fled the Nazis in 1940, her aesthetic was forged in early work with Merce Cunningham, Erwin Piscator, and Jasper Johns: Rosenthal is a postmodern Bernhardt. Her bald head, grand-dame postures, black lipstick, and large presence produce an on- and off-stage persona that refuses easy gender categorization. Finding cosmic significance in personal matters, and vice versa, Rosenthal makes her own life a spectacle. Ockman could have been talking about Rosenthal when she writes that Bernhardt's violating "the codes of accepted femininity but also the sheer bravado with which she did so" contributed to her cultivation of an unconventional image, compounding "the confusion between life and performance."[71]

Rosenthal staged the shearing of her hair in a 1981 performance titled *Leave Her in Naxos*. After answering intimate questions from an interviewer about her love life, Rosenthal ended the piece by having her head shaved by an assistant, her luxuriant red tresses falling onto the stage floor in lifeless, lustrous clumps. Then Rosenthal was buried under a mound of fake snow. She likened the procedure to a ritual of dying from which she could emerge reborn. If the title mocked Theseus for abandoning Ariadne by asserting that she would not pine for him, the head-shaving inverted another ancient narrative, suggesting a sort of anti-marriage ceremony through which Rosenthal could unite with a new vision of self.

Since then Rosenthal has expanded her work to take on animal rights, the environment, technology, the entire cosmos, but always orbiting them around personal experience, and channeling them through the body. The personae she takes on in dozens of pieces created over the last two decades range from a giggling upper-class hostess to a grunting post-nuclear brute, from a confrontational Crone chiding humanity for its cruelty, to an air-borne warrior-diva declaiming text from the Kabbala and from hot-rod magazines while a team of stunt drivers zooms intricate patterns around her.

Global as the concerns of her work have become, Rosenthal's autobiography remains present not only in the anecdotal structures she builds to plot out these issues – in *L. O. W. in Gaia* (1986), the chronicle of her solo vacation in the desert; in *filename: FUTURFAX* (1992) her effort to survive the personal ravages of an America in the throes of apocalypse – but also in the accumulation of her body of work. Each piece builds on the last, and though one need not have seen one to understand the next, being familiar with, for instance, the material in *Charm* (1977), in which she recounts her childhood in a wealthy Parisian home before fleeing in 1940, inflects one's reading of, say, *The Others* (1984), in which she shares the stage with snakes, goats, dogs, and monkeys. Of course Rosenthal makes autobiographical epics about mistreated and endangered species: though she doesn't mention it, we know what would have happened if she hadn't escaped Europe. Her bare head is another reminder.

In *Pangaean Dreams: A Shamanic Journey* (1991) Rosenthal makes the parallel even more explicit. Age 65 at the time, she compares her failing physical state – chronic knee problems, bone fractures – to the breakup of Pangaea, the unified continent that may have existed 250 million years ago. She evokes her own background as a refugee as she imagines herself astride a huge rift in the earth, forced to choose a side to leap onto for safety. She chooses the right "and land[s] petrified on the West rim of the Event, watching the event horizon of my catastrophe, panting and afraid to look down."[72] Speaking at once for the creature severed from geological wholeness and for the adolescent girl schlepped, in a personal continental drift, to Portugal then Brazil then New York, she states:

> I worry about what's left there, on the other side, I make inventories in my head: family, animals, belongings. And also a life structure, architecture of years gone by, of accumulated memories, moraines of

Plate 7 Rachel Rosenthal in *Pangaean Dreams: A Shamanic Journey*, a post-modern Sarah Bernhardt. Photo by Malcolm Lubliner.

habit, sediments of acts shaping character and history. What have I taken with me onto the West Side? Not much: anxiety, nostalgia, longing, an overnight bag.

I can't help hearing strains of klezmer under this plaint, but in discussing the piece Rosenthal is more interested in talking about the experience of refugees from any cataclysm, and more so, about the destruction of native cultures during the westward expansion in this country. She sees a parallel in the North American tectonic plate's splitting off from Pangaea and traveling so quickly that it devoured the previous Pacific plate.[73]

Rosenthal, then, doesn't make the implicit Jew a metaphor in the sense Leslie Fiedler had predicted. Rather, in the same way she maps earthly concerns directly onto her body – experiencing every toxic drop as a personal affront, stretching her stiff limbs as though her own bones were heavy glacial floes – she traces all of history onto her own part in it. Thus she reverses the solipsism of so much solo performance, making a personal art to heal the world.

Beyond trespassing boundaries of gender and nation, Rosenthal dares to challenge the usually uncontested border between humans and other species. In *Rachel's Brain* (1987), to take just one example, Rosenthal attacks the Enlightenment and its promulgation of the mind/body split which celebrates the brain's capacity to make human beings masters over animals. In the opening scene, hilarious and horrific, she appears as Marie Antoinette (whose mind/body split became quite literal). She climbs a ladder and steps up behind a scaffold of stays and hoops into an absurd, parodistically enormous dress. On her head, she balances a foot-high wig of layered rolls, topped off by a triple-masted frigate. The queen announces herself as "the flower of the Enlightenment . . . a higher animal, head severed from body . . . I am a thought machine, *je pense donc je suis.*"[74] As a sort of nemesis to Marie Antoinette, Rosenthal also plays Koko, a hulking gorilla learning to speak sign language. Left to type randomly in the expectation that he will eventually reproduce the Western canon, Koko grunts out his triumphant results: "Therefore not I be not am be am therefore I to to."

In this Hamlet performance, Rosenthal surpasses even Mr Goldberg's astonishing appropriation of the canon. Where Mr Goldberg sheds his visible difference to play the iconic hero in a conventional, if virtuosic, way, Rosenthal puts on the most taboo of differences and forces the iconic hero to conform to Koko. Mr Goldberg takes apart the power of the West to make the Jew other by aping its highest art; the ape fragments that art, recognizing it as a tool of the West's persistent power.

In our own out-of-joint times, Mr Goldberg's "ektink" may offer a liberating, inverting rebuke to fixed identity categories. But Koko's statement, which downright demolishes identity categories, may be a more apt punchline to the story of representing Jewish disappearance and difference now. "Therefore not I be not am be be am therefore I to to" – it's a statement that bursts with citational references to a rich and troubled past, yet – leaving off with that expectant, doubled infinitive – conjures a future in which the act is still to come.

5 Three canonical crossings

CRACKING NATURE'S MOLD: MABOU MINES RE-ENGENDERS *LEAR*

Leaning against a child's toy castle, Kent takes a swig of Budweiser and shakes her head. "I thought that Lear had more affected her elder Goneril than Regan," she says. "It did always seem so to us," replies Gloucester, also sucking on a beer. "But now in the division of the household, it appears not which of her sons she values most." Like a couple of small-town gossips, they await Lear's ceremonial division of her property at her backyard barbecue birthday party. Meanwhile, they introduce us to Gloucester's illegitimate daughter, the leather-clad Elva. Their expository chatter is interrupted when Cordelion runs in, dodging his brother Regan. He fakes to the left and catches a beercan, passed football style by a hooting Goneril. Such is the fanfare that prepares the entrance of Lear, a Southern matriarch in 1950s America, who hopes to divest herself of estate and cares and "unburthen'd crawl toward death."[1]

From the opening moments of the Mabou Mines' production of *Lear* (for which I served as dramaturg), the play takes on the dubious familiarity of a dream reread months after it was recorded. The relentlessly American setting – Georgia in 1957 – immediately dislodges the play from hoary classicism and makes it feel uncomfortably close. At the same time, the reversal of the characters' genders – all the men have been changed to women, and all the women to men (except for the Fool who is played, like a French *folle*, as a man in drag) – makes it startlingly strange and provocative, even paradoxical. After all, to posit a female at the center of *Lear* is to offer a resistant, even parodistic, reading of Shakespeare's grandest tragedy. Yet the text remains virtually unaltered: only pronouns, references to royalty, and sexually marked epithets and images have been changed – with care to sustain the meter as much as possible.

Director Lee Breuer, who once cast Wedekind's *Lulu* as a Motown movie at Boston's American Repertory Theater and converted Sophocles' *Oedipus at Colonus* into a gospel church service, had been seeking a particularly American approach to classical theater for more than a decade. "I don't believe," he has often said, "that doing Shakespeare in this country means being totally fated to imitate the British forever."[2] Here, the setting tries to achieve *King Lear*'s essential tension between myth and contemporaneity in specifically American terms. Maynard Mack points out:

> the primitivism of [*King Lear*'s] atmosphere and the folk-tale cast of the "choosing" episode in the first scene are offset continually by a vivid contemporaneous Elizabethanism. . . . No member of Shakespeare's original audience, hearing Edgar's chatter on the life of farm communities (III, iv), or Lear's on urban knavery (IV, vi), or looking at the symbolic hierarchies of state and family in their "robes and furr'd gowns" (I, i) could doubt for a moment that the play was about a world with which he was deeply and centrally engaged.[3]

The 1950s, Breuer hoped, evoked in late 1980s viewers the qualities of our formative "prehistory," while a Faulkneresque South called forth a world where chivalry, clan wars, and an operative moral code still held sway.

Such transposition has become commonplace in Shakespeare production over the last thirty years or so. *The Winter's Tale* has been transported to the Austro-Hungarian empire, *A Midsummer Night's Dream* to Brazil, *Hamlet* practically everywhere. In the best of such stagings, the placement creates a new context, often by way of analogy, for thinking about the play, its issues, and the contemporary world; in the worst, it detaches the play from any context at all, even as Shakespeare's non-illusory dramaturgy is crammed into an ill-fitting naturalistic frame, where it is cluttered with furniture and stage business.

The Mabou Mines' *Lear* certainly takes a place within this tradition, but does so in disruptive as well as conventional ways. For while often such stagings assert the pan-historical relevance of the Universal Bard, this *Lear* takes that claim to task. The setting in the American South of the 1950s tugs in two directions. In addition to evoking that old, mythic world, it allows Breuer to address some aspects of race relations in the US. A longtime detractor from the notion that "nontraditional casting" means that an audience ascribes no significance to the race, ethnicity, or gender of an actor, Breuer insists that in some contexts, anyway, such invisibility is undesirable, if not impossible. Here, Gloucester is a black

Plate 8 Elva (Ellen McElduff) dupes Edna (Karen Evans-Kandel), "a sister noble," in the Mabou Mines' *Lear*, New York, 1990. Photo by Sylvia Plachy.

neighbor of Lear's. Edna (Edgar) is played by an African-American actor; Elva's (Edmond's) illegitimacy, is marked by her whiteness and blond hair. When Edna throws off her goody-goody crinoline to disguise herself, she turns Tom o'Bedlam into Mad Marie, a dreadlocked Rastafarian. Thus her personal rejection by a duped mother parallels her marginality from the colonialist state. Racism and class hierarchy become legible in this production, adjuncts to the patriarchal order the gender switch reveals.

At the same time, though, the specificity of the setting steers the play toward naturalistic assumptions, encouraging an audience to expect a logic that belongs to a different aesthetic order. Breuer both subverts and strengthens this impulse by invoking the movies: he outfits each actor with a body mike, hoping to elicit a close-up effect, and to reinforce the sense that *Lear*'s world is mythic. (Instead, the microphones make the voices seem disembodied, and even make it difficult to determine who is speaking sometimes. Lacking the technical subtlety Breuer intended, the microphones come across as a garish gimmick – and become a handy touchstone for critical dismissal of the gender reversal.[4])

While *Lear* asserts its membership in a classical tradition, it does so with a defiant claim of its outsider status – as if Breuer is making as noisy a splash as he can when he finally gets to swim in a restricted club. He assembled a cast of downtown superstars: Mabou members Ruth Maleczech (as Lear), Greg Mehrten, Ellen McElduff, and Bill Raymond; the late Ron Vawter of the Wooster Group; Blackeyed Susan and Lola Pashalinski of the Ridiculous Theatrical Company. He commissioned a continuous score by avant-garde composer Pauline Oliveros. Then he piled on high-tech tricks, assorted gadgetry, and pop icons mined from mass culture. But what distinguished *Lear* most of all from mainstream classical theater practices didn't appear on the stage: the process of its creation.

Lear was rehearsed piecemeal, virtually an act at a time, over two years as company members hopskotched across the country for short workshops at small theaters and colleges. Mabou Mines could not possibly have afforded to pay the enormous cast for the full year they needed to mount the play, and they refused outright to squeeze it into a standard four-week rehearsal period to get hired on at a regional theater. After preliminary work in fall 1987 at Atlanta's Theatrical Outfit – talking through the script, staging Act I – *Lear* moved to New Brunswick, New Jersey's George Street Playhouse in January 1988, where scenes (now also from Acts II and III) were presented as a work-in-progress to the largely subscriber audience. Droves walked out during performances and, after the three-week run, most of the theater's artistic staff was fired by its board of directors.

After that, the company finished most of the play in workshops at upstate New York's Storm King theater institute in the summer of 1988, and then at Smith College in the spring of 1989. It wasn't until 1990, when the full production was mounted at the Borough of Manhattan Community College, that all five acts of *Lear* were performed on the same night.

In the meantime, company members went about the typical Mabou Mines business of being a virtually uncharacterizable "theater collaborative" (and *Lear* actors who were not members of Mabou Mines went back to gigs in other productions). Founded in 1970, and named after the Nova Scotia mining town where the group hoped to spend a summer together, Mabou Mines is one of the few avant-garde collectives to have survived for two-and-a-half decades – and has done so perhaps because its collectivity is so loose. (Over the last couple of years, some members have left the group, but it remains intact as a collaborative.)

There is no artistic director, no special guiding aesthetic, and no strictness about division of labor. Most of the members perform, write, direct, design, hang lights and take care of business. A Mabou member might have an idea for developing a new play, or for delving into an old one, and then enlist the members of the group to work on it. Meanwhile, the organizational structure remains in place for technical and financial support. But outsiders (often artists from other disciplines – novelists, filmmakers, painters) are almost always brought in to collaborate. (Composer Philip Glass was a founding member who has since left the group.) And members often work on projects outside the company. (JoAnne Akalaitis, for instance, directed at the American Repertory Theater, the Guthrie, the New York Public Theater, and left the troupe formally before serving for nearly two years as artistic director of the Public Theater.)

Early on, Mabou Mines was seized on as a shining exemplar of American theater's new postmodernism.[5] It wasn't just that, organizationally, the group's identity was fragmented and constantly shifting. The work detonated dialogue, nuked narrative, cited high culture, Hollywood, Hindu, hoola-hoops. No matter what, it required that audiences look and listen in ways never before demanded of them in the theater. In Breuer's environmental staging of Beckett's *The Lost Ones* (1974), for instance, actor David Warrilow recited the monologue ensconced in a foam cocoon. For *Come and Go*, performed on the same bill, Breuer placed the three actors in the back of the theater's balcony, and a slanted mirror on the stage reflected their images toward the audience. Breuer's own fabulistic performance pieces, *Animations* (*The Red Horse*, 1970; *The B. Beaver*, 1974; *The Shaggy Dog*, 1978), with their animal-heroes, emotional cool, theatrical self-consciousness, pop imagery, pun-drunk poetry, and broken but driving narrative, went so far as to kill off character.

Elinor Fuchs sees this "death of character"[6] as a "post-Beckett" turning away from the modern dramatic preoccupation with the workings of consciousness. And for Breuer, *Lear* turned in the same direction. It would be a gross exaggeration, of course, to say that the actors in *Lear* came across as the character-less bodies in space of so much postmodern performance, but Breuer agreed with Jan Kott that Lear points toward a Beckettian world where "there are no characters, and the tragic element has been superseded by the grotesque."[7] Perhaps that's why, in the disjunctive late 1980s, film and theater directors as varied as Tadashi Suzuki, Akira Kurosawa, Jean-Luc Godard, and Robert Wilson[8] had decided it was time to do *Lear*.

It had been some twenty-five years since Maynard Mack had argued that after several centuries of emotional discontinuity, *King Lear* had become deeply in tune with the times:

> After two world wars and Auschwitz, our sensibility is significantly more in touch than our grandparents' was with the play's jagged violence, its sadism, madness, and processional of deaths, its wild blends of levity and horror, selfishness, and selflessness, the pull of the play's apocalyptic undercurrent.[9]

Those undercurrents were now surging up in a giddying tide. The questions *Lear* raises seemed even more at the surface of the culture's political unconscious. In *Lear*'s "little world of man," character is marginalized, language is suspect, humanism is dead.

Obviously, *Lear* is narrative and hence dependent on character, but unlike Shakespeare's other tragedies, *Lear* does not ask us to contemplate the psychologies of its central figures. Instead, our attention is focused on their actions which, as Mack points out, occur without the comfort of explanation. "Instead of scenes recording the genesis or gestation of an action," Mack writes, "*King Lear* offers us the moment at which will converts into its outward expressions of action and consequence."[10] We learn nothing about the characters other than what we witness, and oddly, nothing about their histories.

In Shakespeare's other tragedies, the past is crucial. Everything that gives propulsion to the plot of *Hamlet*, for instance, happens before the action of the play begins. The murder of Hamlet's father and the marriage of Claudius and Gertrude are prior events. Moreover, Hamlet himself has a significant past. He has been other than what we see as we know, for instance, from Ophelia's despair over "what a noble mind is here o'erthrown!" In the case of *Antony and Cleopatra*, there would be no play at all if there were not a previous change in character. We are meant consistently to think of Antony as potentially different from the Antony immediately presented to us.

There is no tension of this kind in *Lear*. The characters live without history in their immediate presentation and behavior. In his setting for the play, Breuer exploits American iconography to achieve immediately identifiable analogues to Shakespeare's pre-modern, almost fairy-tale-like figures such as the loyal servant and the evil child.

Though the characters come to us as recognizable types, in rehearsal they are heavily psychologized (even as Breuer repeatedly admonishes the actors "to find the delicate balance between characterization and lyricism. Don't blow the meter just to make a character point. On the other hand, don't give me a poetry reading"). "You're furious," he says to Karen Evans-Kandel, who plays Edna (Edgar), describing the scene where her bastard sister calls her out of hiding. "You're angry, sullen, probably chewing gum." In the opening scene, he tells Maleczech, "Lear is activating her will before she dies. She's not going to have the right to live in her houses or drive her cars. Not even her own car – which is a '57 Chevy." Once the analogy of period and place is set, Breuer follows it to its logical extremes: Curran delivers a message by bicycle, Regan and Cornwall pull up at Gloucester's with headlights blaring, Gloucester howls in pain when Regan burns her eyes with battery acid.

In this way, Breuer creates a contemporary context for characters who, lacking psychological handles or graspable histories, do what they do because that's what they are – as predictable as the heroes and villains of a western. Thus, visually, Breuer echoes the effects of Shakespeare's language. Goneril and Regan, for instance, do not invite musing about their psychic depths to establish their characters. Shakespeare immediately portrays all we need to know about them with their language in the first scene. We first hear them speak with highly ornate love poetry during Lear's game show of filial devotion. With flowery rhetoric more appropriately addressed to a Petrarchan lover than to a parent, Goneril complies with Lear's unnatural request, leaping onto the porch to drawl:

> Mother, I love you more than word can wield the matter;
> Dearer than eyesight, space and liberty;
> Beyond what can be valued rich or rare;

No less than life, with grace, health, beauty, honor;
As much as child e'er lov'd, or mother found;
A love that makes breath poor and speech unable;
Beyond all manner of so much I love you.

(I, i, 54–60)

With his good-old-boy delivery, this language indeed sounds as euphuistic as a country-western ballad. Without camping it up, actor Bill Raymond almost seems to be crooning a twangy love song called "Dearer than Eyesight."

As Lear offers shares of her estate to her sons, she snakes deliriously across the stage, waltzing to Oliveros's accordion accompaniment and trailed by a comet of her sycophantic family and followers. Only Cordelion stays put. Activity stops dead when Lear holds out a slice of cake to her youngest son. But Cordelion refuses to represent his love falsely; his true feelings cannot be accommodated by the phony vessel of an exaggerated language, "that glib and oily art." Indeed the play repeatedly makes the deconstructive point that language does not express thought or emotion or represent actions faithfully.

Throughout, *Lear* examines the boundaries of structures such as language and their capacity to represent truth. Over and over, the play exposes the inadequacy of imposing artificial structures on human experience. Whether it's Lear's insistence on ceremony, Gloucester's appeals to astrology, or Edgar's continual attempts to steer the tragedy toward a comic form, *Lear* knocks at the frames that describe modern life, that define what is acceptable. Richard Schechner could be describing *King Lear* when he writes, "Accepting such a frame means the end of humanism."[11]

But maybe this finale is not the end of humanism per se, but the end of a humanism that defines the human as the white male, that takes the end of its claim to universalism as an end to the universal it claimed. What is often termed the end of humanism amid the postmodern penchant for declaring things over is, instead, the end of patriarchy.

Schechner describes postmodernism as the end of omnipotence[12] (and others have characterized it as the loss of Western hegemony[13]). Certainly the downward trajectory of old King Lear, as he divests himself of title, power, property, family, and sanity itself is just that. In fact, one could easily do a straight production of the play – that is, without reversing gender – that was "about" the destruction, and destructiveness, of patriarchy. Indeed, Coppélia Kahn goes so far as to describe *King Lear* as "a tragedy of masculinity."[14] In her Chodorow-inspired critique, Kahn suggests that *King Lear* dramatizes a distinctly patriarchal world whose hero continually seeks to be mothered. "I believe that Lear's madness is essentially his rage at being deprived of the maternal presence," she writes.[15]

Though Kahn imagines Lear on a psychoanalytic couch rather than on a stage, her insights point to some of the central, illuminating paradoxes of a gender-reversed Lear. Turning Lear, Gloucester, Edgar, Edmund and so on into women goes beyond the tradition of casting women as Hamlet, where the tragic hero remains a male.[16] Actually changing the sex of the *characters* brings to the foreground assumptions about gender that usually go untested, even unnoticed. While the staging's cinematic style raises questions (central to feminist film theory[17]) about the representability of women, it assures that we see Lear in a socio-political context created by and for men, that we consider gender within existing social relations and don't try to whisk the issue away into an idealized, essentialist vision of goddess-worshipping, mythic female-hood.

Kahn portrays Lear as a misogynistic, emotionally limited, defensive male – an absolute exemplar of masculinity "in a culture that dichotomized power as masculine and feeling as feminine."[18] Nearly 400 years later, in a culture no less defined by this dichotomy, the first question the Mabou Mines production raises, as Breuer puts it, is "what happens when women are the ones with power?" This necessarily encompasses issues of bourgeois feminism. As women have risen toward (but rarely to) the top of corporations and nation states, they have taken on roles defined and traditionally held by men. In doing so, have they adopted the values of these institutions, and if so, inevitably? Or as one disapproving colleague once asked, "What's the point of this production, to show that women can be as bad as men?" Surely Margaret Thatcher has already answered that question amply, but this *Lear* can't escape exposing the corrosive, corrupting effects of power itself. But beyond issues of women in the boardroom, the cross-gender (and, with it, interracial) casting of the Breuer/Maleczech *Lear* contemplates the construction of gender (and other categories) – and does so very much within the play's own terms.

On the heath, seeing Edna disguised as Mad Marie, with her dreadlocks and West Indian accent, clutching a scrap to her body – "my face I'll grime with filth, / Blanket my loins, elf all my hairs in knots" (II, iii, 9) – Lear thinks she recognizes "the thing itself, unaccommodated man" (III, iv, 105).

This was the one place in the text where simply changing "man" to "woman" could not work – precisely because of the question Lear is asking here. As Monique Wittig has written, "The universal has been, and is, continually at every moment, appropriated by men."[19] Seeing Maleczech as Lear yanks universalism out of the tight fists of that male assumption – just as seeing black actors Isabell Monk as Gloucester and Karen Evans-Kandel as Edna (Edgar) takes it away from the assumption of whiteness. Nonetheless, "the thing itself, unaccommodated woman" remains maddeningly specific. (In the end, we settled reluctantly on "unaccommodated one." Interestingly enough, we felt no impulse to change the subject when Elva sends an officer to murder Cordelia. "If it be a man's work," he replies, "I'll do it" (V, iii, 40).)

In this heath scene, *Lear* offers the most pointed expression of one of its most compelling thematic questions: what is it to be human? When Lear, deciding to "unbutton here," strips off the last vestiges of social roles, what remains? This production throws one more element into that stormy question: does gender?

At first, it's impossible to avoid reading the production against a traditional interpretation. For me, at least, the play at first sets up a back-and-forth between what I see on the stage and what I recall in my mind (an experience that parallels the way we compare Gloucester's story to Lear's). Does this transposition work, I'm continually asking myself as, say, a male Cordelion is married off like chattel? Soon, though, the imposing image of the tradition gives way to the live stage experience. The comparisons stop. Lear becomes every inch a woman. (In fact, it's become perfectly natural for me to commit the disruptive act of referring, in this writing, to Lear as she.)

Accepting the facts on the stage, as any engaged spectator eventually must, the audience takes in a world where a matriarch presides. But they are still faced with seeing familiar relationships and events made strange. Even a spectator with no previous knowledge of *Lear* brings assumptions of a patriarchal culture that make the production disjunctive and discomfiting. Nowhere is this effect more striking than in the new intensity of the play's relentless violence.

In its project of testing the boundaries, the ends, of humanism, *Lear* piles brutality upon brutality as if to confront us with the question of how much we, in the audience, are willing to take. What are the limits of *our* humanity? "As we watch in the theater," writes Maynard Mack, "*King Lear* comes to us first of all as an experience of violence and pain."[20] In *Lear*, Michael Goldman adds, "we go not simply from bad to worse, but from worst to worse."[21] Though the production history of *Lear*, he writes, "has been a continuing search for ways to make the play easier for actors and audiences to take," he persuasively argues, "A good production of *Lear* is not easy on its audience."[22]

The problem for productions that take on this challenge has been how to make the action truly painful for an audience that, gorged on the increasingly indistinguishable images of gruesome TV thrillers and sensationalized evening news, remains untouched when an old person's eyes are gouged out or an innocent child is hanged. The Beckett-inspired Peter Brook production in the early 1960s, which starred Paul Scofield, responded by evoking a stunned affectlessness. But, Goldman writes, "*King Lear* is designed to confront torture, not numbness."[23]

In the Mabou Mines *Lear*, the violence is absolutely shocking, partly because it is personal – combat is close, physical, exhausting, full of grunts and cries – and partly because it is performed and suffered by women – who, if involved in fighting at all, are usually portrayed as the victims of male violence. To see Karen Evans-Kandel and Ellen McElduff, for instance, go hand-to-hand with back alley debris such as sticks and bottles for weapons, in the final Edna–Elva duel, is to see violence made palpably grotesque and truly frightening. The fight goes on for a long time, the women dueling with desperation. Elva slams head-first into Edna's belly. Edna dashes her to the ground. They groan, they pant, they sweat, trading punches, kicks, flips, strangleholds, until finally, Edna, horrified, thrusts an icepick into Elva's gut.

The violence – and especially the violent sexuality – of the language in *Lear* takes on serpent's-tooth sharpness in this production as well. When, for instance, Lear rages against female sexuality on the heath, instead of venting the unexamined misogyny of a male Lear, she suggests a tragic disgust with her own biology, even, perhaps, at being forced into a procreative role:

> The fitchew nor the soild horse goes to't
> With a more riotous appetite.
> Down from the waist they are centaurs,
> Though women all above:
> But to the girdle do the Gods inherit
> Beneath is all the fiend's: there's hell, there's darkness,
> There is the sulphurous pit – burning, scalding,
> Stench, consumption, fie, fie, fie! pah, pah!
>   (IV, vi, 124–131)

When Malezcech implores "Dry up in him the organ of increase," pointing menacingly at Goneril (I, iv, 277), Bill Raymond shrivels under her curse, his hand shielding his crotch from her desiccating words. Such imagery serves, ironically, to make the gender switch come easily. Maleczech has said that she slides right into her role without a second thought that it was written as a man. After all, it's precisely such language that enables Coppélia Kahn to "uncover the hidden mother in the hero's inner world."[24] Perhaps one reason for the easy translation is that, as Thomas McFarland points out, "the subject of the play is not the agony of the king, but the agony of the family."[25]

Though the production has not set out to explain the difference between a father's relationship with his daughters and a mother's with her sons, the gender reversal twists the emotional context of the parent–child theme into new places of pathos and depth if only because seeing a mother at the center of a family offers a more accurate description of social relations as they exist.[26] The family struggles seem in some sense ordinary – Cordelion (who is played by Maleczech's real-life teenaged son, Lute Ramblin') recoils from his mother's first-act demands with the silent querulousness of an embarrassed adolescent. And Lear's severing from her son rips through the taboo of motherhood as it is constructed in this culture, with wrenching agony – Lear makes her final entrance huffing under the weight of Cordelion's body, draped lifelessly across her arms. "Howl, howl, howl!" she cries out, her voice collapsing into a gravelly, grief-struck groan.

In the Gloucester subplot, the mother–daughter relationship is intimately established before it, too, is torn asunder. In Gloucester's confrontation with Elva over Edna's letter (I, ii) she teases the false paper out of her illegitimate daughter with playful tickles rather than harsh demands. Later, when Edna takes the blinded Gloucester roaming over the imagined cliffs of Dover, she disguises her voice with the high, pinched tones of a little girl.

Without having to tread near any kind of biological essentialism, these renderings of the parent–child relationships draw specifically on our emotional assumptions about a mother's duties to her children, and vice versa. The filial ingratitude that sets Lear flailing on the heath is measured in different currency by a mother than by a father. If, as Stanley Cavell argues, *Lear* shows the consequences of the "avoidance of love,"[27] a gender-reversed *Lear* shows the consequences of the untested assumption of love. "[King] Lear pervasively assumes at the outset that his status as king and his status as father are the same," writes Thomas McFarland, "and this initial confusion leads him into the fallacious assumption that power and love are interchangeable."[28] If King Lear equates power and love, a female Lear (a female in a patriarchal culture) experiences power in opposition to love. The Mabou Mines *Lear* tests the hidden assumptions of a patriarchal society where to lose power is to become "feminine."

In this production, the Fool, a transvestite, mocks Lear's womanhood

Plate 9 Ruth Maleczech, as Lear, rages into the universal place of tragedy, New York, 1990. Photo by Sylvia Plachy.

as in a traditional production he mocks Lear's kingship. In tottery high heels and a feather boa, Greg Mehrten often imitates Maleczech's gestures and voice (which makes him one of the few Fools I've seen who is actually funny), but also minces and sashays about, speaking with the breathy insistence of a Talullah Bankhead. As the portrayals of the play's central characters appropriate the centrality usurped by men, the Fool continually reminds us of women's marginality by presenting and deconstructing an exaggerated image of femininity. He carries a huge, striped dildo as his coxcomb, making a visual joke of phallic power. But his ridicule of the heterosexist order doesn't go over for long in Georgia. In one of the production's most affecting innovations, Breuer makes of Lear's lament, "And my poor Fool is hang'd" a quick, dark scene of a queer lynching.

Craig Owens observes that modern aesthetics claimed "vision as a privileged means of access to certainty and truth."[29] A feminist critique, which "links the privileging of vision with sexual privilege,"[30] along with the postmodern challenge of the modernist claim, rejects the predominance of the objectifying eye. The eye-gouging of a female Gloucester, who acquires insight only after being blinded, brings this issue into a bloody foreground.

When Edna guides Gloucester to the place where she will try to die, Edna dupes her into "seeing," in her mind's eye, a "horrible steep" ground with the sea raging below. Of course, the stage is flat, but Edna convinces with the power of her evocative words:

> How fearful
> And dizzy 'tis to cast one's eyes so low!
> The crows and choughs that wing the midway air
> Show scarce so gross as beetles; half way down
> Hangs one that gathers sampire, dreadful trade!
> Methinks he seems no bigger than his head.
> The fishermen that walk upon the beach
> Appear like mice, and yond tall anchoring bark
> Diminish'd to her cock, her cock a bouy
> Almost too small for sight. The murmuring surge,
> That on th'unnumber'd idle pebble chafes,
> Cannot be heard so high.
>   (IV, vi, 10–22)

Edna's performative technique is the same as Shakespeare's: in his non-illusionistic, bare-staged theater, where vision was not privileged, this is exactly the way he created place in the mind's eye of an audience. What was represented was not the same as what was shown. When Gloucester takes an imagined leap, the audience takes an imaginative leap.

In the Mabou Mines' *Lear*, what is shown – women occupying the universal place of tragedy – is not what the stage traditionally represents. Here, the audience takes an even bigger leap, across all-too-real social constructions of sexual difference.

PEOPLE DON'T DO SUCH THINGS: CHARLES LUDLAM'S HEDDA

"Don't look for teacups and wallpaper at the American Ibsen Theater,"[31] proclaimed the artistic director, Michael Zelenak, in his opening address for the American Ibsen Symposium the theater sponsored in August, 1984. Zelenak's rousing welcome trumpeted the charge (reiterated by his cavalry of dramaturgs during the three seasons this theater lasted) to rescue Ibsen from twin evils: the drudgery of American realism and what Brecht called the inhibiting factor of classical status.

The tradition of Ibsen production in the US, Zelenak said, has been so much "genuflection to historical xeroxing and has been all but buried in the narrow confines of a realistic/naturalistic coffin – a coffin of course surrounded by Victorian furniture and a box set." But the AIT was determined to find "a production approach that will let the play emerge, not as one of those stuffy classics, but with all the force, energy and vigor of a new work, as if we were the first audience ever to see this play." And this miracle would be achieved without altering or adapting Ibsen's text in any way.

Liberating Ibsen from drawing rooms and freeze-dried directing was a noble aim, to be sure, but, as Zelenak's remarks suggest, the AIT's project was audaciously abstract. It tenaciously adhered to liberal humanist pieties that had long been subjected to contemporary critique. Did AIT really expect that a company in Pittsburgh in the 1980s could offer up Ibsen as if no one had ever heard of him, or as if Ibsen had not lived and created in a particular time and place? The notion that we should, or could, extract a play from context, as though the work of art floats beyond the reach of social reality, underpinned the AIT's aesthetic, indeed its *raison d'être*. Yet the principle remained entirely unexamined. To question it (as I, among others, attempted during some panel discussions at the American Ibsen Symposium) was to be dismissed as "putting politics above art" and, worse, as elevating character and story over the ritual energies of drama.

To insist on drama's panhistorical, transcultural integrity while rejecting story and character, the mechanisms of identification, seems
contradictory. On the one hand, the AIT presciently lined up on the
conservative side of the coming culture wars, championing the
Universal Masterpiece as an entity properly contemplated without any
reference to historical context or political implication. But at the same
time, the AIT promised a postmodern revolution, wielding deconstructive terms as tools for dismantling those box sets cluttering up the
American stage.

In strictly literary terms, this *would* be a contradiction, but in theatrical terms it makes some sense. Indeed, the history of producing the
drama's classics is the history of draping them in the prevailing direc-
torial fashions of the day, and then claiming that the prevailing fashion
best shows off their enduring truths. Joining this tradition, AIT could
enlist the decentering, fragmenting, anti-narrative practices of postmodern staging in the service of modernist assertions about universal
man and the art that expresses his spiritual struggle. Or at least it could
try.

The "universalism" of canonical literature has been abundantly criticized, so there's no need to haul out familiar arguments here, except to
acknowledge that issues addressed by new historicist, feminist, and cultural materialist critics are more easily rendered in writing than in
production. It's one thing to demonstrate in an essay how, say, *A Doll
House* engages Europe's turn-of-the-century debates over the New
Woman. How – or why – a director might do so is a tricky question,
with myriad answers. Still, in newsletter articles and in talks at the Ibsen
Symposium, AIT spokesmen (and they were all men) simply pooh-
poohed such questions, if they even recognized that such questions
exist, as they swept Ibsen out of the box set, far out into the phantom
fjords.

Their anti-contextual, anti-realism stance was expressed most vehemently in discussions and newsletter articles about the AIT's 1984
production of *Hedda Gabler*. Following AIT guru Brian Johnston, who
delivered one of the Symposium's keynotes, AIT staff argued that it was
improper, indeed debasing of Ibsen's Hegelian argument, to regard
Hedda's gender as relevant to the most profound meanings of the play.
As I detailed in Chapter 2, Johnston and his followers maintain that
Ibsen's realism and the social grounding it seems to reflect are inciden-
tal to his higher purposes. Thus, to regard Hedda as a woman is to
remain mired in a degraded form – on "this side of the third empire of
the spirit"[32] – and to miss Ibsen's metaphysical depth. Worse, to assert
that there is any feminist impulse in the play is to wallow in this rank

genre above which Ibsen's plays rise, like a fallen Victorian woman crawling up from the gutter to join the bourgeoisie.

"Hedda is neither a man nor a woman, but a character," announced Leon Katz, another AIT dramaturg, at the Ibsen Symposium's tellingly titled panel, "Ibsen: Feminist or Humanist?" Johnston chimed in: "Hedda is not a woman trapped, but a person trapped." The absurdity of insisting that a character within realism has no gender, and the extent to which "universal" has come to mean male, is revealed by turning such remarks on their heads: it sounds utterly ridiculous to state, for example, "Hamlet (or for that matter, Solness) is not a man, but a human being."

Nonetheless, the AIT staff repeatedly denied that Hedda's gender was at all significant. The best way to make their point was to put a man in the role.

Not just any man. The AIT cast Charles Ludlam, founder and director of New York's Ridiculous Theatrical Company. Their mistake was not letting him also direct the play.

Beginning in the late 1960s and continuing until his death from AIDS in 1987, Ludlam consummately queered classics in a series of plays he wrote, directed, and starred in at the Ridiculous. Combining the lofty and the lowly, Ludlam often remolded canonical works into pop forms, bending genre and gender with outrageous plots, female impersonation, (homo)sexual double entendres, and a presentational performance style made of hammy takes to the audience and elaborately phony *trompe-l'oeil* scenery. In the best of these works, Ludlam achieved an unsettling mix of barbed satire, broad comedy, and brazen emotion.

His queerings of the canon flustered gender and its conventional representations by exceeding the categories of male and female. In *Bluebeard* (1970), a hilarious gothic romp he subtitled "a melodrama in three acts," Ludlam played a mad scientist hellbent on discovering a sexuality beyond the binary. Early in the play he muses with self-loathing:

> Give up your passions, Bluebeard, and become the thing you claim to be. Is to end desire desire's chiefest end? Does sex afford no greater miracles? Have all my perversions and monstrosities, my fuckings and suckings, led me to this? This little death at the climax followed by slumber? Yet chastity ravishes me. And yet the cunt gapes like the jaws of hell, an unfathomable abyss; or the boy-ass used to buggery spread wide to swallow me up its bung; or the mouth sucking out my life! Aaagh! If only there were some new and gentle genital that would combine with me and, mutually interpenetrated, steer me

through this storm in paradise! (The sound of a foghorn.) They said I was mad at medical school. They said no third genital was possible. Yang and yin, male and female, and that's that. (Laughs maniacally.) Science suits a mercenary drudge who aims at nothing but external trash. Give me a dark art that stretches as far as does the mind of man; a sound magician is a demigod.[33]

As Ludlam knows, of course, it's in the theater that such alchemy can be plied. His dark art – art at least presented in the dark – *can* produce sexual combinations and proliferations that make a laughing stock of yin and yang. As creepy and grotesque as the play becomes while Bluebeard pursues new human specimens to experiment on, Ludlam sustains a wry humor that makes sex categories themselves seem sillier and sillier: Bluebird may be evil and crazed, but, Ludlam suggests, he has a point. One Bluebeard victim, Lamia, displays the result of his diabolical diddling to the square, geewhiz boyfriend of Bluebeard's niece. "Eeecht!" he exclaims, seeing the curled chicken claw poking out from beneath her legs. "Is that a mound of Venus or a penis?" And, as the stage directions instruct, "perplexed," she replies, "I wish I knew." Glancing dolefully at his own crotch, Bluebeard presages feminist Lacanian criticism, complaining, "The male genital organ is but a faint relic and shadow, a sign that has become detached from its substance and lives on as an exquisite ornament."

In his profligate pilferings, Ludlam often plundered texts that put questions of representation at their center, and then he spiralled them into further, and funnier, explorations of self and performance, and of self *in* performance. *Stage Blood* (1975) was a surprisingly moving backstage burlesque on *Hamlet*, presented in the style of a nineteenth-century melodrama. Ludlam played the Hamlet-like son in a stage family touring to Mudville, USA. Between snippets from *Hamlet*, played with elaborate pointmaking and with profundity, the company enacts its own Oedipal revenge mystery in the dressing rooms. More textured and nuanced than a mere parody, the comedy takes on familial conflict, sexual preference, and the truth-bearing trickery that is theater itself. In *Secret Lives of the Sexists: The Farce of Modern Life* (1982), Ludlam borrows from Aristophanes' *Thesmophoriazusae*, the quintessential examination of gender as mimetic display. Satirically sniping equally at men's self-importance and feminism's self-righteousness, the play scoffs at various manifestations of gender and sexuality. In one snide reversal, a straight male character poses as gay in order to secure a job in a women's health salon. When plot machinations leave him dangling on a window ledge, a character noticing him exclaims,

"It's just like those plays in the 1950s where the homosexual commits suicide at the end." Another replies, "I love those plays. Why don't they do them like that any more?" And the first speaker retorts, "They still do over at Circle Rep."[34]

But it's in the scene stolen directly from Aristophanes that Ludlam most complicates images of gender. As in *Thesmophoriazusae*, in *Secret Lives* male characters disguise themselves as women to infiltrate a woman-only meeting, where speakers hold forth about their mistreatment by men. One of them is played by a male actor. Ludlam juxtaposes men disguised badly – and therefore comically – as women, a man performing the role of a woman, and women performing women's roles. The conflicting images call into question any claim to an authentic or absolute gender identity. What's more, the main speaker at this feminist rally urges the obliteration of gender categories, by doing away with women altogether. "[Should we] have our sexes changed?" asks her incredulous comrade (played by a man). The speaker replies:

> No. We'd simply give all women a promotion and make them legally men. Some men would have mammary glands and vaginas and some men would carry the seed. This tiny degree of specialization, however, would not be regarded as sufficiently significant to warrant two completely different sexes with different roles and legal status. Those men who bear children would be subsidized during the period of their disability. As long as there are two sexes, there can be no equality!

If, as in most comedies, men and women are restored to rightful couplings in the end, Ludlam's cross-castings and the actors' eye-rollings (not to mention a final vignette revealing a baby's questionable paternity) make mockery of such closure, such common promise of hetero-bliss.

Ludlam frequently commented upon the manufacture of such images by recreating them in his own ridiculous image. From its inception, "ridiculous" theater razzed heterosexism and the dramatic forms that assume, authorize, and celebrate it. Beginning in New York's Lower East Side in the mid-1960s as part of the countercultural surge, Ridiculous theater staked out a flamboyantly queer position through its raucous display of erotic self-affirmation and its celebration of performance as entertainment as well as common mode of mundane activity. Ludlam performed in the première production of the Play-House of the Ridiculous in 1966, founded by writer Ronald Tavel and director John Vaccaro. The three men soon went their separate ways, but Ludlam took with him, and built upon, the rangy rudiments of the Ridiculous:

performances mixing the tawdry with the glamorous, plots meandering into irresolvable convolutions, acting that was aggressively presentational. Most important, as Stefan Brecht notes in *Queer Theater*:

> [Ridiculous] theatre leaves us with an image of social life in its most basic and most salient aspects: the relations between the sexes and political life or organized state power. It presents both of these as the playing of roles. And after showing us the arbitrariness of all role-playing, it points out that the actual roles played (especially those basic and salient ones which between them control the playing of all others) are both evil and ridiculous. Furthermore, they are ridiculous not only by the actual way in which they are played but especially (more basically) in being imposed role-identities, strait-jackets put on us in the bosom of the family and by the power of the state and so transmitted from generation to generation – the inauthentic self-perpetuating variants of one and the same figure, the authoritarian phony.[35]

Ludlam certainly sustained this quintessentially queer impulse over the next two decades, but his genius was to ridicule without nihilism, to take apart traditional theatrical and social forms and offer something exhilarating in their place: new arrangements, both dramatic and sexual, infused with as much nobility as jibe, as much feeling as frenzy. Whether satirizing and recreating glamour movies, Wagnerian opera, American melodrama, French farce, Ludlam appropriated these forms much as Ibsen colonized the well-made play, mastering their mechanisms only to turn them in opposing directions.

When Ludlam played women, he treated femininity in a similar, complex way, revealing it as an effect produced and perpetuated by dramatic and other discursive forms. As a result, his female impersonation never came off as misogynist: it criticized the ideal of femininity as a social construction, not the women compelled to enact it. That's one reason, perhaps, that though Ludlam played male characters in most of his plays, he is often remembered as a drag performer. The other reason is his *Camille*, first produced in 1973 and presented on and off for some seven years.

Ludlam's queering of Dumas fils' *La Dame aux Camélias*, filtered through Garbo's consumptive divinity in the 1937 film, offers some delicious clues to how he might have adapted *Hedda* had the AIT had the courage of its casting quip. Ludlam played doomed Marguerite Gautier, milking for laughs *and* for pathos; he subtitled *Camille* "A Tearjerker."

Just as Ludlam's acting was simultaneously engaging and ironic, his adaptation was both a send-up and, indeed, a tearjerker. He could shift suddenly and seamlessly from high camp to bold conjuring of emotion – and back. When Camille expires at the end, Armand is, of course, grief-stricken. Sentimentality is cranked full up as he weeps at her bedside. Then Camille's old friend offers the parting words that jerk the tears back toward ridicule: "Toodle-loo Marguerite."

Still, as much as the play made fun of hyperromantic histrionics, it also worked as a blatant, bathetic evocation of the pangs of forbidden love – especially queer love. As Armand's father argues, persuading Camille to leave his son, "Think of Armand's career. He will never go through doors you cannot go through. He can't present you to his family and friends. You're killing his right to a normal life." Camille replies, "You're not telling me anything I haven't said to myself a hundred times – but I never let myself go through to the end. (To herself.) A woman once she has fallen can never rise again. (To Duval.) But a man can go back, he can always go back!"[36] (When Ludlam's surviving partner, Everett Quinton, revived *Camille* in 1990, it had become a poignant AIDS play.)

The underlying homoeroticism is especially apparent because Ludlam perpetually emphasizes that he is a man playing a woman, forever denied romantic fulfillment with Bill Vehr's debonair Armand. Ludlam wore a wig of ringlet curls that drizzled down his cheeks; he cooled Marguerite's fevers with a delicate lace fan. Yet his period gown had a plunging neckline, above which Ludlam's chest hair poked out defiantly. He'd strike a languorous Garbo pose, then launch into the most persuasive psychological acting, then gnaw self-consciously on the scenery, then speak directly to the audience in his own voice. Ludlam maintained all these levels of performance, joining them around the image of acting itself as the only salvation – an assertion he repeatedly ironized and undercut. As Camille tells Nichette,

> I came up from grinding poverty and it stinks. . . . I'll never go back! There are only two ways a woman may rise from the gutter and become a queen: prostitution or the stage. And believe me, Nichette, I'd rather peddle my coosie in the streets than become an actress![37]

In a moment that acknowledges the queer spectacle of *Camille* without dropping a beat of its vamping sentiment, Marguerite lies languidly in bed, coughing daintily, then with rude hacking honks. Ludlam regains his decorous decadence with some bats of his eyelashes, then importunes Marguerite's faithful maid. "I'm cold. Nanine, throw another faggot on the fire." Nanine says, "There are no more faggots in the house." Ludlam bolts up in bed, peers at the audience like he's on a split-second reconnaissance mission, and then sinks back under the covers to say, "plaintively" (as stage directions instruct), "No faggots in the house? Open the window, Nanine. See if there are any in the street."[38]

It's tantalizing to imagine how Ludlam, Scribean wizard and sophisticated gender bender, might have queered *Hedda Gabler*, with its inherent critique of two twined artifices, the well-made play and the well-made woman. Having regarded the play as a "bedroom farce played for high stakes,"[39] might he have flirted with Judge Brack, camping on remarks about Brack's entrance through the back door? Swooned for the memories of Lovborg's demi-monde stories like a young gay man who missed the disco years? Would Hedda's inability to exist within the bourgeois boundaries enclosing women have resonated in new ways? Wearing an obviously cheap wig, would Hedda's jealousy of Thea's hair have offered a comment on the constructedness of femininity? What would Ludlam have done with those pistols? And what silly song would he have had Hedda play before that fatal shot? Would he have made good on his threat to "do the entire role with a Norwegian accent" or to "mention her lesbianism"?[40]

The AIT didn't dare wonder. Ludlam's pastiches and poses challenged the AIT's insistence on the venerated masterpiece, with its universal evocation of spiritual yearning. To sustain that vision, *Hedda* would have to remain holy – and wholly hetero. From AIT's metaphysical point of view, to have put the play in Ludlam's hands would have been like giving a delicate glass orb to a soccer player: it wouldn't matter how deftly and beautifully he would use it, they couldn't stand to see it get shattered.

Instead, they asked Mel Shapiro to direct, introducing a third aesthetic, completely at odds with AIT's *and* Ludlam's.

At first glance, the production looked like it might have been a Ridiculous take on *Hedda Gabler*: It had a film noir setting – plush velvet furniture, Aunt Julia wearing a narrow wine-colored gown with a wide sash at the hips, Lovborg in pleated pants and a wide red and gray tie, Tesman in an argyle sweater-vest, Hedda in purple elbow-length gloves, a red wig, and a slinky dress with a fur collar. It's easy to imagine that Ludlam might have used film noir's smoky atmosphere of subterfuge and sexual intrigue to exaggerate and comment upon the play's sense of mystery and repression, and to give Hedda sway to vamp.

But Shapiro seemed to use the temporal transplant (as so many Shakespeare directors use the device) in a more tepid way: to claim the

Plate 10 Charles Ludlam's Hedda Gabler takes aim at the well-made play at the American Ibsen Theater, Pittsburgh, 1984.

play as meaningful in a new mode, to lend it a familiarity that shakes off classical encrustrations even as it asserts the play's classical capacity to be translated to any period and place. This can crack through caked layers of conventional interpretation to open up a new vision of a play, but can also function, in Brecht's disparaging terms, "to annihilate distance, fill in the gap, gloss over the differences"[41] between one historical moment and another. Specifically, the film noir images in the AIT *Hedda* plucked the play out of the dreaded nineteenth-century drawing room and set it down where a primping, even bitchy, femininity would not, presumably, seem out of place. Ludlam's exaggerated Joan Crawfordisms – draping himself over a chaise-longue, clinging to a doorframe with an arm flung upward along the jamb, sniping at Aunt Julie like a peevish shrew – would seem organic to this movieland milieu.

The trouble was, none of the other actors inhabited the same world. Natty costumes notwithstanding, all the actors but Ludlam performed in standard American TV-Stanislavski – and that, apparently, is exactly how Shapiro directed them. In interviews with local Pittsburgh papers, Shapiro (traditional, longtime director of Shakespeare and other canonical authors) discussed *Hedda Gabler* in familiar terms, detailing characters' inner compulsions and subtextual pains, and his efforts to "bring buried truths to light."[42] Casting Ludlam, he said, would help to do this because, he asserted, Hedda's problem is that she is "trapped in the wrong body."[43]

That psychological explanation is not only appallingly naive about sexual politics, it operates in a different aesthetic universe from the one promoted at AIT. The dramaturgs didn't want audiences to *understand* Hedda as a troubled psyche; that, said dramaturg Rick Davis contemptuously, is to engage in "the shallowest and least implicative of all the possible aesthetic responses."[44] They preferred showing that Hedda was blazing into a high art form while all around her remained irredeemably stuck in a well-made play. So during the post-performance panel discussion, they were delighted to hear a spectator say that Ludlam seemed to be doing his own thing, that he was disconnected from everyone else on stage.

The audience may have been persuaded of AIT's ultra-aesthetic reading of *Hedda*, especially with all the panelists and newsletter articles telling them how to respond, but the production was curiously unengaging. With Hedda in a world of her own, there can be no emotional connection, neither between her and other characters, nor between her and spectators. Her actions, then, have no consequences, or at least none that matter, and the play comes off as an academic demonstration of a glib postmodern take.

Hedda was, in effect, invisible to the other characters, her outrageous mannerisms and nasty temper going unnoticed. Tesman and the others just went about their petty business almost as if she wasn't there, as though her outbursts were as ordinary as weather. In the opening scene, for instance, Tesman picks Hedda up and twirls her around as Julie remarks on how filled out Hedda looks. Hedda not only extricates herself from his embrace, she runs gasping to the doorway, sticking her head out to gobble up some air. Later, when Lovborg arrives and chats with Tesman, Hedda lounges on a cushion downstage center, arching her back and tucking her legs like the Whiterock girl; from this perch, she glares at Tesman with venom. No one reacts. When they do respond to Hedda, they seem to see someone quite different from the character the audience sees. And the action simply doesn't make sense.

By the time that gunshot sounds in the last scene, it produces neither shock among the characters nor a tragic sense of inevitability among the audience. It merely creates an opportunity to show Hedda in one final pose: the upstage inner curtain is flung open, so we see Hedda, with her back to the audience, slumped languorously in a stuffed chair, her arm hanging down, dangling a pistol. She, at least, has done it beautifully. Despite the final tableau, this is the coldest *Hedda Gabler* I've ever seen.

As Michael Zelenak had promised, there was no wallpaper – indeed, hardly any walls. The upstage flats were cut open, revealing a scrim of blue sky. Side walls were suggested with structural fragments. There was no surface on which to hang the old general's portrait, so it did not appear. This setting might have served an operatic *Hedda*, making palpable the tension between two representational modes. But such tension went slack under the weight of the soap-opera acting turned in by all the actors but Ludlam.

Because Ludlam's performance was not supported by the rest of the production, it seemed merely campy, as his Camille emphatically had not. Detached from the play's emotional life, this Hedda could be nothing but poses of haughty disdain, and not only Hedda's disdain for Tesman and company. The competing styles unwittingly suggested Ludlam's disdain for Hedda – and, in turn, the AIT's disdain for women.

EPIC FORNICATIONS: BLOOLIPS AND SPLIT BRITCHES DO TENNESSEE

When word got out in 1990 that Bloolips and Split Britches – the queens and queens, respectively, of gay and lesbian theater – were working together on *A Streetcar Named Desire*, rumors started flying: they were doing this play because all four actors wanted to play Blanche DuBois. Bloolips' Paul Shaw and Bette Bourne gushingly agreed that Blanche, with her fripperies and fainting spells, is, as Bourne put it, "a drag queen's dream."[45] And Split Britches' Lois Weaver had always wanted to commandeer the fluttering femme of her native South. But Weaver's partner Peggy Shaw, proving the rumor false, wasn't at all interested. She wanted to play Stanley Kowalski.

So, before the production even opened in early 1991 (first in London, then in New York), this rumor played campily on *Streetcar*'s iconic status within queer culture and beyond. Indeed, the abiding potency of *Streetcar*'s most recognized images became the focus of the Bloolips–Split Britches[46] collaboration, which they called *Belle Reprieve* (a none-too-subtle pun on Belle Reve, the family estate Blanche has lost to creditors). The four actors built the ninety-minute performance in improvisational rehearsals, some starting with plot elements of *Streetcar*, some with a line or a prop – paper lanterns, a trunk full of fancy things, a birthday cake, a bathtub, and so on.

The result refers to *Streetcar*, but is not really an adaptation, much less a production, of it. Retaining barely a handful of lines from Williams's text, Bloolips and Split Britches composed a four-part invention on themes the script evoked for these avatars of homo, pomo performance: the influence of heterosexuality on gay and lesbian eroticism; the mythological power of cinematic icons; the appeal of butch–femme and macho–sissy role-playing in lesbian and gay subcultures; the whole messy meaning of gender itself. There's also a tapdance or two.

As for the three-way duel over who would play Blanche, that was easily decided: Bette Bourne claimed that his shoulders most resembled Vivien Leigh's and he garnered the role. Peggy Shaw pumped up her already formidable biceps to play Stanley. Weaver, assigned to Stella, immediately reveled in what she always admired in the character, "her unconflicted pleasure in sex." And Paul Shaw was cast as Mitch. That was a big stretch, he allowed; he'd been on stage for years, but always in a frock.

Through some ten years of their own work at WOW, the lesbian theater space they co-founded in New York, Peggy Shaw and Weaver staged, celebrated, parodied, interrogated, and reversed butch–femme costumes in autobiographical cabaret (*Anniversary Waltz* – Weaver telling her coming out tale, portraying herself as Katherine Hepburn, waiting for a woman to sweep in as her Spencer Tracy; Shaw imagining herself as James Dean); fractured fairy tales (*Beauty and the Beast*, with Deb Margolin, which offered a metaphoric fable for Shaw and

Weaver's butch–femme roles); and non-linear multi-layered drama (Holly Hughes's *Dress Suits to Hire* in which Shaw, up till then always the heavy butch, sang torch songs in evening gowns, her shoulders massing beneath spaghetti straps, her calves like steel rods rising out of stilettos). Other plays have addressed themes of censorship and spectacle (*Little Women: The Tragedy*, with Margolin) and of rage and its representations (*Lesbians Who Kill*, written by Margolin).

Like other work at WOW, one of the most radical aspects of Split Britches' plays is that they take lesbianism as a given, not as something to be disclosed as a plot's driving secret, nor debated, say between mother and daughter, as its central agon. Heterosexuality is not only not compulsory on WOW's stage, it is nonexistent. As a result, the lesbian performer (and, thus, spectator) is not defined against some "norm" and singled out by her "otherness." (Nor is "woman" defined against "man" since men do not exist either, except sometimes as characters played by women in mock-reluctant drag, or, when a "real" man is required, by the metonymically convenient suitcoat on a hanger.) Split Britches honed its art in this community theater, becoming one of the most sophisticated, best known, and most widely touring lesbian troupes in America, and the one most frequently cited in academic writing on lesbian performance.[47]

Decidedly queer – refusing heterosexuality, fracturing conventional narratives, exposing the mutability of social roles, juicily displaying lesbian desire – Split Britches' work is also resolutely feminist (though its naughty sensuality and butch–femme imagery have long put it beyond the pale of cultural feminism). It pointedly examines – and reimagines – the place of women within material and representational economies.

Over roughly the same period, the all-male, London-based Bloolips wrought whimsical fairyworlds in show-bizzy shows like *Get Hur* and *Gland Motel*. Theirs is a celebratory, self-reflexive music-hall style. Plots string together song opportunities and hilariously flamboyant costume changes for the troupe's dimestore divas. The actors hold forth in gowns dangling with rhinestones or tea strainers, skirts made of umbrellas or shiny scouring pads, headdresses of flower pots. In one show, when a character's buns are admired, they light up like a lantern.

Playing in, and on, a performance tradition where every theatrical trick is done, undone, and undone again, Bloolips uses drag to celebrate queerness, not to mock or reify women's second-class social status. They work against the custom that takes frou-frou sequined drag queens to be a joke, a misogynist mockery made of tawdry tinsel and bedecked bitchiness that, like blackface, is a kind of dressing down by dressing up. Misogynistic drag, like racist blackface, reassures, making fun of the socially subservient class by parodying it, always reminding the viewer that the power-granting penis remains – what a relief! – just beneath the skirts. Bloolips sidesteps this sort of slumming by not playing women at all. Wearing clownwhite and bold slashes of glittery eyeshadow, they declare themselves fairies, sissies, and queens, ridiculing category and making hash of convention.

The loving, lived spirit that underlies this use of drag informs the fun Bloolips pokes at *theatrical* convention too. They haul out the cheesiest stage gimmicks and then carry them off with such precise timing and skill that they manage to venerate what they mock. In *Gland Motel*, for example, Cleopatra sings about how Caesar threw her into the Nile as fabric waves appear upstage and are waggled from the wings. Cleo, of course, "swims" behind them for a good long time, only to be upstaged by a plastic ducky that scurries along the surface after she dives out of sight. Then, after you're sure the joke can't be milked any further, the ubiquitous piano player pulls out a shotgun and picks off the duck, causing the wave operators to drop their strings and run away. That, of course, reveals Cleo crouching up stage and having to scamper off with the duck-on-a-stick, muttering her hope that no one will notice.

Split Britches, too, often discloses the mechanics of simple stage illusion: cut-out clouds mass into a heaven in *Little Women: The Tragedy*, bearing the cross-hatches and angle measurements diagrammed in a seventeenth-century scenery manual's instructions for how to build them. Like Bloolips, they draw an analogy between stage invention and social persona, delighting in the phantasmagoria both conjure up by revealing their devices. Yet Split Britches constructs plays of disjunctive progressions, each scene made with intricate, diurnal detail, then leading by some allusive or imagistic logic to the next, but without adding up to the grand action of a conventional plot. Bloolips' shows, on the other hand, meander, but remain tethered to a narrative throughline (otherwise, who could tell that they were meandering?). And if Split Britches uses butch–femme imagery and performance to indict the sex–gender system, Bloolips uses a clownish, almost ethereal drag (and male privilege) to dismiss that system altogether, to act as though it doesn't exist.

Interlacing Split Britches' ethos of the everyday with Bloolips' *shmatte*-glamour aesthetic, and then wrapping the warp and woof around Williams produced, to borrow Blanche's phrase, epic fornications, in several senses: *Belle Reprieve* messed with a masterpiece, multiplied combinations of sexual couplings, wrought endless gender-fucks, rendered hetero licentiousness strange. The company deconstructed *Streetcar* with dynamite, assembling in its place an exploration of the relationship between narrative and social conformity, between the yoked constraints of naturalism and naturalized notions of gender. Thus *Belle Reprieve* produced an exciting proliferation of genders, pointing to realms beyond the binary.

The program listed the four characters:

Mitch.........a fairy disguised as a man
Stella........a woman disguised as a woman
Stanley.......a butch lesbian
Blanche.......a man in a dress[48]

To complicate matters further, in the performance Blanche describes herself as a drag queen, and Stanley is always referred to with male pronouns. Throughout *Belle Reprieve* the company dances on these indeterminacies, sometimes literally. In one number, Stanley croons a solo, while Mitch and Blanche (dressed for the moment in mechanics' overalls) provide backup. "I'm a man," sings Stanley, flexing beneath a torn undershirt. The two men join in the chorus: "I'm a man, spelled M-A-N, ow ow ow ow ow." Mitch and Blanche seem awkward, fake, even dainty as they try to preen in macho poses, while Stanley struts with the assured strength of a construction worker.

Gender instability is rendered especially transgressive in an early scene where Blanche's crossing of vestments is figured as a border crossing. Questioned by a guard, represented by Stanley, Blanche's sexuality and gender are brutally policed. Stanley rummages roughly through Blanche's trunk, yanking out feather boas and chiffon scarves, demanding to see her passport. Its photograph, he asserts, does not look at all like Blanche. Her reply: "I believe nature is there to be improved upon." Later, Blanche refreshes herself in the tub, shaving her beard while singing a poignant lament for the lost world of gay bathhouses. Later still, Stanley stands in the same spot, shaving her face in echoing motions. Over and over, the assumptive ground of gender conformity wobbles, gives way, disappears. During *Belle Reprieve*'s run, Peggy Shaw raked in adoring fan mail from gay men.

Given gender's fluidity, its unreliability, virtually any given pairing on stage can be read simultaneously as homo- and heterosexual – and even more pleasurably as an oscillating current of eroticism that requires no opposing poles to produce a charge. Stella and Blanche share a sisterly moment, with Stella telling a made-for-TV little sister's remembrance of how she admired her older sibling, and imitated her bearing and carriage: an ironic twist on the supposition that a transvestite might study a woman to learn her behavior. Using language from one of Williams's

Plate 11 A proliferation of genders: Peggy Shaw, Bette Bourne, Lois Weaver, and Paul Shaw (Precious Pearl) in *Belle Reprieve*, 1991. Photo by Sheila Burnett.

stage directions describing Blanche (as well as the evocative phrase "gentleman caller"), Stella remembers:

> I used to follow her into the bathroom. I loved the way she touched her cheek with the back of her hand. How she let her hand come to rest just slightly between her breasts as she took just one last look in the mirror. I used to study the way she adjusted her hips and twisted her thighs in that funny way when she was changing her shoes. Then she would fling open the bathroom door and sail down the staircase into the front room to receive her gentleman callers.

Blanche joins the reminiscence, then pulls off a robe to reveal that she, like Stella, is wearing a cheerleader's outfit, and the two sing a ditty that blatantly sexualizes their relationship:

> . . . Under the covers, the pillows and laces
> We both can share, those soft cotton places
> Lying together like spoons in a drawer
> Then turning over to have an explore
> . . . Lean on a pillow and look in my eyes
> Spreading our knowledge and sharing our thighs . . .

Is it a lesbian scene? An incestuous one? Does it break an even touchier taboo by suggesting an intimate encounter between a lesbian and a drag queen? Is heterosexuality projected onto the exchange simply because the actors are a woman and a man? Such questions come up again and again: Stanley and Mitch parody paroxysms of male homosocial competition, each topping the other's declarations of blustery masculinity:

> *Stanley:* I'm gonna eat my car! I'm gonna eat dirt!
> *Mitch:*   I'm gonna eat a tree! Eat your whole leg!
> *Stanley:* I'm gonna eat the sun and then I'll sweat!

And then the two fall to arm wrestling, as though the contest were a carnal consummation.

The most affecting love scenes, though, parallel Williams's pairings, and come off queerest of all precisely because they follow the frame of his ultra-hetero couplings – Mitch–Blanche, Stanley–Stella – and render it superfluous. In a reversal of stereotypes, the love scene between the men is tender and whimsical; the scene between the women, steamily explicit.

In the former, Blanche luxuriates in a tub of tulle bubbles as Mitch is lit behind an upstage scrim, perched on a ladder and strumming a ukelele. His fairy-tale song describes his courtship of Bette/Blanche. The chorus goes:

I'm a supernatural being, I'm your sweetie-pie
And I've come here from somewhere far, away up in the sky
I'm here to play a song tonight by Rimsky-Korsakov
And if you play your cards right we might even have it off.

Come-on notwithstanding, the enchanting innocence of the scene's form – the scrim, the uke, the nursery-like rhyme – contrasts an earlier exchange between Stanley and Stella that strains to the point of union:

Stella: . . . I know that your tension is sexual, and it's a desire that I share in, but not for your pleasure, for my own. I'm lookin' for it, I might not find it in you, I might find it somewhere else, as a matter of fact, and there's nothing you can do about it. You don't satisfy me, you're not real.
Stanley: Are you saying I'm not a real man?
Stella: I'm saying you're not real. You're cute. Could be much cuter if you weren't so obvious.
Stanley: Then it wouldn't be me. I am not subtle.

Their banter escalates, but is soon overcome by the piano player, who sings a blues tune while Stanley and Stella dance in a sinewy, sinuous embrace. Stella pulls at Stanley's t-shirt, ripping it apart, and they strike the famous conciliatory pose of Brando and Kim Stanley – Brando on his knees with his head buried in her belly. Unlike the film, though, here it's Stella who makes the aggressive next move, jumping up and wrapping her legs around Stanley, throwing Stanley's shirt to the ground as they exit.

As this moment so viscerally demonstrates, *Belle Reprieve* can deconstruct the frantically maintained masculinity and femininity that undergird heterosexuality because these qualities are so palpably present in *Streetcar*. The 1951 film performances of Brando and Leigh, especially, offer the most extreme renderings of the feminine and masculine, taking Williams fully at his word when he describes Blanche as "dainty" and "delicate" with "something about her uncertain manner . . . that suggests a moth." As for Stanley, Williams waxes over the "animal joy in his being . . . implicit in all his movements and attitudes" and "his power and pride of [being] a richly feathered male bird among hens" – he is a "gaudy seed bearer."[49] Indeed, Williams's characters, especially the film versions, have been hypostatized into emblems of American manhood and femininity of the Cold War period, Brando and Leigh becoming icons of the self-made brute and the fragile femme fatale he can't help but destroy. As Bette Bourne quipped in an interview, "Well, it would all be very different if Ernest Borgnine had played Stanley."

Indeed, *Belle Reprieve* refers specifically to film's power to infiltrate the spectator's sexual imagination, especially when it comes to the display of woman as the object of male desire. In a direct invocation of feminist film theory, *Belle Reprieve*'s Stella challenges the audience toward the beginning of the play: she is revealed behind a scrim in a sultry pose, sucking on a bottle of coke. Moving out front, she confronts the "male gaze." Of course she is capable of doing so precisely because this is *not* a film. She looks right out into the audience and in a testy tone, she asks:

> Is there something you want? What can I do for you? Do you know who I am, what I feel, how I think? You want my body. My soul, my food, my bed, my skin, my hands? You want to touch me, hold me, lick me, smell me, eat me, have me? You think you need a little more time to decide? Well, you've got a little over an hour to have your fill.

But of course Stella's promise is a tease; the play's constant rupture of both theatrical illusion and gender conformity thwarts that soppy state of scopophilic dreaminess that film induces. This Stella's sexuality is aggressively her own to satisfy.

It's possible to make a case that on stage *Streetcar* itself can produce similar disruptions, especially now, when, as David Savran suggests, in the wake of Richard Foreman, Robert Wilson, Mabou Mines, and the Wooster Group, American theater may be "prepared to accommodate a Tennessee Williams who is not simply an eccentric realist."[50] In his pioneering work, *Communists, Cowboys, and Queers*, Savran rereads Williams and Arthur Miller, historicizing both as American writers coming to grips with, or against, culturally and state-enforced imperatives of political and sexual containment in the 1940s and 1950s. Williams's plays, he argues, "disrupt orthodox modes of genderization by cutting diagonally across the binary oppositions between masculinity and femininity, heterosexuality and homosexuality."[51] Savran doesn't discuss *Streetcar* in detail. It's clear enough, though, that the "dislodging [of] the present moment from the flux of time and causality"[52] he discerns in Williams's dramatic structures, and the force of eroticism he identifies in the plays as "the source of a transgressive and liberating energy,"[53] blare out of *Streetcar*. So much so, perhaps, that one may wonder whether a contemporary, queer (Savran would say "camp"[54]) production of the play might achieve the same sex–gender critique *Belle Reprieve* accomplishes.

It's curious that contemporary American directors have not yet sought to transport Williams beyond the strictures of a Milleresque realism that his plays so blatantly labor to resist. Perhaps the film versions of the plays still exert too much sway, forever determining how current generations of directors, anyway, can imagine his torpid yet turbulent worlds. Or perhaps the damage done by biographical critics who diagnose Williams's characters with their author's homosexuality quashes queer approaches, as though deciphering what Edgar Hyman called the "Albertine strategy" ("metamorphosing a boy with whom the male protagonist is involved into a girl")[55] were the last, limiting word.

Instead of producing readings like Hyman's, which lead only away from the play, contemporary queerings, such as those Savran proposes, might help move Williams out of relentlessly realistic scenery, into a theatricalized space that talks back to the plays. In more presentational productions than we're used to, we might be able to hear new overtones in familiar speeches. Blanche, for instance, famously declares: "I don't want realism, I want magic! Yes, yes, magic! I try to give that to people. I misrepresent things to them. I don't tell the truth. And if that is sinful, then let me be damned for it! – *Don't turn the light on!*" Yes, yes, she is a woman desperate to retain an ideal she has repeatedly fallen far short of, trying to eke out a space where kindness and desire can coexist. And sure, she sounds like a drag queen (especially when she adds, "A woman's charm is fifty percent illusion"). But she also describes the predicament of the mid-century American playwright, writing self-reflexively against the glare of a prevailing form.

Belle Reprieve itself may help point the way to a more revelatory Williams. For one thing, casting an actual drag queen as Blanche reveals how impossible, how flattening, it would be to read Blanche as such in a production of *Streetcar*: it just makes no sense, despite what Hyman and his epigones argue.[56] If a transvestite Blanche discovered she'd married a homosexual boy, there would have been no cataclysm in her life – and thus no play. Besides, such a reading seeks to "solve" the play in pop-psychological terms, instead of granting Blanche (not to mention a drag queen) the mystery that makes her interesting.

But more than that, through its very resistance to the original play – and, one might say, *Streetcar*'s resistance to radical queers like Split Britches and Bloolips – *Belle Reprieve* confronts the extent to which Williams does rely on realism. Just as the suffocating form of the well-made play forces Hedda to do the thing that people just don't do, just as all those homosexuals kill themselves at the end of those plays, as Charles Ludlam quips, that are still presented at Circle Rep, within the narrative form Williams retains, Blanche must get raped and go crazy. *Belle Reprieve* is as much about the company's inability to *do* the last couple of scenes in *Streetcar* as it is a celebration of the proliferating perversities that rejecting narrative affords.

As the title suggests, *Belle Reprieve* sets out to offer the characters a reprieve from stifling constraints by placing them within a liberating, non-narrative form. Rather than remain subjected to a narrative order that leads inevitably to violence against women, the characters in *Belle Reprieve* break down the structure.

In a hilarious outburst toward the end of the play, as the actors are tapdancing in life-sized paper lanterns, Blanche breaks out of the line, tears off her tawdry outfit and demands:

> *Blanche:* I want to do a real play. With real scenery, white telephones, French windows, a beginning, middle, and an end. What's wrong with a plot we can all follow? There isn't even a drinks trolley.
> *Stanley:* Okay, you want realism? I'll give you realism.
> *Blanche:* You mean like in a real play?
> *Stanley:* If that's what you want.
> *Blanche:* With Marlon Brando and Vivien Leigh?
> *Stanley:* You think you can play it?
> *Blanche:* I have the shoulders.
> *Stanley:* I have the pajamas. Okay. Let's go for it. "It's just you and me now, Blanche."

For the first time in the ninety-minute performance, the actors actually begin to perform a scene from *Streetcar*, playing it in front of a backdrop painted in imitation of the famous Thomas Hart Benton rendering of *Streetcar* (but without the people in it). Almost immediately Blanche, frightened, retreats to the non-narrative margins. And Stanley understands because, as this beer-drenched butch explains to the fluttering queen: "We're in this together. . . . We are the extremes, the stereotypes. We are as far as we can go." And then the two share a little music-hall number about falling in love. They are soon joined by Mitch and Stella, and then they all deliver a song-and-dance finale, praising the "glama" and the "drama" of the theater they "love, love, love."

Still, it's not just the formal fact of *Streetcar* that propelled Bloolips and Split Britches to detonate it into their own postmod romp (nor just that they couldn't get the rights to the play). As post-Stonewall queers, they possess a temperament tremendously at odds with the one brooding within Williams's plays. It's summed up best, perhaps, in an emblematic line from *Orpheus Descending*: "We're all of us sentenced to solitary confinement inside our own skins," Val says. That's the last sentiment one could attach to Split Britches or Bloolips. Rather, they stage themselves in a delicious display of how *liberating* it can be to live in our skins, sensual, sentient, alive to the world.

Epilogue
Not just a passing fancy: notes on butch

I didn't realize, when I decided to talk about butchness, that I was creating a serious conundrum for myself, one that would not have arisen if I simply had to write "Notes on Butch" for publication. The fact that I'd have to stand up, delivering – perhaps one can even say, performing – this paper was to magnify a mundane question into both a theoretical and practical dilemma: what was I going to wear? Given my themes – the way butchness both reveals gender as performance-like and reveals the limits of the theatrical metaphor – I knew that whatever I pulled out of my closet would be a costume: that is, it would be read as having some direct relation to what I had to say. My garments could substantiate my points, contradict them, call my authority into question, assert my authenticity.

Would I wear a suit and tie as prideful affirmation of my own butchness, or as compensation for my lack of it? Loop a string of dimestore pearls through that tie to suggest, through mixing iconography, that such identities are provisional? Would I just not think about it and don my everyday academic garb, slacks and a blazer, which in this context might appear more butch than usual? Or, perhaps, in this context, appear *less* butch than usual, and seem like a cop-out, a shameful refusal to knot that tie or snap those cufflinks on? Maybe I'd wear a little black dress with fishnets and pumps, just to keep things provocatively confusing (though I'd have to borrow the entire get-up and practice walking in advance so I wouldn't trip over my highheels on my way to the podium).

Obviously, like actors who have multiple ways of interpreting a particular moment in a play, I had to make a single choice, and in doing so, it seems, I had to do away with the possibility of expressing all the options that had been open to me. Luckily, since I could write my own script, I could have it both ways: of course I made a choice, which by now is not only self-evident but also extremely self-conscious. (Stirrup

pants, a unisex button-down shirt, a blazer, a flowery necktie, wingtips.)
At the same time, I could call attention to my choice as a way of suggesting that what you see isn't always everything you might get. It's a
point worth stating because it's one that's made by butchness and by a
particular kind of theatricality.

I want to look at what butchness and that kind of theatricality have
in common and at what kind of theater metaphor works best for
describing butchness specifically, and, by extension, all manifestations
of gender presentation, and I want to look at what happens when this
already theatrical image is put on a stage.

In considering butchness as performance, it's important to emphasize
that I'm addressing butchness as a style of self-presentation, as a way of
asserting or displaying oneself – one's lesbian self – in 1990s America.
I won't be focusing on butchness as a sexual identity or as a sexual
practice (though these can certainly be related to butch presentation,
even if they aren't necessarily related by cause and effect, and sometimes have no relation at all). I won't be discussing the historical
functions of butch roles, their manifestations in other cultures, the vast
differences between, say, 1950s American working-class bar butches
and 1920s elegant Left Bank salon butches, or the psychoanalytic meaning of butch representation. (There is, though, a growing body of
literature that takes up these subjects.[1]) Instead, I'm interested specifically in how different theories of acting, based on Brecht, Boal,
contemporary performance art, might be used to understand the power
of the butch image.

It was, after all, through theater that I first understood how butchness helps reveal gender's intimate relationship to performance and
performativity, though that's not how I would have articulated the
insight at the time. As a stage-struck adolescent it was instantly clear to
me that I was something of a gender outlaw. I understood this because
it was so obvious to me that I couldn't hope to get a lead part in a
school play any more than I could expect to make the cheerleading
squad or be elected homecoming queen. I saw that only certain kinds
of girls could play the certain kinds of dramatic parts available to
girls. And, with my jock swagger and not quite budding breasts, I certainly wasn't one of those girls. (Recognizing the limits of these parts
awakened my feminist consciousness, too.) Luckily, I didn't much care
that I didn't fit that mold. I was far happier to play on the field hockey
and softball teams, and to labor as a backstage techie, which allowed
me to clip a tapemeasure on my belt, tie a crescent wrench to my jeans,
and wear workboots to school. (This was junior high as baby butch
heaven!)

Watching rehearsals day after day of some Huck Finn play or another, I saw adolescent life repeating itself: girls practiced giggling with each other, gawking at boys, and gagging themselves; boys practiced impressing each other, impressing girls, and impressing themselves. At first I took the impossibility of my being cast in the play to mean that there was no part for me in the real-life order of the boy–girl universe, either. (Funny how that didn't upset me too much.) But as I studied theater more intently, I came to a more startling revelation: that I *could* be cast in one of those girl parts if only I learned to act well enough. I figured this out just around the time that female schoolmates started putting on mascara and holding back in class. I decided I could never be that good an actor.

Butchness is the sometimes conscious, sometimes intuitive, refusal to play a part in the heterosexist binary (which doesn't mean that butches never have male lovers). Often referred to as a kind of role-playing, butchness can more accurately be described as the denunciation of a given role. It ranges: there are "hardcore" butches and "Saturday night" butches; "stone" butches and "soft" butches. Butches who so define themselves because they are turned on by turning on femmes and butches who fall for other butches. There are butches who pass as men, butches who opt for female-to-male hormonal and surgical transsexualism, butches who turn femme, butches who never even think about being butch. The most useful way of defining butch, Gayle Rubin suggests, is "as a category of lesbian gender that is constituted through the deployment and manipulation of masculine gender codes and symbols."[2] In other words, dykes with such objects or attributes as motorcycles, cumberbunds, wingtips, money, pronounced biceps, extreme chivalry. Straight women with such objects or attributes are just straight women with motorcycles, cumberbunds, biceps, etc. The difference is audience. Butches present their butchness for women – whether femmes, other butches, or themselves, or all three. Some declare their desire through their appearance. Some self-consciously participate in codes that, at least under certain social conditions, make lesbians visible to each other. Some would say they're simply expressing outwardly who they inwardly know themselves to be. In any case, those motorcycles, biceps and so forth are layered with meaning by the lesbian butch. For her, they are not only things, but signs.

Like gender in general, butchness is learned behavior that feels natural, but the fact of learning it is often self-conscious. Fifties butches often tell of being tutored by older butches in everything from how to buy a suit to how to behave in bed. In a campy exaggeration of that tradition, one weekend afternoon in the mid-1980s at the WOW Cafe, the predominantly lesbian women's theater in New York's Lower East Side, Peggy Shaw, a member of the Split Britches company, offered free Butch Lessons. She gave tips on such butch basics as lighting your date's cigarettes, cruising, and choosing a tie.

Adopting and often transforming traits traditionally associated with men, butches threaten masculinity more than they imitate it; they colonize it. Making aggression or toughness or chivalry or rebelliousness their histrionic own, butches reveal the arbitrariness with which such traits are said to belong to men. Rather than copying some "original" image of masculinity, butches point to the embarrassing fact that there is no such thing: masculinity is an artifice no matter who performs it. It's for this reason that butches are often victims of the worst lesbian bashings. Certainly femme lesbians, or any lesbians, enrage straight men for preferring women lovers over them. What's more, femmes confound straight assumptions about sexuality and that's enraging, too. But butches confound assumptions about gender, and that is even more infuriating for it challenges straight men's frantically assembled certainty about their sexuality and power.

This dynamic is clearest in the most macho and most homosocial world of the military, where women – regardless of their sexuality – are considered man-hating dykes because they remove themselves from the category of sexual object by virtue of their uniforms, physical ability, and yes, often their lesbianism. Of course not all women in the military are butches or even lesbians (though, like farm women, they can confuse even the most seasoned dyke). But they illustrate how any women encroaching on male privilege and presentation will be punished. A common remark from male recruits when one of their colleagues' girlfriends comes to the base for a visit is: "How nice to have some real women around here." And when military men just can't stand it any more that the women around them every day are not present for the purpose of the men's entertainment and pleasure, there's always a Tailhook to set things – shall I say? – straight.

The extent to which bashers are most incensed by butches for blurring the lines between male and female genders is most apparent in their violent promises to restore butches to their "proper" role. Typical butch-bashing begins with a rhetorical question, followed by the threat to answer: Are you a man or a woman? We'll show *you*. One man walking past me on upper Broadway one day after I'd gotten a particularly severe haircut strode right up into my face and barked: "Hey, Whadda you? A boy or a girl?" (To which the only appropriate reply seemed to be, "Hey, Whadda *you*? A shmuck or an asshole?")

Being butch isn't simply to flunk basic gender training; it's to scoff at the whole curriculum. And doing so reveals the artificiality of that entire system. If a butch can construct her appearance in a way that seems totally authentic and internally consistent to her, then isn't that what all people are doing when it comes to gender presentation? In other words, if one woman can flout the expected or "normal" appearance and behavior of women, doesn't that mean anyone can flout them? Doesn't that mean that gender is performance?

Of course it is a kind of performance, but gender isn't *merely* performance. We may self-consciously choose our clothing for effect, but few people wake up each morning and decide which gender to put on for the day. It's too simple to say that gender is *all* role-playing, even in the sense Erving Goffman has developed in his theory of social interaction.[3] For Goffman seems to forget that there's no self that preexists our roles, or that the roles we play are not separate from us, as they are, say, for a conventional actor. If in this context the analogy to an actor is to be at all useful, then we can't invoke the naturalistic, Stanislavskian actor who develops her role, performs it, and leaves it behind when she steps off the stage. Rather, we have to think about the actor of the experimental theater from the 1970s on – the actor who tries not to make a distinction between herself and her role, whose role, in fact, is not a dramatic character, but her own self as framed by the time and task she has on stage, the sort of actor, in other words, who came to be known as a performance artist.

It's not easy to draw a line between authenticity and artificiality when looking at this type of performer. Her "real self" (and I'll leave the defining of that to philosophers and psychoanalysts) is not hidden or put in abeyance by a part she's playing; it is the persona that stays with her on stage as she dances, tells a story, utters insensible words, moves about. And yet this persona is to some extent crafted for presentation, at the same time as it is constituted by that presentation. In sum, how do you tell the performer from the performance, artificial as it may be?

Gender, certainly, is a performance more like this than like the performance of an actor playing, say, Hedda Gabler. It's not a role that is easily discarded, or even easily taken on, though it is heavily regulated. It accrues gradually, yet does not attach itself to some blank, some actor cast in a play she's not yet read; it comes into being by virtue of being performed. Judith Butler has been clarifying this point in various essays and in her book *Gender Trouble*. She writes: "[G]ender is not a performance that a prior subject elects to do, but gender is *performative* in the sense that it constitutes as an effect the very subject it appears to express."[4] Elsewhere she argues:

gender cannot be understood as a *role* which either expresses or disguises an interior "self," whether that "self" is conceived as sexed or not. As performance which is performative, gender is an "act," broadly construed, which constructs the social fiction of its own psychological interiority."[5]

Butches produce that act in a special way, which can be understood, I think, by looking at some other performance models. This isn't to say that butches feel any less "real" in their gender presentations than people who follow the rules. I offer myself as an example: I'm not, for the sake of making a political point, acting like I can't wear a dress and heels comfortably, I really can't! I'd feel, and look, like I was in drag, and I'm not even all that butch. To say that butchness is consciously constructed at times is not to say that it can be easily thrown off, or that it's as simple as putting on a leather jacket and boots. (Though a leather jacket and boots can go a long way.) But because it operates outside of what Butler calls the "regulatory fiction" of gender, it reveals that regulatory fiction for what it is. Butch reminds its audience of what it is not. Which is another way of saying that butchness, if not by intention, at least in effect, might be epic acting.

Brecht defined epic acting this way (well, not quite this way – I'm changing his pronouns):

> When [an actor] appears on stage, besides what she actually is doing she will at all essential points discover, specify, imply what she is not doing; that is, she will act in such a way that the alternative emerges as clearly as possible, that her acting allows the other possibilities to be inferred and only represents one of the possible variants. . . . Whatever she doesn't do must be contained and conserved in what she does.[6]

Brecht said that the epic actor must show her character in quotations, and suggested that a good way for an actor to practice epic acting was by playing the opposite sex.

The purpose of this acting style, of course, is to make the familiar strange, to reveal social conventions that have become invisible or "natural" and to show how they have been artificially constructed. Elin Diamond has written persuasively of the implications this theatrical theory can have for feminist representation in the theater,[7] even though the particular social conventions Brecht was interested in didn't include gender, much less its particularly oppressive hold on women.

Still, it seems to me that the butch doesn't adopt masculinity, as most stereotypes would have it, but puts quotation marks around it. (This is a very different process from the parodying of femininity that drag queens perform. Sontag said that camp puts quotation marks around things, too, but she uses the image in a different way from Brecht. In camp, quotation marks punctuate parody, in epic theater, irony.[8]) Thus the butch reveals the conventions of masculinity while at the same time her self-presentation allows the possibility of femininity, the role she is refusing, to be inferred. That's why she is so intolerable: at once the butch demonstrates the choice she's refusing and claims the ground she can't have.

This is the tempting contradiction the *V-effekt* of her epic acting reveals. And it's what makes her sexy. The butch's eroticism comes not from her looking like a man, but from her not being one – that is, from her transgression, from the disruption so wittily captured in Deborah Bright's "Dream Girls" photomontages.

Of course once a butch steps over the invisible line into passing for male, her acting is no longer epic. The ironic quotation marks are replaced with earnestness; the alternative is no longer implied.

Historically, there are numerous examples of women who passed for male in order to travel safely, find work, live with the women they loved, get through the day without being beaten up. This type of transvestism is what Marjorie Garber disparagingly calls the "progress narrative," cross-dressing for success. She resents this use of transvestism as "an instrumental strategy rather than an erotic pleasure and play space" for failing to recognize the transvestite as the "figure that disrupts."[9] But why is Garber's abstraction the privileged way of disrupting? Doesn't it count when a woman disrupts her own oppression by dressing as a man?

Garber prefers to see the transvestite as the grand signifier of boundary crossing, that which creates and reflects what she calls a "category crisis." The transvestite, she argues, shakes up our conventional notions of male and female, and unsettles other categories, such as nationality, race, and religion as well by, she writes, "put[ting] in question identities previously conceived as stable, unchallengeable, grounded, and 'known.'"[10]

The butch, I believe, unsettles these categories more successfully than the transvestite – if, that is, the transvestite is passing successfully. For if s/he is passing successfully, what is being trans-ed? To accomplish the disruption Garber insists on, transvestites must allow their beholders a moment to catch themselves in a recognition, a moment of being struck with the realization: She's really a man! or He's really a woman! It's Wittgenstein's duck–rabbit again: we must notice ourselves seeing-as. Which, again, is exactly what Brecht asks us to do in the theater.

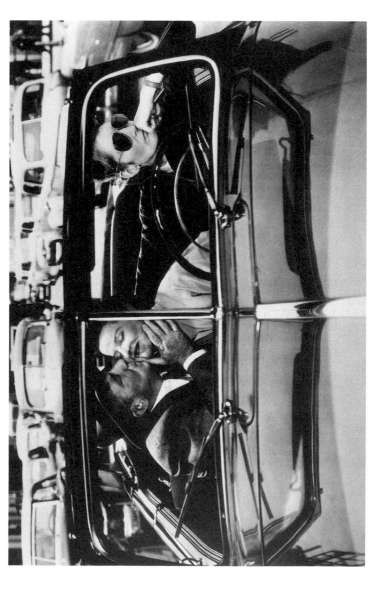

Plate 12 In her photomontage series, "Dream Girls," Deborah Bright captures, in fantasy film scenes, the conventions of masculinity that the butch reveals.

The acting model that best describes passing is Augusto Boal's idea of invisible theater, described in his book *Theater of the Oppressed*. A Brazilian director influenced by Paolo Freire, who used theater techniques to teach literacy and community empowerment, Boal developed a series of guerilla theater exercises and tactics for intervening in public life. Invisible theater, he explains, is

> the presentation of a scene in an environment other than the theater, before people who are not spectators. . . . During the spectacle, these people must not have the slightest idea that it is a "spectacle" for this would make them spectators.[11]

What Boal had in mind was the creation of some kind of ruckus or confrontation in which the undercover actors would demonstrate some lesson to the unwitting spectators, and perhaps draw them into the action. The actors, in other words, would function as catalysts to some event and discussion, that would set people thinking in new ways about, say, the distribution of wealth.

The passing butch can do this, if that is her intention – though a butch passing to keep a job or stay alive may have more pressing things on her mind. But it is in Boal's sense of invisible theater that I understood my single experience of passing for male.

In 1991 I attended a workshop titled Drag King for a Day (which had been advertised in the issue of the *Movement Research* magazine that had gotten the NEA's knickers in a twist[12]). Eleven women took turns for an afternoon as John Armstrong, a preoperative female-to-male transsexual, meticulously colored strips of stage makeup hair to match what we had on our heads and then pasted the fuzz above our lips, on our chins, or along our jawlines. He showed us how to flatten our breasts by wrapping Ace bandages around and around our torsos (my Jogbra did the trick). We loosened our belts a notch to make our waistlines fall, slicked back hair, put on vests. I clinched the transformation by knotting my necktie on the first try. We giggled at each other and at ourselves in the mirror. Some of us stuffed a sock into our pants.

Performance artist Diane Torr – now Danny with a thick moustache and a dark suit – led us in movement exercises. We swaggered, we slumped, we took up space. We dropped our voices into our diaphragms, and talked in slow, measured tones – as if, Torr coached, "you know you have thousands of years of philosophy behind every word and people are bound to listen." We grunted, we grumbled, and we practiced not smiling. Passing for male, said Torr, "is an exercise in repression."

I ventured out onto Lexington Avenue in the blazing light of the afternoon sun, terrified that I'd be discovered. The spirit gum itched like crazy under my brand new moustache. I didn't dare wipe the sweat that trickled down my cheek for fear of smudging off my 5-o'clock shadow. But in no time I hit my stride – a lumbering, loping, masculine stride. I wasn't half-way down the block before the self-consciousness slipped away. Not just the self-consciousness of being in disguise, but the every-day self-consciousness that women carry in the street, the self-consciousness of being on display. Now, as I sauntered along in my heavy shoes and butch black jacket, no one looked. I walked right past – men hanging out on corners, men strolling by on the sidewalk, men lingering in doorways. They didn't even see me. For once my shoulders didn't tense in anticipation of some "hey-baby" lewdness. I had become invisible.

The ad had promised "the adventure of a lifetime." But what was most remarkable about being dressed as a man for twelve hours was how *un*remarkable it felt. I'd expected the frisson of putting one over on the guys, the thrill of catching a glimpse of male privilege and power, the eroticism of maintaining a secret in public, the eeriness of feeling that I'd "become" my brother (whom I resemble even without a moustache). All those emotions were stirred. But what I felt most was ease and comfort.

It was so easy to pass, in fact, that I almost took the subway home at 2 a.m., until I remembered that I was still 5–2 and 115 pounds and that men, too, get mugged. The cabdriver asked me what I thought about those Mets.

What turned the experience into invisible theater in Boal's sense were some conversations I had with some men.

The dozen of us from the workshop spent the evening together, first going for drinks and dancing at a queer bar frequented by transvestites. (That's where I screwed up my courage to go to the men's room, swaggered safely into a stall, pulled down my pants and watched my crotch-stuffing, wadded up, red cotton sweatsock leap out, roll under the door, and land by a urinal. So much for the phallus as signifier.) I spent a happy couple of hours, learning to boogie to Motown without swiveling my hips.

Later we headed downtown to a lesbian bar where lots of gay boys hang out to prove how cool they are. By then a lot of our group had tired of their itchy whiskers, had yanked them off and gone cruising for girls, but I was in for the long haul. I sat at the bar quaffing a Rolling Rock and chatting with gay guys as they came along. Like one of Boal's undercover actors, I asked them about why they'd come to this bar, using invisible theater to provoke a discussion they otherwise would never have. (They'd never respond to a woman asking such questions.) Why, when there were more than fifty gay men's bars in New York, had they decided to come to one of two lesbian bars, since they clearly weren't there to shmooze with the women? Most responded as if this question had never occurred to them before, but I prodded, and they replied, thinking things over, weighing their words, wondering aloud why they had come. Some said they *had* come to converse with the women, and were disappointed that more of them weren't interested in socializing with *them*; others said they appreciated the relief of being away from the heavy cruising of men's bars. But one of the guys who told me that was the one who asked me if we might get together later. It was time to draw the curtain on my invisible theater by revealing myself. Why do *you* come here, he asked me. I stroked my moustache and answered matter-of-factly: "I'm a lesbian."

What happens to the highly theatrical activities of butchness, gender, and passing, though, when they are put in a theatrical frame, when they are made the subject of drama?

I've already mentioned Peggy Shaw, the big butch Split Britches actor who is every feminist critic's favorite example. The company's major works have been written about amply – not only because the group tours to colleges across the country, but because their work so neatly demonstrates, and sometimes even refers to, principles of contemporary queer and performance theory. I want briefly to talk about a piece they performed for one summer night in 1992 at Dixon Place, the downtown performance space where new work is developed and tested. I don't recall whether the piece even had a name; there certainly wasn't any program.

The short performance was created by Shaw and her partner of more than a decade on stage and off, Lois Weaver, shortly after they'd finished a run of *Belle Reprieve*, their collaboration with the drag troupe Bloolips based on *A Streetcar Named Desire* (see Chapter 5). The piece at Dixon Place was a kind of scaling down, a chance for Shaw and Weaver to get used to working alone again, as well as a chance for them to incorporate some of the themes they'd developed in *Belle Reprieve* and make them work even when there weren't any men – or drag queens – in the show with them.

The result was a complex and poignant examination of butch–femme taken to its extremes. Weaver and Shaw had long played with these roles. (Indeed, they traded them briefly in *Anniversary Waltz*, a compendium of skits celebrating their tenth anniversary. This exchange, and the celebration of their relationship, though heavily camped up, led to accusations by one lesbian critic after another that they'd produced an "assimilationist" work and denuded "butch–femme" of its sexual content by reducing it to a set of costumes. I found the show ironic enough to beat those charges; it was both charming and liberatory.)

The Dixon Place piece begins with Weaver coming on stage naked in all her buxom bleached-blondeness, and calmly welcoming the audience. She then performs a strip-tease to the "Take it All Off" song, but strips her femme clothing *on*, one little piece at a time: stockings, black bustier, strapless dress (which a spectator is recruited to zip up). The brilliance of the strip is that the more Weaver puts on, the sexier she becomes.

Shaw follows with a monologue, adapted from *Belle Reprieve*:

> I was born this way. I didn't learn it at theater school. I was born butch. I'm so queer I don't even have to talk about it. It speaks for itself. It's not funny. Being butch isn't funny. Don't panic. I fall to pieces in the night. I'm just thousands of parts of other people all mashed into my body. I'm not an original person. I take all these pieces, snatch them off the floor before they get swept under the bed, and manufacture myself. When I'm saying I fall to pieces, I'm saying Marlon Brando was not there for me. James Dean failed to come through. Where was Susan Hayward when I needed her? And how come Rita Hayworth was nowhere to be found? I fall to pieces at the drop of a hat. Take your pick of which piece you want and when I pull myself back together again I'll think of you. I'll think of you and what you want me to be.[13]

In both solo turns, the roles are established as a layered system of signs, created by the piling on of pieces from popular culture, from the dominant heterosexist world. Weaver's soft nakedness and Shaw's declaration "I was born this way" assert a femme and butch essentialism, which are immediately distanced and commented upon by the pieces that make their costume – whether stockings and bustier, or gestures and mannerisms borrowed from Brando or Hayworth. Butch and femme are not just the costume; but they're nothing without the costume.

But that's not all. Weaver and Shaw dance together and almost immediately another butch, an even butcher butch (Leslie Feinberg), cuts in to dance with Shaw (though Shaw would kill me if she heard me call someone a butcher butch). The two glide awkwardly yet tenderly around the floor, stumbling as each tries to lead the other, as they talk about their discomfort: "What if someone sees us dancing together? They might think I'm a femme!" The line is hilarious in its implausibility, yet absolutely honest, and heart-breaking, in its expression of panic.

The anxiety is palpable, like at a junior high prom. Shaw and Feinberg fumble and trip, searching for the way to make their smooth moves smooth. The scene is intensely erotic.

The exchange is complex in another way: Shaw, a seasoned performer whose street and stage life are largely blurred, represents herself on stage as a butch whose butchness is self-conscious, but no less real for being self-conscious: that is, it's Brechtian. Feinberg, long-time activist, novelist, and pre-Stonewall bar butch, sways across the stage without the mediation of any self-conscious performance frame. The simple fact of the stage provides one distancing frame, of course, but that irony is not as thick or as nuanced as the ironies surrounding Shaw. The contrast, never remarked upon, raises impossible questions: Which is the more desirable butch – more desirable to have, more desirable to be like, or both? Which is the "realer" butch? This, of course, is the question vexing the performers, but at a totally different level than for us. For them, at least as characters in a script, the question is ontological; for them, as performers whose real lives are enmeshed in their performance, the question is existential; for us, the audience, the question is social, sexual, political, aesthetic.

Because it subverts male privilege, butchness can be the most dangerous queer image, and that's exactly why it is increasingly invisible even as gays and lesbians find ourselves in the news for good or ill. And that's why, when it does appear, it's tamed, even commodified. Though proportionally three times as many women as men are kicked out of the military for being homosexual, lesbians are never mentioned when the generals get hysterical over the prospect of gay guys in the shower. (If they're so afraid of a few fags, I wonder, what business do these brass have protecting America, much less democracy?) And butches are increasingly absent in the ever more pleading efforts of some gay activists to prove that we are just like straights. Think of the page-one photo in the *New York Times* the day domestic partnerships were introduced in New York City: Wow! A lesbian couple on the cover of the *Times* – both of them in little black dresses and pearls. Or think of the we're-just-like-you rhetoric around the April 1993 gay-rights March on Washington. Butches are left out of the picture.

In the 1990s, as a recent *New York Magazine* cover story ecstatically explained, lesbians are looking sharp.[14] And thus we overcome the myth of the "mannish" lesbian, banishing, in one ironic swoop, both butches and the lesbian-feminist flannel crunchies of the 1970s, who themselves once drove butches out of the lesbian community.

The effect of our being so fashionable is the de-dyking of butchness. While butchness vanishes from mainstream images of lesbians, a faux butchness, its parameters carefully delineated, is all over the straight world. Model Brooke Shields poses in backward baseball cap and 5 o'clock shadow for the cover of a New York fashion mag under the title "Pretty Butch."[15] Straight female college students wear splashy neckties purchased from men's shops.

In part this occurs because women, at least in the corporate world – or, more accurately, fashion designers of clothing for those in the corporate world – have acknowledged women's relative liberation by tailoring their power suits after men's traditional business attire, making sure, of course, there's still a slit at the thigh, or a flounce at the neck, or, best of all, a little cleavage peeping through. Still, Radclyffe Hall could almost walk through Wall Street in her famous duds today without much notice – except that her shoes might give her away. (When it comes to physical labor, women's attire has almost always, of necessity, been the same as men's.)

But of course, this is only costume. Butchness, like any full performance, involves stance, gesture, movement, vocal intonation, and, most important, intention. And there's no danger that the intention will ever be appropriated.

Notes

INTRODUCTION: HOW EASY IS A BUSH SUPPOS'D A BEAR

1 All quotations from *Thesmophoriazusae*, unless otherwise noted, are taken from David Barrett's translation in *Aristophanes: The Wasps/The Poet and the Women/The Frogs*, London, Penguin Books, 1964. Barrett's version is somewhat bowdlerized and I have filled in aspects of the action he leaves out on the basis of material provided by Zeitlin and Taaffe (see below).

2 Froma I. Zeitlin, "Travesties of Gender and Genre in Aristophanes' *Thesmophoriazousae*," in H.P. Foley (ed.), *Reflections of Women in Antiquity*, New York, Gordon & Breach, 1981, p. 177. In this essay Zeitlin explores the relationship of transvestism and parody to mimesis, and my thoughts on the play are suffused with her ideas. She, however, takes her analysis in a different direction, focusing on the misogyny implicit in the play; I don't dispute her, I'm simply more interested in examining the theatrical event. Similarly, Lauren K. Taaffe focuses on gender and genre in her reading of *Thesmophoriazusae* in *Aristophanes & Women*, London, Routledge, 1993, but uses the "male gaze" to elucidate her points – a strategy I find gratuitous, if not misleading.

3 Arthur Pickard-Cambridge, *Dithyramb, Tragedy and Comedy*, Oxford, Clarendon Press, 1962, p. 129. I am grateful to Framji Minwalla for drawing this work to my attention.

4 Marjorie Garber, *Vested Interests: Cross-Dressing and Cultural Anxiety*, New York, Routledge, 1992, p. 39.

5 See, for example, Sue-Ellen Case, "Classic Drag: The Greek Creation of Female Parts," *Theatre Journal*, vol. 37, 1985, pp. 317–28; Lesley Ferris, *Acting Women: Images of Women in Theatre*, New York, New York University Press, 1989; Helen Foley, "The Conception of Women in Athenian Drama," in Foley (ed.), *Reflections of Women in Antiquity*, pp. 127–68; Taaffe, *Aristophanes and Women*.

6 See Michael Fried, "Art and Objecthood," in Gregory Battock (ed.), *Minimal Art: A Critical Anthology*, New York, E.P. Dutton, 1968, and *Absorption and Theatricality: Painting and Beholder in the Age of Diderot*, Berkeley, University of California Press, 1980.

7 Bruce Wilshire, *Role-Playing and Identity: The Limits of Theatre as Metaphor*, Boston, Routledge & Kegan Paul, 1981, p. x.

8 See, to cite only a few examples, Simone de Beauvoir, *The Second Sex*, New

York, Vintage Books, 1951; Bonnie Bullough and Vern L. Bullough, *Cross Dressing, Sex and Gender*, Philadelphia, University of Pennsylvania Press, 1993; Elizabeth Burns, *Theatricality: A Study of Convention in Theatre and in Social Life*, New York, Harper & Row, 1973; Judith Butler, *Gender Trouble: Feminism and the Subversion of Identity*, London, Routledge, 1990 and "Performative Acts and Gender Constitution: An Essay in Phenomenology and Feminist Theory," in Sue-Ellen Case (ed.), *Performing Feminisms: Feminist Critical Theory and Theatre*, Baltimore, Johns Hopkins University Press, 1990; Jill Dolan, "Gender Impersonation on Stage: Destroying or Maintaining the Mirror of Gender Roles?" *Women and Performance*, vol. 2, no. 2, 1985, pp. 4–11; Erving Goffman, *The Presentation of Self in Everyday Life*, Garden City, Doubleday, 1959; Esther Newton, *Mother Camp: Female Impersonators in America*, Chicago, University of Chicago Press, 1972; Joan Rivière, "Womanliness as Masquerade," in V. Burgin, J. Donald, C. Kaplan (eds), *Formations of Fantasy*, London, Methuen, 1986 (Rivière's essay was originally published in 1929); Wilshire, *Role-Playing and Identity: The Limits of Theatre as Metaphor*.

9 For the original elaboration of the term, see Adrienne Rich, "Compulsory Heterosexuality and Lesbian Existence," in A. Snitow, C. Stansell, S. Thompson (eds), *Powers of Desire: The Politics of Sexuality*, New York, Monthly Review Press, 1983, pp. 177–205.

10 See J. L. Austin, *How to Do Things with Words*, Cambridge, MA, Harvard University Press, 1975. See also Derrida's famous critique of Austin's idea of performative speech acts in "Signature, Event, Context," in *Glyph*, nos 1 and 2, 1977, pp. 172–97 and Judith Butler's careful use of the concept for "gender performativity" in *Gender Trouble*.

11 This definition is Judith Butler's, from *Bodies That Matter: On the Discursive Limits of "Sex"*, New York, Routledge, 1993, p. 2.

12 For a further discussion of this trend, see, Jill Dolan, "Geographies of Learning: Theatre Studies, Performance, and the 'Performative'," *Theatre Journal*, vol. 45, 1993, pp. 417–41. She notes, for instance, that the University of California-Riverside's annual conference, "Themes in Drama," was renamed a few years ago, "Unnatural Acts: Theorizing the Performative." See also the schedule from the latest meeting of the Modern Languages Association for panels on such subjects as "Performing Postcoloniality," and "Text as Performance."

13 Dolan, "Geographies of Learning," p. 431.

14 Gayle Rubin. "The Traffic in Women: Notes on the 'Political Economy' of Sex," in Rayna R. Reiter (ed.), *Toward an Anthropology of Women*, New York, Monthly Review Press, 1975, pp. 199–200.

15 Candace West and Don H. Zimmerman, "Doing Gender," *Gender & Society*, vol. 1, no. 2, June 1987, pp. 125–51. I am grateful to Tony O'Brien for passing along this article to me.

16 Taaffe, *Aristophanes & Women*, points out a number of such critics, p. 85.

17 See Ferris, *Acting Women*, p. 23. On the Thesmophoria itself, see W. Burkert, *Structure and History in Greek Mythology and Ritual*, Berkeley, University of California Press, 1979, and Burkert, *Greek Religion*, J. Raffan (trans.), Cambridge, MA, Harvard University Press, 1985.

18 Taaffe, *Aristophanes & Women*, pp. 77–78.

19 This translation is Taaffe's, *Aristophanes & Women*, p. 82.

20 Taaffe, *Aristophanes & Women*, p. 84.
21 This translation is Taaffe's, *Aristophanes & Women*, p. 92.
22 Ferris, *Acting Women*, p. 27.
23 Zeitlin, "Travesties of Gender and Genre," p. 195.
24 Sue-Ellen Case, *Feminism and Theatre*, New York, Methuen, 1988, p. 7.
25 Case, *Feminism and Theatre*, p. 19.
26 See Helene Foley (ed.), *Reflections of Women in Antiquity*, for essays on misogyny in ancient Greece, and D. Cohen, "Seclusion, Separation, and the Status, of Women in Classical Athens," *Greece & Rome*, 36, 1989, pp. 3–15; Foley, "Sex and State in Ancient Greece," *Diacritics*, vols 4–5, 1975, pp. 31–6.
27 Teresa de Lauretis, "The Technology of Gender," in *Technologies of Gender*, Bloomington, Indiana University Press, 1987, p. 2.
28 See, for instance, Sue-Ellen Case, *Feminism and Theatre*; Case (ed.), *Performing Feminisms: Feminist Critical Theory and Theatre*; Jill Dolan, *The Feminist Spectator as Critic*; Lynda Hart (ed.), *Making a Spectacle: Feminist Essays on Contemporary Women's Theatre*, Ann Arbor, University of Michigan Press, 1989; Hart and P. Phelan (eds), *Acting Out: Feminist Performances*, Ann Arbor, University of Michigan Press, 1993; Laurence Senelick, *Gender in Performance: The Presentation of Difference in the Performing Arts*, Hanover and London, University Press of New England, 1992.
29 There have been important theoretical discussions of realism and its limitations for a feminist theater practice. See, for instance, Jill Dolan, "Personal, Political, Polemical: Feminist Approaches to Politics and Theater," G. Holderness (ed.), *The Politics of Theatre and Drama*, New York and London, St. Martin's Press and Macmillan, 1992; and "'Lesbian' Subjectivity in Realism: Dragging at the Margins of Structure and Ideology," in *Performing Feminisms*. Many of the essays in the volumes mentioned above take performance art and other non-naturalistic presentations as their examples. Still, realism remains the basis of much theoretical work, and it is rarely historicized. I take up these issues more specifically in my chapter on Ibsen.
30 See J. L. Styan, *Drama, Stage, and Audience*, Cambridge, Cambridge University Press, 1975, and *Elements of Drama*, Cambridge, Cambridge University Press, 1960.
31 For good feminist summaries of and commentaries on Lacan see Jane Gallop, *The Daughter's Seduction: Feminism and Psychoanalysis*, Ithaca, Cornell University Press, 1982, and *Reading Lacan*, Ithaca, Cornell University Press, 1985; E. Ann Kaplan, *Women & Film: Both Sides of the Camera*, New York, Methuen, 1983; Kaja Silverman, *The Subject of Semiotics*, New York, Oxford University Press, 1983; Julia Kristeva, *Desire in Language*, New York, Columbia University Press, 1980.
32 Kaplan, *Women & Film*, p. 13.
33 Case, *Feminism and Theatre*, p. 15. See also Dolan, "Gender Impersonation on Stage: Destroying or Maintaining the Mirror of Gender Roles?" *Women & Performance*, vol. 4, 1987.
34 Herbert Blau, "Universals of Performance; or, Amortizing Play," *Substance*, vols 37–38, 1983, p. 148.
35 Butler, *Gender Trouble*, p. 138.

36 In an important essay, "Mimesis, Mimicry, and the 'True-Real'," *Modern Drama*, vol. 32, no. 1, 1989, Elin Diamond comes to a similar conclusion. She writes, "Mimesis has little to do with stable mirror reflection that realism inspires, but rather suggests . . . a trick mirror that doubles (makes feminine) in the act of reflection." As a result, theater can be recognized as "a privileged site for feminist analysis because of, not in spite of, its long association with mimetic practice and theory." I differ from Diamond simply in the choice of tool used to pry open the issue. She proposes that "mimesis can be retheorized as a site of, and means of, feminist intervention [through the] intertexts of [Luce] Irigaray and [Julia] Kristeva," and she makes a good case for that proposal. My suspicion, though, is that Irigaray and Kristeva are not needed to make the point, and that their Lacanian foundations (not to mention their dense jargon) can even be counterproductive.

37 Laura Mulvey, "Visual Pleasure and Narrative Cinema," *Screen*, vol. 16, no. 3, Autumn 1975, pp. 17–18.

38 Kaplan, *Women & Film*, p. 15.

39 Case, *Feminism and Theatre*, p. 119.

40 Kristina Straub, "The Guilty Pleasures of Female Theatrical Cross-Dressing and the Autobiography of Charlotte Charke," in Straub and Julia Epstein (eds), *Body Guards: The Cultural Politics of Gender Ambiguity*, New York, Routledge, 1991, pp. 144 and 143.

41 Mikel Dufrenne, *The Phenomenology of Aesthetic Experience*, E. Casey (trans.), Evanston, Northwestern University Press, 1973, p. 15.

42 Case, Dolan, and others reject the white heterosexual male as the assumed universal spectator, as they should, but invoke a construct called "the feminist spectator," as they must.

43 All quotes with Fierstein are from an interview I conducted with her in New York City on 12 October 1993.

44 Judith Fetterly, *The Resisting Reader: A Feminist Approach to American Fiction*, Bloomington, University of Indiana Press, 1978.

45 John Willet (ed.), *Brecht on Theater*, New York, Hill & Wang, 1964, p. 44.

46 Ludwig Wittgenstein, *Philosophical Investigations*, G.E.M. Anscombe (trans.), New York, Macmillan, 1958, 3rd edn, pp. 193–208.

47 Wittgenstein, *Philosophical Investigations*, p. 213.

48 Laurel Richardson and Verta Taylor (eds), *Feminist Frontiers III*, New York, McGraw-Hill, 1993, p. 2.

49 Ann Powers, "Class Conflicts: A Vindication of the Rights of Women's Studies," *Voice Literary Supplement*, October 1993, p. 11.

50 Phillip Stubbes, *The Anatomie of Abuses* (1583), facsimile, Arthur Freeman (ed.) New York, Garland, 1973.

51 Butler, *Bodies That Matter*, p. 283, n. 15.

52 Lanoue credits Sonny Graf with this story.

1 MUCH VIRTUE IN IF: SHAKESPEARE'S CROSS-DRESSED BOY-ACTRESSES AND THE NON-ILLUSORY STAGE

1 All quotations from Shakespeare plays come from the Arden editions: *As You Like It*, The Arden Edition of the Works of William Shakespeare, Agnes Latham (ed.), London, Methuen, 1975; *Twelfth Night*, The Arden

Edition of the Works of William Shakespeare, J. M. Lothian and T. W. Craik (eds), London, Methuen, 1975.

2 In the production that played in Stonybrook, New York in 1991, the actor playing Celia was a bit squat, wonderfully intense, and quite serious in her/his doting on Rosalind. But in the version that played in Brooklyn, in 1994, Celia was played by a taller, lither actor who played "girlishness" with more laugh-grabbing self-consciousness – almost campily. I preferred the earlier performance, and it made the stronger impression on me. This essay responds primarily to that 1991 production.

3 See, among many others, Janet Adelman, "Male Bonding in Shakespeare's Comedies," in P. Erickson and C. Kahn (eds), *Shakespeare's "Rough Magic": Renaissance Essays in Honor of C. L. Barber*, Newark, University of Delaware Press, 1985, pp. 73–103; Catherine Belsey, "Disrupting Sexual Difference: Meaning and Gender in the Comedies," in J. Drakakis (ed.), *Alternative Shakespeares*, London, Methuen, 1985; Juliet Dusinberre, *Shakespeare and the Nature of Women*, New York, Macmillan, 1975; Peter Erickson, *Patriarchal Structures in Shakespeare's Drama*, Berkeley and Los Angeles, University of California Press, 1985; Clara Claiborne Park, "As We Like It: How a Girl Can Be Smart and Still Popular," in C.R.S. Lenz, G. Greene, and C.T. Neely (eds), *The Woman's Part: Feminist Criticism of Shakespeare*, Urbana, University of Illinois Press, 1980, pp. 106–9; Phyllis Rackin, "Androgyny, Mimesis, and the Marriage of the Boy Heroine on the English Renaissance Stage," *PMLA*, vol. 102, 1987, pp. 29–41; Valerie Traub, *Desire & Anxiety: Circulations of Sexuality in Shakespearean Drama*, London and New York, Routledge, 1992.

4 Joel Fineman, "Fratricide and Cuckoldry: Shakespeare's Doubles," in M. Schwartz and C. Kahn (eds), *Representing Shakespeare: New Psychoanalytic Essays*, Baltimore, Johns Hopkins University Press, 1980, p. 92.

5 Interview with Declan Donnellan, 20 September 1994.

6 Jonathan Dollimore, *Sexual Dissidence: Augustine to Wilde, Freud to Foucault*, Oxford, Clarendon Press, 1990, p. 282.

7 Barbara Freedman, *Staging the Gaze: Postmodernism, Psychoanalysis, and Shakespearean Comedy*, Ithaca, Cornell University Press, 1991, p. 43.

8 Susan Zimmeran, "Introduction," *Erotic Politics: Desire on the Renaissance Stage*, New York and London, Routledge, 1992, p. 8.

9 Jean Howard, "Scripts and/versus Playhouses: Ideological Production and the Renaissance Public Stage," in Valerie Wayne (ed.), *The Matter of Difference: Materialist Feminist Criticism of Shakespeare*, Ithaca, Cornell University Press, 1991, pp. 221–36.

10 See Lawrence Stone, *The Family, Sex, and Marriage in England, 1500–1800*, abridged edition, New York, Penguin Books, 1977; David Underdown, *Revel, Riot, and Rebellion: Popular Politics and Culture in England, 1603–1660*, Oxford, Oxford University Press, 1987.

11 David Underdown, "The Taming of the Scold: The Enforcement of Patriarchal Authority in Early Modern England," in A. Fletcher and J. Stevenson (eds), *Order and Disorder in Early Modern England*, Cambridge, Cambridge University Press, 1985, p. 119.

12 See Linda Woodbridge, *Women and the English Renaissance: Literature and the Nature of Womankind, 1540–1620*, Urbana and Chicago, University of Illinois Press, 1986; and K. Henderson and B. McManus (eds), *Half*

Humankind: Contexts and Texts of the Controversy about Women in England, 1540–1640, Urbana and Chicago, University of Illinois Press, 1985.

13 Reported by John Hale in his *The Civilization of Europe in the Renaissance*, London, Atheneum, 1994, p. 454.

14 Ania Loomba, *Gender, Race, Renaissance Drama*, Manchester, University of Manchester Press, 1989, p. 132.

15 Quoted in Paul Johnson, *Elizabeth I: A Study in Power and Intellect*, London, Weidenfeld & Nicolson, 1974, p. 320.

16 N.E. McClure (ed.), *The Letters of John Chamberlain*, Philadelphia, American Philosophical Society, 1939, quoted in Woodbridge, *Women and the English Renaissance*, p. 143.

17 Both pamphlets are published in Henderson and McManus (eds), *Half Humankind*. For commentary, see: Barbara Bowen, *Gender in the Theater of War: Shakespeare's Troilus and Cressida*, New York, Garland Publishing, 1993; Jean Howard, "Cross-Dressing, the Theatre, and Gender Struggle in Early Modern England," in L. Ferris (ed.), *Crossing the Stage: Controversies on Cross-Dressing*, London, Routledge, 1993, pp. 20–46; Constance Jordan, *Renaissance Feminism: Literary Texts and Political Models*, Ithaca, Cornell University Press, 1990; Woodbridge, *Women and the English Renaissance*.

18 John Rainolds, *Overthrow of the Stage-Plays*, New York, Johnson Reprint Corp., 1972, pp. 96–7.

19 William Prynne, *Histrio-mastix: The Player's Scourge or Actor's Tragedy*, 1633, New York, Garland Publishing, 1974.

20 Marjorie Garber, *Vested Interests: Cross-Dressing and Cultural Anxiety*, New York and London, Routledge, 1992, p. 63.

21 See commentary in Henderson and McManus (eds), *Half Humankind*, and Woodbridge, *Women and the English Renaissance*, pp. 139–51.

22 The phrase, "The Patriarchal Bard," is the title of Kathleen McLuskie's generative essay in J. Dollimore and A. Sinfield (eds), *Political Shakespeare: New Essays in Cultural Materialism*, Ithaca and Manchester, Manchester University Press, 1985, pp. 88–108.

23 Matthew H. Wikander, "As Secret as Maidenhead: The Profession of the Boy-Actress in *Twelfth Night*," *Comparative Drama*, vol. 20, no. 4, 1986, p. 351.

24 Wikander, "As Secret as Maidenhead," p. 350.

25 Katherine E. Kelly, "The Queen's Two Bodies: Shakespeare's Boy Actresses in Breeches," *Theatre Journal*, 1990, p. 92.

26 Howard, "Cross-Dressing, the Theater, and Gender Struggle," p. 37.

27 Howard, "Cross-Dressing, the Theater, and Gender Struggle," pp. 29–30.

28 Northrop Frye introduces the phrase in *A Natural Perspective: The Development of Shakespearean Comedy and Romance*, New York, Columbia University Press, 1965, to refer to self-consciously familiar, formulaic, even hackneyed, plot devices that take attention off the question of what will happen to focus on how it happens, and that heighten a sense of play and lead to an interest in convention itself.

29 See, for instance, Dusinberre, *Shakespeare and the Nature of Women*; Park, "As We Like It: How a Girl Can Be Smart and Still Popular"; and Traub, *Desire & Anxiety*.

30 See, for instance, Lisa Jardine, "Twins and Travesties: Gender, Dependency, and Sexual Availability in *Twelfth Night*," in S. Zimmerman (ed.), *Erotic*

Politics, pp. 27–38; Susan Zimmerman, "Disruptive Desire: Artifice and Indeterminacy in Jacobean Comedy," in Zimmerman, pp. 39–63.

31 See, for instance, Dollimore, *Sexual Dissidence*, pp. 284–306; Peter Stallybrass, "Transvestism and the 'Body Beneath': Speculating on the Boy Actor," in Zimmerman, pp. 64–83.

32 Traub, *Desire & Anxiety*, p. 126.

33 Michael Feingold, "Mythical Problems," review of Mark Lamos's production of *Measure for Measure* at Lincoln Center, New York City, *Village Voice*, 21 March 1989, p. 98.

34 Noting the numerous questions in the text, Maynard Mack points out that *Hamlet* takes place in the "interrogative mode." See "The World of Hamlet," *Yale Review*, vol. XLI, 1952, pp. 502–23.

35 Stallybrass, "Transvestism and the 'Body Beneath'," p. 74.

36 Stallybrass, "Transvestism and the 'Body Beneath'," p. 77.

37 Stallybrass, "Transvestism and the 'Body Beneath'," p. 71.

38 Bertolt Brecht, *The Messingkauf Dialogues*, John Willett (trans.), London, Methuen, 1965, p. 58.

39 Barbara Bowen, "*Twelfth Night*: Shakespeare's Doubly Redoubled Play," unpublished manuscript generously provided by the author.

40 See, for instance, C. L. Barber, *Shakespeare's Festive Comedy: A Study of Dramatic Form and its Relation to Social Custom*, New York, Princeton University Press, 1963; Coppélia Kahn, "The Providential Tempest and the Shakespearean Family," in C. Kahn and M. Schwartz (eds), *Representing Shakespeare: New Psychoanalytic Essays*, Baltimore, Johns Hopkins University Press, 1980, pp. 217–43; Marjorie Garber, *Coming of Age in Shakespeare*, London, Methuen, 1981 (which emphasizes Olivia's maturation toward the choice of an appropriate love object).

41 See Judith Butler, *Gender Trouble: Feminism and the Subversion of Identity*, New York, Routledge, 1990; *Bodies That Matter*, New York, Routledge, 1993.

42 Similarly, the production makes use of a red clown's nose to indicate and play upon class differences and disruptions. Touchstone dons it when he enters the role of court fool; Jacques uses it later when retelling his encounter with Touchstone; Corin pops it onto his face still later to signal that he is getting the last laugh when Touchstone mocks his naive paean to pastoral.

43 I eventually did see an all-woman *As You Like It*. It was presented by the Looking Glass Theatre in New York in September 1995, directed by Anne Beaumont. It was one of the most badly acted and least thought-through productions I've ever seen. Despite an advertisement counseling potential spectators to "check your gender at the door," from what they presented on stage, the company didn't seem to have any interest at all in gender questions. Rosalind was a prissy ingenue all the time, even when disguised as Ganymede; the production overall felt like the sort of thing one might see at a girls' boarding school. So I'm still waiting for an all-woman *AYLI* that might shake up the layers of gender conundrums in new ways.

44 For discussion of the use of Shakespeare as a tool of colonialism see, among others, Loomba, *Gender, Race, Renaissance Drama*; Dollimore and Sinfield (eds), *Political Shakespeare: New Essays in Cultural Materialism*, Ithaca, Cornell University Press, 1985; Gary Taylor, *Reinventing*

Shakespeare: A Cultural History from the Restoration to the Present, New York, Weidenfeld, 1989.

45 Telephone interview with John K. Clemens, Hartwick Humanities in Management Institute, Oneonta, New York, 11 December 1993, and study-guide materials provided by the institute.

46 In *Ain't I a Woman? Black Women and Feminism*, Boston, South End, 1981, bell hooks notes, "In a racially imperialist nation such as ours, it is the dominant race that reserves for itself the luxury of dismissing racial identity while the oppressed race is made daily aware of their racial identity," p. 138.

47 Postcard advertisement for *House of Lear*, May 1993.

48 Dollimore, *Sexual Dissidence*, p. 285.

2 THE NEW DRAMA AND THE NEW WOMAN: RECONSTRUCTING IBSEN'S REALISM

1 This and all subsequent quotations from Ibsen's plays are from Rolf Fjelde's translations in *Ibsen, The Complete Major Prose Plays*, New York, New American Library, Plume, 1978.

2 Clement Scott quoted in Michael Egan (ed.), *Ibsen, The Critical Heritage*, London, Routledge & Kegan Paul, 1972, pp. 114 and 227.

3 *Shaw's Dramatic Criticism 1895–98*, selected by John F. Matthews, New York, Hill & Wang, 1959, p.192.

4 For critiques of the masculinist assumptions within the "objective" see Donna J. Haraway, *Simians, Cyborgs, and Women, The Reinvention of Nature*, New York, Routledge, 1991, and Ruth Bleier (ed.), *Feminist Approaches to Science*, New York, Pergamon Press Inc., The Athene Series, 1986.

5 Richard Gilman, "Seeing Hedda Whole," *The Repertory Reader*, newsletter of the American Ibsen Theater, vol. 1, no. 3, Spring 1984. Gilman calls Ibsen's style "naturalism" in this passage. Although "naturalism" and "realism" are often used synonymously, I prefer to maintain the historical distinction, and, at the very least, to recognize naturalism as a subset of realism. As reactions against romanticism, both share the purpose of representing contemporary life and of avoiding an overemphatic idealism. Drawing everyday characters, they reject the division of humanity into the wholly heroic and the completely villainous. Naturalism more particularly strives to do away with any reference to or reliance on supernatural forces in the working out of a drama, to avoid rhetorical speech, and to put a "slice of life" on the stage.

6 Brian Johnston, *To the Third Empire, Ibsen's Early Drama*, Minneapolis, University of Minnesota Press, 1980, p. 274.

7 Robert Brustein, "The Fate of Ibsenism," *Critical Moments: Reflections on Theatre and Society 1973–1979*, New York, Random House, 1980, p. 132.

8 Robert Brustein, *The Theatre of Revolt, Studies in Ibsen, Strindberg, Chekhov, Shaw, Brecht, Pirandello, O'Neill and Genet*, New York, Atlantic-Little Brown, 1962, p. 105.

9 Michael Meyer, *Henrik Ibsen, Volume 2, The Farewell to Poetry 1862–1882*, London, Granada Publishing, 1971, p. 266.

10 Johnston, "The Turning Point in *Lady from the Sea*," in *Text and Supertext in Ibsen's Drama*, University Park and London, Pennsylvania State University Press, 1989, p. 223. For an insightful, inspiring feminist reading of this play, see Elinor Fuchs, "Marriage, Metaphysics, and the *Lady From The Sea* Problem," *Modern Drama*, vol. 35, September 1990, pp. 434–44.

11 An oft-repeated phrase at the American Ibsen Theater Symposium, Pittsburgh, PA, l984. For further details see Chapter 5.

12 Lona Hessel, in *Pillars of Society*, Fjelde (trans.) *Ibsen*, p. 117.

13 Henry James, quoted by Richard Gilman, *The Making of Modern Drama*, New York, Farrar Strauss & Giroux, 1972, p. 68.

14 Ibsen quoted in Brustein, "The Fate of Ibsenism," *Critical Moments*, p. 135.

15 While living in Rome, Ibsen argued in a scandalous tirade that the city's Scandanavia Club accept women as voting members and permit them to serve as librarians. He signed an 1884 petition calling for passage of a Norwegian bill that would establish separate property rights for married women – commenting that "To consult men in such a matter is like asking wolves if they desire better protection for the sheep" (Ibsen, in E. Sprinchorn (ed. and trans.), *Letters and Speeches*, New York, Hill, 1964, p. 228). His notes to *A Doll House* affirm, "A woman cannot be herself in modern society. It is an exclusively male society, with laws made by men and with prosecutors and judges who assess feminine conduct from a masculine standpoint" (quoted in Meyer, *Volume 2*, p. 254). And when an Italian translator/producer wanted to put a conciliatory ending on the play, Ibsen scornfully replied, "It was for the sake of the last scene that the whole play was written" (*Letters*, p. 300). Those who assert that Ibsen was not a full ally of the women's movement typically quote his statement made to the Norwegian Women's Rights League, which honored him in 1898 on his seventieth birthday. He said, "Whatever I have written has been without any conscious thought of making propaganda. I have been more the poet and less the social philosopher than people generally seem inclined to believe. . . . My task has been the description of humanity" (*Letters*, p. 337). Templeton notes that Ibsen made this disclaimer many years after writing the play. In any case, Ibsen's statement is relative, he didn't say that he had been *nothing* of a social philosopher – just not *entirely* one. Addressing the woman question wasn't his *whole* purpose, only part of it.

16 Joan Templeton, "The *Doll House* Backlash, Criticism, Feminism, and Ibsen," *PLMA*, vol. 104, no. 1, January 1989, p. 32.

17 Templeton, "The *Doll House* Backlash, Criticism, Feminism, and Ibsen," p. 32.

18 Jill Davis, "The New Woman and the New Life," in V. Gardner and S. Rutherford (eds), *The New Woman and Her Sisters, Feminism and Theater 1850–1914*, Ann Arbor, University of Michigan Press, 1992, pp. 17–36.

19 This cartoon is reproduced and discussed in V. Gardner's Introduction to *The New Woman and Her Sisters*, pp. 5–6.

20 George Bernard Shaw, "Appendix to the *Quintessence of Ibsenism*," in E. J. West (ed.), *Shaw on Theatre*, New York, Hill & Wang, 1958, p. 5.

21 Perhaps the most telling – and hilarious – indication of the equation of "man" with "human being" occurred in an 1880 translation of *Doll House* into English. The translator, T. Weber, rendered some of the final scene like

this: "Helmer: You are first of all a wife and mother. Nora: . . . I believe that I am first of all a man, I as well as you – or at all events, that I am to try to become a man" (quoted in Meyer, *Volume 2*, p. 270).

22 Meyer, *Volume 2*, p. 264.

23 Brian Johnston, *The Ibsen Cycle, The Design of the Plays from* Pillars of Society *to* When We Dead Awaken, University Park, PA, University of Pennsylvania Press, 1992 revised edition, p. 370.

24 Gerhard Gran, in *Samtiden*, 1891, pp. 75–7, quoted by Michael Meyer, *Henrik Ibsen, Volume 3, The Top of a Cold Mountain 1883–1906*, London, Granada Publishing, 1971, p. 156.

25 Clement Scott, in *Truth*, quoted by Michael Meyer, *Volume 3*, p. 173.

26 Brian Johnston, *Cycle*, p. 368.

27 Benjamin Bennett, *Modern Drama and German Classicism*, Ithaca, Cornell University Press, 1979, p. 305, quoted in Johnston, *Cycle*, p. 369.

28 Johnston, *Cycle*, p. 362.

29 William Archer, "The Theatre," *World*, 27 April 1892, p. 22, quoted by Tracy C. Davis, "Acting in Ibsen," *Theatre Notebook* vol. 39, no. 3, 1985, p. 115.

30 William Archer, "Lyric Theatre, Ibsen in Italian," *Daily Graphic*, 10 June 1893, p. 7, quoted by T. Davis, "Acting in Ibsen," p. 116.

31 Quoted in J. L. Styan, *Modern Drama in Theory and Practice 1, Realism and Naturalism*, Cambridge, Cambridge University Press, 1981, p. 24.

32 Templeton, "The *Doll House* Backlash, Criticism, Feminism, and Ibsen," p. 34.

33 Else Host, "Nova," *Edda*, 46, 1946, p. 28, quoted and trans. by Templeton, "The *Doll House* Backlash, Criticism, Feminism, and Ibsen," p. 29.

34 Herman Weigand, *The Modern Ibsen, A Reconsideration*, New York, Holt, 1925, pp. 68, 64, quoted by Templeton, "The *Doll House* Backlash, Criticism, Feminism, and Ibsen," p. 29.

35 Johnston, *Cycle*, pp. 110–11.

36 Tracy C. Davis, *Actresses As Working Women, Their Sexual Identity in Victorian Culture*, London, Routledge, 1991, p. 134.

37 T. Davis, *Actresses*, p. 135.

38 T. Davis, "Acting in Ibsen," p. 113.

39 William Archer, "A Doll's House," *The Theatrical "World" for 1893*, p. 158, quoted in T. Davis, "Acting in Ibsen," p. 116.

40 *Hedda Gabler*, pp. 713, 753.

41 Johnston, *Cycle*, p. 145.

42 Elinor Fuchs, "Mythic Structure in Hedda Gabler, The Mask Behind the Face," *Comparative Drama*, Fall, 1985, pp. 209–21.

43 Brian Johnston, *Cycle*, pp. 144–5.

44 Rolf Fjelde's "Introduction" to *Hedda Gabler*, 1965, p. 690.

45 Lou Salomé, in Siegfried Mandel (ed. and trans.), *Ibsen's Heroines*, New York, Proscenium Publishers, Inc., Limelight Edition, 1989.

46 Gail Finney, *Women in Modern Drama, Freud, Feminism, and European Theater at the Turn of the Century*, Ithaca, Cornell University Press, 1989, p. 151.

47 Meyer, *Volume 3*, p. 154.

48 Rick Davis, "Buried Truths to Light, Mel Shapiro on *Hedda Gabler*, Charles Ludlam, and other Classics," *The Repertory Reader*, newsletter of

the American Ibsen Theater, vol. 1, no. 3, Spring 1984. For a fuller discussion of this production see Chapter 5.

49 All quoted in Meyer, *Volume 3*, 1971, pp. 156–7.

50 Joseph Donahue, "Women in Victorian Theatre, Images, Illusions, Realities," p. 123, in L. Senelick (ed.), *Gender in Performance, The Presentation of Difference in the Performing Arts*, Hanover, NH, Tufts University, University Press of New England, 1992, pp. 117–40.

51 Gay Gibson Cima, *Performing Women: Female Characters, Male Playwrights and the Modern Stage*, Ithaca, Cornell University Press, 1993, p. 48.

52 Cima, *Performing Women*, p. 49.

53 Cima, *Performing Women*, p. 57.

54 Henrik Ibsen, *Four Major Plays*, James W. McFarlane (ed. and trans.), New York, Oxford University Press, 1981, p. 251.

55 Rick Davis promoted this view at the Ibsen Symposium in August 1984 at the American Ibsen Theater in Pittsburgh. See Chapter 5.

56 Edward Gordon Craig, *On The Art of the Theatre*, New York, Theatre Art Books, 1957 (first published 1911), p. 290.

57 Styan, *Modern Drama in Theory and Practice 1*, p. 15.

58 Gayle Rubin coined this phrase to describe "the set of arrangements by which a society transforms biological sexuality into the products of human activity, and in which those transformed sexual needs are satisfied" ("The Traffic in Women, Notes on the Political Economy of Sex," p. 159, in R. Reiter (ed.), *Toward an Anthropology of Women*, New York, Monthly Review Press, 1975, pp. 157–210.

3 MATERIALIST GIRL: *THE GOOD PERSON OF SZECHWAN* AND MAKING GENDER STRANGE

1 John Fuegi, *Brecht and Company: Sex, Politics, and the Making of the Modern Drama*, New York, Grove, 1994.

2 See: Robert Brustein, "In the Company of Women" (in which, unlike other critics, Brustein praises the book for being "vigorously researched and scholarly," while deriding it only for its "angry ideological agenda"), *New Republic*, 10 October 1994, pp. 34–6; Erika Munk, "When the Shark Bites," *The Nation*, 31 October 1994, pp. 501–4; Ronald Speiers, *New York Times Book Review*, 4 August 1994, p. 1+ and "Reading Brecht, Writing Brecht," letter to the editor of *New York Review of Books*, 12 January 1995, pp. 51–2; John Willett, "Bashing Brecht vs. Reading Brecht," *Theater*, vol. 25, no. 2, 1994, p. 41 and letter to the editor of *New York Review of Books*, 12 January 1995, p. 52; Carl Weber, "Has Mr. B's Private Life a 'Use Value'?," *Theater*, vol. 25, no. 2, 1994, pp. 38–40. In a review in the Fall 1987 *Theater Three* (pp. 102–8), Weber pointed out serious errors in fact and interpretation in the warm-up for *Brecht and Company*, Fuegi's book on Brecht as a director, *Bertolt Brecht: Chaos According to Plan*.

3 Michiko Kakutani, "Lifting the Memory of Slavery into the Realm of Myth," *New York Times*, 8 October 1993, p. C32.

4 James Lyon, *Brecht in America*, Princeton, NJ, Princeton University Press, 1980.

5 All quotations from *The Good Person of Szechwan* come from the Ralph Manheim translation in Manheim and Willett (eds), *Brecht: Collected Plays, Volume 6*, New York, Vintage Books, 1976.

6 Gay Gibson Cima, *Performing Women: Female Characters, Male Playwrights and the Modern Stage*, Ithaca, Cornell University Press, 1993, p. 123.

7 Bertolt Brecht, *Brecht on Theatre: The Development of an Aesthetic*, John Willett (ed. and trans.), London, Methuen, 1973, p. 46.

8 Iris Smith, "Brecht and the Mothers of Epic Theater," *Theater Journal*, vol. 43, 1991, p. 501.

9 Peter W. Ferran, "Notes Toward Composing Music for Brecht's *The Good Person of Szechwan*," unpublished manuscript, generously provided by the author, p. 5. My thoughts on *Good Person* are influenced tremendously by his article and by helpful conversations with him while I developed the essay. For a thorough discussion of the function of this and other songs, see Peter Ferran, "Musical Composition for an American Stage Brecht," *Brecht Today/Brecht Heute*, the yearbook of the International Brecht Society, vol. 22, forthcoming 1997.

10 Brecht, "Notes" on *Good Person* in *Collected Plays, Volume 6*, p. 375.

11 Walter Benjamin, "What Is Epic Theatre? [Second version]," *Understanding Brecht*, New York, Verso, 1983, pp. 18–19.

12 *Brecht on Theatre*, p. 204.

13 *Brecht on Theatre*, p. 44.

14 *Brecht on Theatre*, p. 45.

15 Bertolt Brecht, *Journals 1934–1955*, Hugh Rorrison (trans.), John Willett (ed.), New York, Routledge, 1993, p. 86.

16 *Journals*, p. 86.

17 Walter Kerr, "Will Brecht Ever Come True?," *New York Times*, Sunday, 15 November 1970, Arts Section, pp. 1 and 5.

18 *The Good Person of Sichuan*, The National Theatre Version, Michael Hofmann (trans.), London, Methuen, 1989, p. 16.

19 *Brecht on Theatre*, pp. 121–9.

20 Cima, *Performing Women*, p. 101.

21 See, for example, Sue-Ellen Case, "Homosexuality and the Mother," in J. Fuegi, G. Bahr and J. Willett (eds), *Brecht: Women and Politics: Brecht Yearbook*, vol. 12, Detroit, Wayne State University Press, 1983, pp. 65–74.

22 "Notes" on *Good Person* in *Collected Plays, Vol. 6*, p. 372.

23 Sarah Lennox, "Women in Brecht's Works," *New German Critique*, no. 14, Spring 1978, p. 86.

24 Anne Herrmann, "Travesty and Transgression: Transvestism in Shakespeare, Brecht, Churchill," *Theatre Journal*, vol. 41, no. 2, 1989, p. 146.

25 *Journals*, p. 70.

26 Walter Sokel, "Brecht's Split Characters and His Sense of the Tragic," in Peter Demetz (ed.), *Brecht*, Englewood Cliffs, NJ, Prentice Hall, 1962, pp. 127–37.

27 John Fuegi, "The Alienated Woman: Brecht's *The Good Person of Setzuan*," in S. Mews and H. Knust (eds), *Essays on Brecht: Theater and Politics*, Chapel Hill, University of North Carolina Press, 1974, p. 194.

28 Fuegi, "The Alienated Woman," p. 194.

29 *Journals*, p. 76.
30 Fuegi, "The Alienated Woman," p. 193.
31 Cima, *Performing Women*, p. 95.
32 Case, "Homosexuality and the Mother," p. 66.
33 Herrmann, "Travesty and Transgression," p. 147.
34 For an important discussion of the *Lehrstücke*, to which this discussion is much indebted, see Peter W. Ferran, "New Measures for Brecht in America," *Theater*, vol. 25, no. 2, 1994, pp. 9–24. I am grateful that the author supplied me with an advance copy of the essay.
35 Quoted in "Editorial Note," in *Collected Plays, Volume 6*, p. 375.
36 Brecht, "The Job," in *Short Stories 1921–1946*, Yvonne Kapp, Hugh Rorrison, Antony Tatlow (trans), Willett and Manheim (eds), London and New York, Methuen, 1983, p. 112.
37 "The Job," pp. 115–16.
38 Quoted in "Editorial Notes," in *Short Stories*, p. 235.
39 "The Job," p. 114.
40 The phrase was originated by Marjorie Garber in *Vested Interests: Cross-Dressing and Cultural Anxiety*, New York, Routledge, 1992, see especially pp. 67–71.
41 *Journals*, p. 25.
42 *Journals*, p. 71.
43 Quoted in Ferran, "Notes Toward Composing," p. 4, from Ernst Schumacher, "Er wird bleiben," in *Neue Deutsche Literatur*, Berlin, 1956. Schumacher's essay is translated as "He Will Remain," in Hubert Witt (ed.), *Brecht as They Knew Him*, New York, International Publishers, 1974, pp. 215-28. I prefer Ferran's translation of this passage.
44 G. W. Brandt, "Realism and Parables (from Brecht to Auden)," in J. R. Brown and B. Harris (eds), *Contemporary Theatre*, London, Edward Arnold, 1962, p. 34
45 *Journals*, p. 30.
46 *Journals*, p. 69.
47 *Journals*, p. 30.
48 David Z. Mairowitz, "Brecht's Women: A Synopsis/Proposal," in *Brecht Yearbook*, 1983, p. 208.
49 Iris Smith, "Brecht and the Mothers of Epic Theater," p. 503.
50 Ferran said this in a conversation with me in July 1993.
51 Ekkehard Schall made this remark at an impromptu lecture-demonstration on epic acting at the "Brecht: 30 Years After" conference in Toronto, October 1986.
52 *Brecht on Theatre*, p. 197.
53 This is a central concept of epic acting, and Brecht elaborates on it throughout *Brecht on Theatre*. See especially, "Alienation Effects in Chinese Acting," pp. 90–9, "Short Description of a New Technique of Acting which Produces an Alienation Effect," pp. 136–47, "A Short Organum for the Theatre," pp. 179–205.
54 Janelle Reinelt, "Rethinking Brecht: Deconstruction, Feminism, and the Politics of Form," in M. Silberman, J. Fuegi, R. Voris, C. Weber (eds) *The Brecht Yearbook 15*, Madison, University of Wisconsin Press, 1990, p. 101.
55 Elin Diamond, "Brechtian Theory/Feminist Theory: Toward a Gestic Feminist Criticism," *The Drama Review*, vol. 32, no. 1, 1988, p. 84.

56 Diamond, "Brechtian Theory/Feminist Theory," p. 85.
57 Diamond, "Brechtian Theory/Feminist Theory," p. 89.
58 John Willett, *The Theatre of Bertolt Brecht*, London, Methuen, revised, 1977, p. 85.
59 Karen Laughlin, "Brechtian Theory and American Feminist Theatre," in Pia Kleber and Colin Visser (eds), *Reinterpreting Brecht: His Influence on Contemporary Drama and Film*, Cambridge, Cambridge University Press, 1990, p. 152.
60 Laughlin, "Brechtian Theory and American Feminist Theatre," p. 152.
61 *Brecht on Theatre*, p. 71.
62 Kathie Sarachild, "Consciousness-Raising: A Radical Weapon," in *Feminist Revolution*, New Paltz, NY, Redstockings, 1975, p. 134.
63 Case, "Homosexuality and the Mother," p. 72.
64 Kroetz made this remark at a panel on contemporary German playwriting at the "Brecht: 30 Years After" conference in Toronto, October 1986.
65 *Brecht on Theatre*, pp. 272–4.
66 Karin Struck, quoted by Renate Möhrmann, "The influence of Brecht on Women's Cinema in West Germany," in Pia Kleber and Colin Visser (eds), *Reinterpreting Brecht*, p. 161.

4 QUEERING THE CANON: *AZOI TOOT A YID*

1 I am grateful to Bob Komaiko, from whom I first heard this joke. He still tells it better than anyone.
2 On the feminization of the male Jew, see: Sander Gilman, *The Jew's Body*, New York and London, Routledge, 1991; Jay Geller, "The Unmanning of the Wandering Jew," *American Imago*, Summer 1992, and "(G)nos(e)ology: The Cultural Construction of the Other," in Eilberg-Schwartz (ed.), *People of the Body: Jews and Judaism from an Embodied Perspective*, Albany, State University of New York Press, 1992, pp. 243–82; David Biale, *Eros and the Jews: From Biblical Israel to Contemporary America*, New York, Basic Books, 1992; Paul Breines, *Tough Jews*, New York, Basic Books, 1990.
3 Edward P. Vining, *The Mystery of Hamlet*, Philadelphia, Lippincot & Co., 1881, p. 61.
4 It's common nowadays for people not familiar with the etymology of the word "anti-Semitism" to suggest that it has nothing to do with Jews. Jews aren't really Semites, they say, so the term has no application. Leaving aside the question of what it means to "really be" a Semite, the fact is the term was created especially for Jews. As Sander Gilman writes in *The Jew's Body*, p. 5: "Coined by Wilhelm Marr as part of the scientific discourse of race in the nineteenth century, it is half of the dichotomy of 'Aryan' and 'Semite' which haunted the pseudoscience of ethnology during this period and beyond. . . . The very choice of the label 'anti-Semitism' was to create the illusion of a new scientific discourse for the hatred of the Jews and to root this hatred in the inherent difference of their language. And their language was believed to reflect their essence."
5 Sander Gilman made these remarks at a talk introducing a showing of the Nazi propaganda film *Jud Süss* at New York's Jewish Museum, November 1996.
6 For accounts in English of the Yiddish Theater see: Nahma Sandrow,

Vagabond Stars: A World History of the Yiddish Theater, New York, Limelight, 1986; Irving Howe, *World of Our Fathers*, New York, Simon & Schuster, 1976, especially pp. 460–98; Luba Kadison and Jacob Buloff, with Irving Genn, *On Stage, Off Stage: Memories of a Lifetime in the Yiddish Theatre*, Cambridge, MA, Harvard University Library, 1992; David Lifson, *The Yiddish Theatre in America*, New York and London, Thomas Yoseloff, 1965; Lulla Rosenfeld, *Bright Star of Exile: Jacob Adler and the Yiddish Theatre*, New York, Thomas Y. Crowell Company, 1977; Hutchins Hapgood, *The Spirit of the Ghetto*, New York, Shocken Books, 1972; Ida Kaminska, *My Life, My Theater*, Curt Leviant (ed. and trans.), New York, Macmillan, 1973.

7 See Howe, *World of Our Fathers*, p. 467; Lifson, *Yiddish Theatre*.

8 Alain Finkielkraut, *The Imaginary Jew*, K. O'Neill and D. Suchoff (trans), Lincoln, University of Nebraska Press, 1994, p. 83.

9 Linda Nochlin, "Starting with the Self: Jewish Identity and its Representations," in L. Nochlin and T. Garb (eds), *The Jew in the Text: Modernity and the Construction of Identity*, London, Thames & Hudson, 1995, p. 10.

10 For details, see the recent biography of Bernhardt, Arthur Gold and Robert Fizdale, *The Divine Sarah: A Life of Sarah Bernhardt*, New York, Vintage Books, 1991.

11 Gilman, "Salome, Syphillis, Sarah Bernhardt, and the Modern Jewess," in *The Jew in the Text*, p. 115.

12 For a sensitive, Freudian-based reading of how the race/gender system produces Jewish difference through Bernhardt, see Ann Pellegrini, *Performance Anxieties*, New York, Routledge, 1996, especially Chapter 2, "Entr'acte: Portrait d'une Autre Dora," pp. 39–47.

13 Max Beerbohm, "Hamlet, Princess of Denmark," 17 June, 1899, in Max Beerbohm, *Around Theatres*, London, Rupert Hart-Davis, 1953, pp. 34–7.

14 William Winter quoted in Bernard Grebanier, *Then Came Each Actor*, New York, David McKay Company, Inc., 1975, p. 261.

15 Grebanier, *Each Actor*, pp. 261–2.

16 Unsigned review, *Birmingham Gazette*, 24 June 1899, quoted in Jill Edmonds, "Princess Hamlet," in V. Gardner and S. Rutherford (eds), *The New Woman and her Sisters: Feminism and Theatre 1850–1914*, Ann Arbor, University of Michigan Press, 1992, p. 70.

17 Clement Scott, *Some Notable Hamlets*, New York and London, Benjamin Blom, 1969 (reprint from 1905), p. 18.

18 Anonymous interview with Sarah Bernhardt, *Daily Chronicle*, 17 June 1899.

19 See Carol Ockman, "When Is a Jewish Star Just a Star? Interpreting Images of Sarah Bernhardt," in *The Jew in the Text*, pp. 121–39. Ockman is careful to point out that six-pointed stars and other such imagery didn't *always* signify Jewishness, but that when it did, it combined with other images "to convey her inappropriate behavior," p. 135.

20 Ockman, "Jewish Star," p. 124.

21 Marie Colombier, *Memoirs of Sarah Barnum*, quoted in Ockman, "Jewish Star," p. 125.

22 Ockman, "Jewish Star," p. 138.

23 George Bernard Shaw, "Duse and Bernhardt," in *Shaw's Dramatic Criticism (1895–98)*, John Matthews (ed.), New York, Hill & Wang, 1959, p. 82.

24 Unsigned obituary of Sarah Bernhardt, "The Idol–Woman and the Other," *The Times* (London), 28 March 1923, quoted in Pellegrini, *Performance Anxieties*, p. 41.

25 Pellegrini notes that Victorien Sardou's first play for Bernhardt, *Fedora* (1882), was set in Eastern Europe (*Performance Anxieties*, p. 42). It's worth adding that the play is set in Russia per se, not in the Jewish Pale of Settlement to which Jews were generally restricted. Still, the mechanical plot hinges on whether the hero has committed murder out of jealousy, or out of ideological compulsion as a Nihilist; belonging to the Nihilists was a frequent accusation leveled against Jews in the Pale, and, as noted below, is used by Claudius against his nephew in the Yiddish adaptation of *Hamlet*.

26 *Der Folks Advokat*, 30 November 1888, quoted in Lifson, *Yiddish Theatre*, p. 56. His ellipses.

27 Sheva Zucker, Introduction to "Yiddish Literature and the Female Reader," in Judith R. Baskin (ed.), *Women of the Word: Jewish Women and Jewish Writing*, Detroit, Wayne State University Press, 1994, p. 70.

28 Shmuel Niger, "Yiddish Literature and the Female Reader," Sheva Zucker, (trans. and abridged) in Baskin (ed.), *Women of the Word*, p. 72.

29 Niger, "Female Reader," p. 80. By the time Jews had become well assimilated into America, the feminized image of the man of the *shtetl* re-emerged. Unlike the hero of Sholom Aleichem's "Tevya the Dairyman" stories, which formed the basis for *Fiddler on the Roof*, the Tevya of the musical comedy prays in the language of the *tkhines*.

30 The Hebrew–Yiddish conflict would escalate as the Zionist movement insisted on the revival of Hebrew as a spoken language. Throughout this infamous war, Hebrew and Yiddish were thoroughly gendered as male and female, respectively; the Zionist movement itself was, among other things, an effort of male self-transformation toward, as Max Nordau famously put it, "Muskeljudentum" – a muscular Judaism. In 1930s Palestine, the militant Brigade for the Defense of the Language tried to stamp out public usage of Yiddish. See Benjamin Harshav, *Language in Time of Revolution*, Berkeley, University of California Press, 1993. See also: Naomi Seidman, *A Marriage Made in Heaven: The Sexual Politics of Hebrew and Yiddish*, Berkeley, University of California Press, 1997, which was published when this book was already in production, so can merely be acknowledged here as a pioneering, incisive work.

31 Jacob Adler, *Arbeiter Zeitung*, 29 July 1892, quoted in George O'Dell, *Annals of the New York Stage* vol. XV, 1891–1894, New York, Columbia University Press, 1949; reprinted New York, AMS press, 1970, p. 403.

32 Quoted in Sandrow, *Vagabond Stars*, p. 139.

33 Quoted in Sandrow, *Vagabond Stars*, p. 141.

34 Howe, *World of Our Fathers*, p. 495.

35 Lifson, *Yiddish Theatre*, p. 167.

36 Howe, *World of Our Fathers*, p. 493.

37 Howe, *World of Our Fathers*, p. 449.

38 Ben Siegel, *The Controversial Sholem Asch: An Introduction to his Fiction*, Bowling Green, OH, Bowling Green University Popular Press, 1976, p. 22.

39 All quotations from *God of Vengeance* come from Joachim Neugroschel's 1996 translation. I am grateful to him for supplying me with a copy of the

translation prior to its publication in *The Pakn-Treger*, the Magazine of the National Yiddish Book Center, Winter 1996/5756, number 23, pp. 16–39.

40 Jenna Weissman Joselit, *Our Gang: Jewish Crime and the New York Jewish Community, 1900–1940*, Bloomington, University of Indiana Press, 1983, p. 15. See also, Edward J. Bristow, *Prostitution and Prejudice: The Jewish Fight Against White Slavery 1870–1939*, New York, Oxford University Press, 1982.

41 Joachim Neugroschel, "The Drama of Translation," *The Pakn-Trager*, Winter 1996/5756, Number 23, p. 42.

42 Daniel Boyarin, *Carnal Israel*, Berkeley, University of California Press, 1993, see especially pp. 134–66.

43 Sholem Asch quoted in Binyomin Weiner, "Judging Vengeance," *The Pakn-Treger*, Winter 1996/5756, p. 12. I am grateful to Binyomin Weiner for permitting me to see this article prior to its publication, and to Diane Simon for sending it to me.

44 "God of Mercy" by David Frischmann, from *Teatervelt*, Warsaw, 1908, Binyomin Weiner (trans.), *The Pakn-Treger*, Winter 1996/5756, pp. 44–5.

45 Though these days "kosher" tends to be used only to describe a set of religious dietary practices (except for the slang use, as in a "kosher deal"), it still carries some force in no-longer-Yiddish-speaking Jewish communities. The filmmakers Alisa Lebow and Cynthia Madansky are currently working on a film about Jewish lesbians; its title is *Treyf*.

46 See, especially, Kaier Curtin, *"We Can Always Call Them Bulgarians": The Emergence of Lesbians and Gay Men on the American Stage*, Boston, Alyson Publications, 1987, pp. 25–42.

47 Judge McIntyre quoted in *New York Tribune*, 24 May 1923.

48 Walter Benn Michaels, "The Souls of White Folk," in *Literature and the Body: Essays on Populations and Persons*, ed. E. Scarry, Baltimore, Johns Hopkins University Press, 1988. See also, Walter Benn Michaels, "Race into Culture: A Critical Genealogy of Cultural Identity," *Critical Inquiry*, vol. 18, Summer 1992, pp. 655–85.

49 This appellation for Cahan, the publisher, editor, journalist, and novelist, comes from the actor Jacob Buloff, quoted in Kadison and Buloff, *On Stage, Off Stage*, p. 64.

50 Quoted in Weiner, "Judging Vengeance," p. 14.

51 Percy Hammond, "The Theatres," *New York Tribune*, 20 December 1922.

52 See Leonard Dinnerstein, *The Leo Frank Case*, New York, Columbia University Press, 1968, p. 98.

53 Burns Mantle, "Father in Double Role Gets Ovation," *New York Daily News*, 21 December 1922. The review's subtitle is even more telling in its revulsion for Rudolf Schildkraut and the people he represents: "Sire of Jewish Actor Stars in Ugly Drama."

54 James Craig, "The God of Vengeance," *Mail*, 20 December 1922.

55 Kenneth MacGowan, "The New Play," *Globe*, 20 December 1922.

56 Maida Castellun, "The Stage," *Call*, 21 December 1922.

57 "Truth," *New York Telegraph*, 31 December 1922.

58 Jonathan Boyarin, *Thinking in Jewish*, Chicago, University of Chicago Press, 1996, p. 112. Boyarin makes this point as part of a nuanced and eloquent critique of the general failure to *historicize* Jewish exclusion from Europe, see pp. 108–39.

59 I have developed this argument in two articles, "The Eternal Queer: In the Symbolic Landscape of Homophobia, We Are the Jews," *Village Voice*, 27 April 1993; and "Homo*feh*bia: Jews and Gays: The Shande That Dares not Speak Its Name," *Village Voice*, 29 June 1993.

60 Tyrone Guthrie, preface, in Mendel Kohansky, *The Hebrew Theatre*, New York, KTAV, 1969, p. v.

61 I am grateful to Donald Margulies for sending me a copy of his script-in-progress, and to the director, Gordon Edelstein, for talking it over with me.

62 I discussed plans for the production with Gordon Edelstein in November 1996.

63 Leslie Fiedler, "What Can We Do About Fagin? The Jew-Villain in Western Tradition," *Commentary* May 1949, p. 418.

64 I have developed this argument in "Wrestling with *Angels*: A Jewish Fantasia," in D. Geis and S. Kruger (eds), *Approaching Millennium: Essays on Tony Kushner's Angels in America*, Ann Arbor, University of Michigan Press, forthcoming, 1997.

65 See Kushner's *It's an Undoing World, or Why Should It Be Easy When It Can Be Hard: Notes on My Grandma for Actors, Dancers, and a Band*, in *Conjunctions*, vol. 25, special issue on The New American Theater, 1995, pp. 14–32.

66 For a pioneering, compelling analysis of how and why the JAP stereotype emerged in post-war America, see Riv-Ellen Prell, "Why Jewish Princesses Don't Sweat," in H. Eilberg-Schwartz (ed.), *People of the Body: Jews and Judaism from an Embodied Perspective*, Albany, State University of New York Press, 1992, pp. 329–59.

67 Pellegrini, *Performance Anxieties*, p. 18.

68 See: Pellegrini, *Performance Anxieties*; Gay Gibson Cima, *Performing Women: Female Characters, Male Playwrights, and the Modern Stage*, Ithaca, Cornell University Press, 1993. Cima not only barely mentions Rosenthal, but when she does, she mischaracterizes her work as "committed to lesbian . . . concerns" (p. 117). There is also a book published in France called *Arcade: Belles et bêtes* that features Rosenthal on its cover, but doesn't mention her in its text.

69 Miller, quoted in Dinitia Smith, "Step Right Up! See the Bearded Person!" *New York Times* 9 June 1995, pp. C1 and 23.

70 *Juggling Gender* is a 30-minute film about Miller made by Tami Gold. It is distributed by Women Make Movies, (212) 925-0606. See also, "Transgressive Hair: The Last Frontier," in *Lilith*, Spring 1995, pp. 22–3.

71 Ockman, "Jewish Stars," p. 121.

72 Rachel Rosenthal, *Pangaean Dreams*, text published in *Movement Research*, 1993.

73 Rosenthal made such comments in conversations with me in July 1991, and in notes in *Movement Research*.

74 Quotations from *Rachel's Brain* come from my notes taken at a performance at Dance Theater Workshop in New York City, October 1986.

5 THREE CANONICAL CROSSINGS

1 All quotations from *King Lear* come from the Arden edition, edited by Kenneth Muir, London, Methuen, 1972. Alterations of the text were made

by Lee Breuer, Ruth Maleczech, me, and other members of the company.

2 All quotations from Lee Breuer and Ruth Maleczech are based on my own notes from rehearsals and from conversations over the course of rehearsals and performances.

3 Maynard Mack, *King Lear in Our Time*, Berkeley, University of California Press, 1965, p. 23.

4 Predictably, the most vicious and dismissive review came from the notoriously misogynistic, avant-garde-hostile critic, John Simon, "Diminished 'Dilemma,' Lethal 'Lear'," *New York Magazine*, 5 February 1990, pp. 84–5. He complained that the microphones, "being of the cheap kind, look like life-support tubes stuck into their noses," adding, "As these assorted no-talents whisper or shriek into their microphones (you never know who is speaking), the moribund production makes at least a fairly compelling argument for euthanasia." See also Frank Rich, "Mabou Mines Creates a 'King Lear' All Its Own," *New York Times*, 26 January 1990, p. C3; "Goings On About Town: The Theatre," *The New Yorker*, 12 February 1990, p. 4.

5 See Elinor Fuchs, "The Death of Character," *Theater Communications*, vol. 5, no. 3, March 1983; Richard Schechner, "The End of Humanism," *Performing Arts Journal* 11, 1979, pp. 9–22; Bonnie Marranca, "The Self as Text: Lee Breuer's Animations," in *Theaterwritings*, New York, PAJ Publications, 1984, pp. 42–59.

6 Fuchs, "The Death of Character," p. 1.

7 Jan Kott, "*King Lear* or *Endgame*," in *Shakespeare Our Contemporary*, New York, W.W. Norton, 1964, p. 130.

8 In his production, Robert Wilson cast a woman, Marianne Hoppe, as Lear. Though she did nothing to disguise herself as a man, the character's gender was not changed. For a detailed description of this production, see Erika Fischer-Lichte, "Between Difference and Indifference: Marianne Hoppe in Robert Wilson's *Lear*," in L. Senelick (ed.), *Gender in Performance: The Presentation of Difference in the Performing Arts*, Hanover, Tufts University, University Press of New England, 1992, pp. 86–98.

9 Mack, *King Lear in Our Time*, p. 25.

10 Mack, *King Lear in Our Time*, p. 91.

11 Schechner, "The End of Humanism," p. 10.

12 Schechner, "The End of Humanism," p. 11.

13 See Andreas Huyssen, *After the Great Divide: Modernism, Mass Culture, and Postmodernism*, Bloomington, Indiana University Press, 1986; Hal Foster (ed.), *The Anti-Aesthetic: Essays on Postmodern Culture*, Seattle, Bay Press, 1983.

14 Coppélia Kahn, "The Absent Mother in *King Lear*," in M. Ferguson, M. Quilligan, and N. Vickers, (eds), *Rewriting the Renaissance: Discourse of Sexual Differences in Early Modern Europe*, Chicago, University of Chicago Press, 1985, p. 36.

15 Kahn, "The Absent Mother in *King Lear*," p. 41.

16 There was, reportedly, a gender-reversed production of *Hamlet* at California State University at Sacramento in 1989, directed by Juanita Rice.

17 See Mary Anne Doane, "Women's Stake in Representation: Filming the Female Body," in *October*, no. 17, 1981, pp. 22–36; E. Ann Kaplan, *Women and Film: Both Sides of the Camera*, New York, Methuen, 1983; Teresa de Lauretis, *Alice Doesn't: Film, Semiotics, Cinema*, Bloomington, Indiana

University Press, 1984 and *Technologies of Gender*, Bloomington, Indiana University Press, 1987; Laura Mulvey, "Visual Pleasure and Narrative Cinema," *Screen*, vol. 16, no. 3, 1975, pp. 6–18; M.A. Doane, P. Mellencamp, and L. Williams (eds), *Re-Vision: Essays in Feminist Film Criticism*, Frederick, MD, University Publications of America in association with American Film Institute, 1984.

18 Kahn, "The Absent Mother in *King Lear*," p. 47.
19 Monique Wittig, "The Mark of Gender," in *The Poetics of Gender*, Nancy K. Miller (ed.), New York, Columbia University Press, 1986, p. 66.
20 Mack, *King Lear in Our Time*, p. 87.
21 Michael Goldman, *Shakespeare and the Energies of Drama*, p. 100.
22 Michael Goldman, "*King Lear*: Acting and Feeling," in Lawrence Danson (ed.), *On King Lear*, Princeton, Princeton University Press, 1981, p. 28.
23 Goldman, *Shakespeare and the Energies of Drama*, p. 96.
24 Kahn, "The Absent Mother in *King Lear*," p. 35.
25 Thomas M. McFarland, "The Image of the Family in *King Lear*," in Danson, *On King Lear*, p. 99.
26 Of course, biological families aren't the only ones that can evoke such powerful responses. Reginald Jackson's forthcoming adaptation, called *House of Lear*, casts the tragic hero as the mother of a fashion house in New York's African-American community.
27 Stanley Cavell, "The Avoidance of Love: A Reading of *King Lear*," in *Must We Mean What We Say?*, Cambridge, Cambridge University Press, 1976, pp. 267–353.
28 McFarland, "The Image of the Family in *King Lear*," p. 100.
29 Craig Owens, "The Discourse of Others: Feminists and Postmodernism," in H. Foster (ed.), *The Anti-Aesthetic: Essays on Postmodern Culture*, Park Townsend, Washington, Bay Press, 1983, p. 70.
30 Owens, "The Discourse of Others," p. 70.
31 All quotations from speeches and panel discussion at the American Ibsen Theater in Pittsburgh, 9–11 August 1984, come from my notes taken at the event.
32 Johnston was quoting Ibsen's *Lady from the Sea* when invoking this phrase at the symposium – and in his book, *To the Third Empire*, Minneapolis, University of Minnesota Press, 1980.
33 Charles Ludlam, *Bluebeard*, in *The Complete Plays of Charles Ludlam*, New York, Harper & Row, 1989, p. 118.
34 Ludlam, *Secret Lives of the Sexists*, *Complete Plays*, p. 654.
35 Stefan Brecht, *Queer Theatre*, London and New York, Methuen, 1986, p. 55.
36 Ludlam, *Camille*, *Complete Plays*, p. 239.
37 *Camille*, p. 236.
38 *Camille*, p. 246.
39 Charles Ludlam, "*Hedda* Journal," in Ludlam, S. Samuels (ed.), *Ridiculous Theatre: Scourge of Human Folly*, New York, Theatre Communications Group, 1992, p. 169.
40 Ludlam, *Scourge*, p. 169.
41 Bertolt Brecht, "Appendices to the Short Organum," in John Willett (ed. and trans.), *Brecht on Theatre*, New York, Hill & Wang, 1964, p. 276.
42 Mel Shapiro, quoted in *American Theatre*, October 1984, p. 25.
43 Mel Shapiro, quoted in *AIT: The Repertory Reader* (newsletter of the

American Ibsen Theater), vol. 1, no. 3, Spring 1984, p. 3.

44   Rick Davis,"The Histrionic Hedda," *AIT: The Repertory Reader*, Spring 1984, p. 7.

45   All quotations from Bette Bourne, Precious Pearl (Paul Shaw), Peggy Shaw, and Lois Weaver come from interviews I conducted with them in February 1991.

46   Weaver and Shaw were actually two-thirds of Split Britches; the third member, Deb Margolin, did not participate in *Belle Reprieve*; Bloolips is a company of six men; Bourne and Paul Shaw are two of its constants.

47   See, for instance, Sue-Ellen Case, "Toward a Butch-Femme Aesthetic," in L. Hart (ed.), *Making a Spectacle: Feminist Essays on Contemporary Women's Theatre*, Ann Arbor, University of Michigan Press, 1989, pp. 282–99; and "From Split Subject to Split Britches," in E. Brater (ed.), *Feminine Focus: The New Women Playwrights*, New York, Oxford University Press, 1989, pp. 126–46; Jill Dolan, *The Feminist Spectator as Critic*, Ann Arbor, UMI Research Press, 1988, especially pp. 72–6; Vivian Patraka, "Split Britches in *Little Women: The Tragedy*: Staging, Censorship, Nostalgia, and Desire," *The Kenyon Review*, no. 15, Spring 1993, pp. 6–13.

48   All quotations from *Belle Reprieve* (whose text changed over the course of production) come from my notes taken at several performances, and from the unpublished manuscript generously supplied by the company.

49   Tennessee Williams, stage directions in *A Streetcar Named Desire*, New York, Signet, 1947, p. 15 (Blanche) and p. 29 (Stanley).

50   David Savran, *Communists, Cowboys, and Queers: The Politics of Masculinity in the Work of Arthur Miller and Tennessee Williams*, Minneapolis, University of Minnesota Press, 1992, p. 98.

51   Savran, *Communists, Cowboys, and Queers*, p. 116.

52   Savran, *Communists, Cowboys, and Queers*, p. 92.

53   Savran, *Communists, Cowboys, and Queers*, p. 96.

54   See Savran, *Communists, Cowboys, and Queers*, p. 118. He uses the term here specifically after Sontag to mean a celebration of artifice and extravagance, and a theatricalization of social roles, where instead of offering reversals, a camp reading will transpose, recognizing that "all gender is masquerade and all costume is a form of drag."

55   Stanley Edgar Hyman, "Some Trends in the Novel," *College English*, October 1958, p. 3.

56   See, for instance, Stephen S. Stanton, "Introduction," in Stanton (ed.), *Tennessee Williams: A Collection of Critical Essays*, Englewood Cliffs, NJ, Prentice-Hall, 1977; Nancy M. Tischler, *Tennessee Williams: Rebellious Puritan*, New York, Citadel, 1961. Savran powerfully condemns the "virtual ubiquity of the 'Albertine strategy' as a guide to interpreting Williams" (*Communists, Cowboys, and Queers*, p. 116).

EPILOGUE: NOTES ON BUTCH: NOT JUST A PASSING FANCY

1   See Sue-Ellen Case, "Toward a Butch-Femme Aesthetic," in Lynda Hart (ed.), *Making a Spectacle*, Ann Arbor, University of Michigan Press, 1989; Madeline Davis and Elizabeth Lapovsky Kennedy, *Boots of Leather,*

Slippers of Gold: The History of a Lesbian Community, New York, Routledge, 1993; Leslie Feinberg, *Stone Butch Blues*, Ithaca, New York, Firebrand, 1993; Teresa de Lauretis, "Film and the Visible," in Bad Object Choices (ed.), *How Do I Look*, Seattle, Bay, 1991; Joan Nestle (ed.), *The Persistent Desire: A Femme-Butch Reader*, Boston, Alyson, 1992.

2 Gayle Rubin, "Of Catamites and Kings: Reflections on Butch, Gender, and Boundaries," in Nestle (ed.), *The Persistent Desire*, p. 467.

3 See Erving Goffman, *The Presentation of Self in Everyday Life*, Garden City, Doubleday, 1959.

4 Judith Butler, "Imitation and Gender Insubordination," in Diana Fuss (ed.), *Inside/Out: Lesbian Theories, Gay Theories*, New York, Routledge, 1991, p. 24.

5 Judith Butler, "Performative Acts and Gender Constitution: An Essay in Phenomenology and Feminist Theory," in Sue-Ellen Case (ed.), *Performing Feminisms: Feminist Critical Theory and Theatre*, Baltimore, Johns Hopkins University Press, 1990, p. 279.

6 Bertolt Brecht, *Brecht on Theatre: The Development of an Aesthetic*, John Willett (trans. and ed.), New York, Hill & Wang, 1964, p. 137.

7 Elin Diamond, "Brechtian Theory/Feminist Theory: Toward a Gestic Feminist Criticism," *The Drama Review*, vol. 32, no. 1, 1988, pp. 82–94.

8 See Susan Sontag, "Notes on 'Camp'," in *Against Interpretation*, New York, Dell, 1966.

9 Marjorie Garber, *Vested Interests: Cross-Dressing and Cultural Anxiety*, New York, Routledge, 1992, pp. 67–71.

10 Garber, *Vested Interests*, p. 16.

11 Augusto Boal, *Theater of the Oppressed*, New York, Urizen, 1979, pp. 143–4.

12 *Movement Research Performance Journal*, no. 3, Fall 1991. The journal was a publication of Movement Research, an organization in New York City offering workshops, performance series, and services for performing artists. A full-page ad by an activist group featured a 10-inch square photograph of female genitalia with the caption, "Read My Lips Before They're Sealed," and encouraged readers to contact New York senators to urge them to vote against the abortion "gag rule." Movement Research received some National Endowment for the Arts funding and the agency charged that MR had misused its funds and demanded that the group return $1,113, the amount of NEA money, the agency somehow calculated, MR had spent on the journal.

13 From *Belle Reprieve* by Bette Bourne, Paul Shaw, Peggy Shaw, and Lois Weaver. Unpublished manuscript generously supplied by the authors.

14 Jeannie Kasindorf, "Lesbian Chic," *New York*, vol. 26, 10 May 1993, pp. 30–7. See also Sylvia Rubin, "The New Lesbian Chic," *San Francisco Chronicle*, 22 June 1993, B, 3:4.

15 *Paper Magazine*, October 1990. On the inside, a four-page spread features Shields modeling men's fashions.

Index

204 *Index*

PN 1650 .W65 S65 1997
VISUAL STUDIES
Solomon, Alisa, 1956-

Re-dressing the canon

'a *brilliant,* bold, mar- velously *entertain- ing,* necessary book'

Tony Kushner

What can theater teach us about the performance-like qualities of gender, and what can gender teach us about the workings of theater? In re-dressing the canon, Alisa Solomon returns to the dramatic canon to investigate such questions, finding feminist and queer fissures within the performance conventions of patriarchal drama.

re-dressing the canon offers a theater-based re-examination of canonical drama, considering works by, among others:

Aristophanes

Shakespeare

Ibsen

Brecht

Yiddish Theater

Mabou Mines

Split Britches

Ridiculous Theater

Rachel Rosenthal

Combining performance criticism with performance theory in an engaging, jargon-free prose style, re-dressing the canon bridges the boundary between theory and practice in a brilliant and unique analysis for our times.

Alisa Solomon is a theater critic, teacher, and dramaturg in New York City. She is Associate Professor of English/Journalism at Baruch College-City University of New York, and of English and Theater at the CUNY Graduate Center. She is a staff writer at the VILLAGE VOICE.

Theater Studies

ISBN 0-415-15721-8

ROUTLEDGE

9 780415 157216

11 New Fetter Lane, London EC4P 4EE
29 West 35th Street, New York NY 10001
PRINTED IN GREAT BRITAIN

photograph: Ruth Maleczech as Lear by Sylvia Plachy, 1990
design: richard carney